RIGHT SIDE UP

RIGHT SIDE UP

The Fall of Paul Martin and the Rise of Stephen
Harper's New Conservatism

PAUL WELLS

McCLELLAND & STEWART

Library and Archives Canada Cataloguing in Publication

Wells, Paul (Paul Allen)
    Right side up : the fall of Paul Martin and the rise of Stephen Harper's new conservatism / Paul Wells.

"Douglas Gibson books"
ISBN 13: 978-0-7710-8919-0
ISBN 10: 0-7710-8919-8

1. Martin, Paul, 1938-.   2. Harper, Stephen, 1959-.   3. Canada – Politics and government – 2006-.   4. Canada – Politics and government – 1993-2006.   5. Canada. Parliament – Elections, 2006.   I. Title.

FC635.W43 2006   971.07'2   C2006-902167-8

We acknowledge the financial support of the Government of Canada through the Book Publishing Industry Development Program and that of the Government of Ontario through the Ontario Media Development Corporation's Ontario Book Initiative. We further acknowledge the support of the Canada Council for the Arts and the Ontario Arts Council for our publishing program.

Typeset in Janson by M&S, Toronto
Printed and bound in Canada

A Douglas Gibson Book

This book is printed on acid-free paper that is 100% recycled, ancient-forest friendly (100% post-consumer recycled).

McClelland & Stewart Ltd.
75 Sherbourne Street
Toronto, Ontario
M5A 2P9
www.mcclelland.com

1 2 3 4 5   10 09 08 07 06

To Mom and Dad, who taught me everything

"Tout commence en mystique et finit en politique."
— Charles Péguy, *Notre Jeunesse* (1910)

CONTENTS

RUBICON CROISSANTS

⇧

It begins, as great adventures so often do, in a conference room on the Vancouver International Airport hotel strip, at a Canadian Alliance breakfast meeting on competitiveness policy. There's a pastry tray and some pitchers of orange juice at the back. Just like in Homer.

The date was Saturday, September 8, 2001. In Newark and Baltimore and Laurel, Maryland, teams of hijackers were convening at very similar hotels in the last stages of preparation for the 9/11 attacks. The events of that murderous Tuesday would, of course, rock the world. Quite incidentally, they would also briefly throw Canadian political reporters off the story that had kept us amused for most of 2001: the relentless collapse of the Canadian Alliance under Stockwell Day. But on this bright Saturday the convulsions of the Alliance were still damned good copy.

Barely a year earlier Stock Day had seemed the very sunny incarnation of Western conservative renewal: young, photogenic, with a record of achievement as Alberta's treasurer. But Day was surprisingly tentative and unprepared in his first weeks in the House of Commons. So wily old Jean Chrétien called a snap election and briskly cleaned the younger man's clock. After that Day just seemed to *implode*. His shaky judgment, his fondness for vendetta, and his inability either to plan or to improvise left him wall-eyed and stammering as more and more MPs started to leave the caucus or dare Day to kick them out.

Day took Art Hanger's dare on May 2; the law-and-order Calgary MP was the first to be expelled from the Official Opposition caucus. Hanger soon had company: Jim Gouk, Jay Hill, Gary Lunn, Grant McNally, Val Meredith, Jim Pankiw, and Chuck Strahl left on May 2. Andy Burton, Brian Fitzpatrick, and Monte Solberg in late June. Deb Grey and Inky Mark in early July. But the more Day tried to contain the revolt, the faster it grew. Finally, on July 17, Day forestalled a caucus confidence vote he would certainly have lost by calling for the Alliance to select a new leader. Day might or might not be a candidate for that job. But at least there was some kind of chance that the party would see the back of him.

Not all the rebels found that the folks back home were behind their little adventure. Several of the insurrectionists polled their constituencies and found their local party members were angrier with them than at Day. In return for a promise not to bad-mouth the leader again, Day offered amnesty and safe passage back to the Alliance caucus. Two days later, on September 10, five of the rebels – Burton, Fitzpatrick, Gouk, Hanger, and Solberg – would return on those terms. But the other seven would soon form a parliamentary coalition with Joe Clark's tiny Progressive Conservative caucus. So the forces of Canadian conservatism were split into – what? Three factions? Four? Three and a half? Five divided by four, except on Tuesdays and in months with an 'n'? – well, many factions, anyway.

And here, into the midst of the turmoil, comes Stephen Harper. On paper he was just one of several invited guest speakers at this snoozer Saturday-morning economic-policy conference. But nobody was fooled. Harper had already announced, two weeks earlier, that he would soon resign from his current job as president of the National Citizens' Coalition, a little pressure group devoted to complaining non-stop about the size and expense of Canada's assorted governments.

So here was Harper leaving his job just as Day put his own up for grabs. Reporters may not know much about competitiveness policy, but we're pretty good at adding two and two. So the parking lot outside the hotel was a maze of television satellite trucks and feeder cables. There were almost as many reporters at the back of the conference room as there were windbreaker-clad, pastry-munching Alliance competitiveness wonks at the front.

Before us all stood Stephen Harper, forty-two years old. Taciturn, self-assured, and, if you must know, a bit woozy. An inner-ear infection was keeping him out of airplanes. An Alliance staffer had driven him through the Rockies from Calgary, like Hannibal minus the elephants.

Most of the reporters in the room had had occasion to chat with Harper, but not lately. "We had an active strategy from about February until he declared he was in the race: He didn't do a single media interview," a close friend of Harper's said later. "Complete radio silence. It wasn't possible for him to talk without addressing the Day thing, without saying something about it. And he was, frankly, quietly organizing a team and doing things that he needed to do. Which is a pattern in Harper's life: You don't need to be in the media to be politically successful."

He wouldn't formally launch his campaign for the Alliance leadership until December 2. But in its modest way this was his coming-out party. His speech that morning was both valedictory and a call-to-arms. In 1993, he reminded his audience, Canada was a mess of high taxes, deficits, debt, and unemployment. Two years later all that had changed. How did it get so bad in the first place? "There was no political option unequivocally committed to fighting this direction and providing Canadians with an alternative."

The Progressive Conservatives had demonstrated no real interest in smaller government. Certainly the Liberals hadn't bothered to hold their feet to the fire. Nothing changed until Reform was founded in 1987 – "or, to be honest with ourselves, more accurately until the Reform Party made the decision to become a national party in 1991."

The Liberals would return to their free-spending ways unless somebody serious stood up to them, Harper said. Which meant somebody besides Joe Clark's Progressive Conservative rump. "Frankly, Joe Clark wasn't elected to stop big government. The Canadian Alliance was. If you don't do it, nobody will."

What about merging the two parties, an idea Clark and the Alliance rebels were flirting with? "The fact of the matter is that in a practical day-to-day sense your two parties remain divided on core issues of fiscal and economic conservatism as often as they are not."

Not that the Progressive Conservatives were lepers, precisely. "They have a range of opinion and you've got to talk to those people. But don't sell your own record short."

As he had done before, as he would do so often again, Stephen Harper was trying to thread a needle. He liked conservatives best when they formed a national party. To make sure the party was national in scope, the Alliance – heir to Reform – needed to "talk to" the old-line, clubbable Conservatives. But there was no point to electoral advantage if it did not pursue some more lasting end, some more potent mix of conservative policies. "This party is about policy or it is about nothing."

And what was the policy end to which Harper was urging conservatives? He offered only hints. He cited research suggesting a nation's government is simply wasting money if it spends more than 30 per cent of a nation's gross domestic product. "Canada is fifty cents on the dollar above that level." That is, Canada's various levels of government were spending closer to 45 per cent of GDP.

This is the kind of statement that news reporters never write about. It's full of numbers; it's abstract; it's theoretical. But if Harper's words had any meaning, the implication of what he was saying was breathtaking. Total federal spending in 2001 was about $120 billion. So Harper was calling, at least in theory, for $40 billion in cuts to government spending.

In the brief scrum after his speech, Harper didn't elaborate on that last comment, or on much else. But in less than a half hour he had hinted at the techniques he would bring to his second stint as an elected politician, the one that would be made to count. He would not speak until ready. He would speak quietly and carry big ambitions. He would be flexible in method – surprisingly, almost maddeningly so at times – but he would never lose sight of the long game, which was to transform Canada, if it would let him, into a profoundly different place.

⇧

I had seen him before, of course, but I didn't really know him. Even today, more than a decade after I met him, I still don't. Stephen Harper is hard to know. Ever since he became the young policy director of the Reform Party after its founding convention in 1987, and especially after he and fifty-one other Reform candidates won their tickets to Ottawa in the 1993 election, Harper had been like those floaters that appear in your field of vision on a bright sunshiny day. What *are* those things, anyway? Dust motes? Blood vessels? No way to tell. You never stop seeing them, but every time you try to actually stare at one, it scoots off to the side.

Every reporter on Parliament Hill, where the Montreal *Gazette* sent me to work in 1994, soon learned to call Harper for intelligent, quotable commentary on any number of topics. The lovingly catalogued failings of Chrétien's Liberal government were a favourite subject, but he was also good on economics, the subject he had studied at the University of Calgary, and on Quebec separatism, the file he had been assigned by Preston Manning, Reform's founding leader.

Reformers weren't the most urbane bunch. One of them, a tiny, black-eyed Saskatchewan farmer named Lee Morrison, dedicated his maiden speech in the Commons to the proposition that he was a "redneck" – his word – and proud of it. (Morrison was actually one of the best-read, funniest, and most well-travelled MPs in the Commons. But he kept it well hidden.) Art Hanger was oddly fascinated by corporal punishment. Darrel Stinson would, at intervals, leap across the Commons floor and challenge his political opponents to fisticuffs. A disconcerting number of these people wore cowboy hats in Ottawa without apparent irony. Even Manning, whose gentle nature and love of Canadian history would eventually win him at least a few admirers in the Press Gallery, was in those early days still wearing coke-bottle glasses and a pinched expression.

Harper was different. Not wildly different, but different enough. More approachable. He'd been born in Leaside, a Toronto suburb, in 1959 and moved west – first to Edmonton when he was nineteen, then to Calgary two years later. He'd studied economics at the University of Calgary, which didn't confer status as lofty as McGill or Queen's or that holy grail of Central Canadian insider status, Trinity College, but was at least an accredited degree-granting institution. He was *with* this crew of Reformers, but not really *of* them. His suits weren't flashy or custom-tailored, but they did fit his lean and slouchy frame like real clothes, not like somebody's idea of a joke. He didn't make a show of being folksy and down-home. Didn't make any show at all, really. He spoke passable French.

Best of all, Harper was capable of insight, which is better than mere book learning and at least as rare on Parliament Hill as anywhere else. Once, in the run-up to the 1995 Quebec secession referendum, I called him to discuss the Parti Québécois's glib assurance that the rest of Canada would offer up an economic association on terms favourable to a seceding Quebec. Harper called this evidence of "the profound unilateralism of the Quebec separatists": the belief that the rest of the world would gather round to cheerfully help the separatists on their way when the great day came. It wasn't just a tactic, Harper said – they actually believed the world was supposed to help them with their little project. It was as compact a critique of separatist logic as any I'd heard.

All of these characteristics made Harper the first-call Reformer for most Ottawa reporters during the first Jean Chrétien government. And when we called, Harper wasn't stingy with his opinions. In fact, when Harper shows up in

Manning's autobiography, *Think Big*, it is often because Manning is complaining about what a flap-jawed gossip his young charge could be. Harper didn't like Manning's choice for national campaign director in 1993, Rick Anderson, and he "was prepared to air his objections in the media," Manning writes. In 1994, Manning came under fire for alleged abuse of his expense account. Harper joined the chorus of critics. "Even though procedures existed for handling any complaints about the use of party funds," Manning writes, "Stephen went to the media."

Today almost no MP serving under Harper would dare mouth off to reporters as freely as Harper did under Manning. If it's any defence, Harper's impatience wasn't contrived. It was real. When he quit the Reform caucus in 1997, he was genuinely frustrated with electoral politics. And if the truth be told, he was getting pretty good at quitting by that point.

In fact, in trying to understand Harper's career, it helps to split it into two parts, with the dividing line running through that breakfast talk on the Vancouver airport hotel strip in 2001. A play in two acts.

Every once in a while throughout the first act, the young Harper quits, storms out, shuts down, or complains about how everyone else is such a disappointment. In the second, he decides to do the work – and impose the discipline and, yes, make the compromises – that will advance his goals in an uncertain world. The Harper of Act II is less acerbic, less biting, less grandly weary of every other political actor in Canada, so in many ways he's a lot less fun. But he is also incomparably more mature, sophisticated – and much more politically formidable.

⇧

A lot happened in his life between 1997, when he went stomping out of politics, and 2001, when he came shuffling back. But it wasn't conviction or maturation that made him change. It was an emergency: the looming collapse of the Reform/ Alliance experiment. There was no time to write a cutting op-ed analyzing everyone else's failure to save political conservatism at the federal level in Canada. If it was to be saved, Harper had to do the hard work himself.

Before he resigned his seat in 1997, Harper had made significant contributions to the growth of Reform. But mostly he was the kind of highly intelligent young man who is quicker with a critique than a solution. It's a common enough trait: insight combined with a lack of patience.

Not that Harper's insight, in itself, didn't come in handy. "He always, right back to university days, was a pretty perceptive evaluator of people," John Weissenberger, one of Harper's best friends, told me over coffee at a Calgary Starbucks. "Pretty good at knowing what slots they could fill, what their strengths and weaknesses were."

Weissenberger is a handsome, soft-spoken geologist at Husky Oil. Unlike just about all of Harper's other close friends, he didn't mind being quoted for this book. The two men met in 1984 when Harper was finishing his B.A. and Weissenberger was starting his Ph.D. in engineering at the University of Calgary. Weissenberger was from Montreal, so like Harper, he was a Calgarian by choice. As late arrivals to that city sometimes do, they took to the city's dominant small-government political philosophy with a vengeance. In their case – remember, after all, they were students – this meant doing a lot of reading.

"We spent a couple of years sort of doing a very broad review of the classic texts of classical liberal economics and political theory," Weissenberger said. "A dozen or two dozen books that we had read and that we discussed. You know, the Austrian school, Hayek, a couple of [William F.] Buckley's books – *God and Man at Yale, Up From Liberalism.* Peter Berger, a guy who wrote a lot of interesting stuff in the eighties, on the transition from the liberal state. Edmund Burke's *Reflections on the Revolution in France.*"

Students of such heady stuff would inevitably have found Brian Mulroney's Toryism pretty thin gruel. And indeed, when an alternative came along – the embryonic Western protest party being formed by Preston Manning and a few others – Harper and Weissenberger didn't need much persuading. "Stephen went to the Vancouver meeting – I couldn't go, unfortunately – in May of 1987," Weissenberger said. "We both resigned from the PCs the same day, in June of '87. And we drove out to the convention in Winnipeg, which was Halloween weekend that year."

It was at Winnipeg that Reform became Reform, the name chosen from thirty alternatives by hundreds of delegates. Harper delivered a prime-time speech to the assembly, an attack on federal politics from a Western perspective. Manning loved the speech, asking one reporter after another whether they had heard it. For the next five years, Harper would be Manning's unofficial lieutenant and most prominent spokesman.

Which is not the same as saying they always agreed. This is obvious to anyone who reads Tom Flanagan's critical biography of Manning and Reform, *Waiting for the Wave.* Flanagan is a University of Calgary political scientist, one of Harper's closest friends, and he has often been one of his closest political allies. With Harper, he was one of Reform's important early strategists. And with Harper, Flanagan was one of Manning's early critics. *Waiting for the Wave* often reads as a history of the

tension between Harper's and Flanagan's conservative ortho-
doxy and Manning's attempts – sometimes naive, sometimes
inspired – to situate Reform in some novel place outside the
old left-right spectrum.

Barely seventeen months after his star turn at Reform's
founding convention, Flanagan writes, Harper sent Manning
a memo containing "a root and branch critique of what he saw
as Manning's strategy." Manning had already moved beyond the
idea of Reform as a Western protest party. But to Harper it was
still too much of a populist movement whose goal was to speak
for the "thinly populated resource-producing regions." Big
problem: the rural resource-producing regions didn't have
enough people or seats to compete realistically for power. Second
big problem: the resource-producing regions had different beefs
against Central Canada. So you couldn't herd voters in those
regions, and the payoff wouldn't be worth the effort in any case.

What was the alternative? A mostly economic conservatism, "a modern Canadian version of the Thatcher–Reagan
phenomenon." The basis of Reform's market should be the
private-sector urban middle class, and the core of its message
should be free markets and low taxes. The party "should tailor
its broader, 'social' agenda to gain a sizeable chunk of the urban
working class and rural sector 'swing' vote, without alienating
its urban private sector middle-class 'core.' The key is to
emphasize moderate, conservative social values consistent with
the traditional family, the market economy, and patriotism."

There are two interesting things about this analysis. Well,
maybe more, but at least two. The first is that right from the
outset, Harper thought the party should make only so much
room for the tenets of social conservatism – explicit appeals to
evangelical Christianity as a basis for political policy, anti-
abortion tub-thumping, suspicion of homosexuals, immigrants,

French Quebeckers, and what have you. Of course there would be plenty of room for social conservatives, and where you draw the line wasn't obvious either then or now. (There's plenty of room for social conservatives in the Liberal Party too: that's why people like Tom Wappel and Paul Szabo and Dan McTeague feel comfortable there.) But too much emphasis on those policies would "alienate" the core audience Harper wanted to attract.

The second interesting thing is Harper's insight into the nature of that core audience. Flanagan, paraphrasing Harper, says it would be stitched together from "those parts of the urban middle class, urban working class, and rural population that can agree on an agenda of market economics and traditional values." Compared to traditional conservatism, this version would be substantially down-market.

"The older model of a conservative party based largely on the middle and upper classes is no longer viable," Flanagan writes, "because so much of the urban middle class (for example, teachers, nurses, social workers, public-sector administrators) is now part of the 'new class,' or 'knowledge class,' as it is sometimes called, and is thus a political class dependent on tax-supported government programs. Political coalitions now divide less along class lines than on the question of public-sector dependence."

As we'll see, Harper would later execute a hairpin turn in the *manner* of his political action, from critiquing other actors to becoming, himself, an important actor. But to a great extent the *ends* of his political action are already visible here: to build a broad coalition aimed not at swells, fat cats, and less-affluent voters who nonetheless depend on assorted grants and subsidies, but at a lunch-bucket crowd of cabbies, skilled tradesmen, young families, and modest entrepreneurs.

For Harper, for the longest time, the big problem was that nobody could get this formula right. That certainly included Manning. In 1992, the Reform leader started to rely heavily on the strategic advice of Rick Anderson, who worked in Ottawa for the sprawling Hill and Knowlton consulting firm. Anderson was a Liberal from way back. As the referendum on the Charlottetown accord approached, it became clear that Anderson wanted Charlottetown passed, a position he had in common with the Chrétien Liberals, the Mulroney Conservatives, the NDP, the editorial boards of just about every newspaper you could name – in fact, almost every card-carrying member of the Canadian elite. But not Stephen Harper and Tom Flanagan.

In the end, with a reluctance that infuriated Harper, Manning opposed Charlottetown and campaigned against it. When it failed to win ratification, he wound up looking pretty smart. But Harper had had enough. Manning's torrid affair with a Liberal in a fancy suit smacked too much of compromise. Harper stopped working on Reform's national campaign and concentrated on winning his own Calgary West seat in the 1993 election. To Manning it was just so much sour grapes: "Stephen had difficulty accepting that there might be a few other people (not many, but a few) who were as smart as he was with respect to policy and strategy."

Still, Harper ran and he won. He joined the great herd of Reform MPs who stormed Ottawa in 1993. But even while he was one of the most valuable players in Manning's rookie caucus, Harper kept up his periodic sniping at Manning's style. In 1994, Reform's executive council handed Harper a public reprimand for his own public criticism of Manning's expense accounts. A year later Harper wrote a long opinion article for the *Globe and Mail* that amounted to a slightly more genteel public version of the critique he had delivered privately to Manning in 1989.

Reform's constitution called for it to dissolve if it couldn't win power by 2000. Manning's method for getting there was riding a series of populist protests against Meech Lake or the GST or the gun registry. "The impression is that the party wants either to form a majority government right away or to pack up and go back to the farm," Harper wrote. What should it do instead? "Accept itself as the principal force of the democratic right in Canadian politics, like the Conservatives in Great Britain, the Republicans in the United States, or the Christian Democrats in Germany." For Harper this actually wasn't as big a change as it might sound: it required "adaptation in organization more than in policy. It means doing what modern national conservative parties do. It means constructing a coherent coalition in a pluralistic democracy."

Harper's article didn't mention Manning by name, but what he was arguing was that Manning was too caught up in the idea that Reform was unique and special. Harper wanted the party to be generic and effective. To "do what modern national conservative parties do." To advance an agenda by, at least every once in a while, *winning*.

Or, on the other hand, not. In October of 1996, seventeen months after he wrote that *Globe* article, Harper announced he wouldn't run for Reform in the next election. "He was fundamentally upset about a party that he didn't think could pursue a conservative road as long as Preston was in charge," a friend of Harper's says today. Principle wasn't all that was driving him. Politicians are more likely to leave Parliament if they have a new family or a job offer; Harper had both. His wife, Laureen Teskey, had given birth to a son in April. And Harper was offered the presidency of the National Citizens' Coalition. For once he could be the boss. Not the boss of much – only a few full-time employees – but still.

At least nobody would publicly reprimand him if he said what he thought. He wasted no time getting things off his chest. In his last days in Parliament, he wrote, with Tom Flanagan, one of the most important and revealing articles of his career. Once again it was an analysis of what had gone wrong. Setting it right would come later.

The article ran under the title "Our Benign Dictatorship" in *The Next City*, an ambitious magazine of modern conservative thought and analysis, since defunct. (In Canada, publications that champion the market are often its early victims.) The dictatorship in question, of course, was the near-continuous reign of the Liberals at the federal level. Not one-party rule, but "a one-party-plus system beset by the factionalism, regionalism, and cronyism that accompany any such system." Sure, John Diefenbaker broke through in 1958 and Brian Mulroney in 1984, but Diefenbaker's "chaotic, populist management style" ruined his chances and Mulroney's coalition collapsed into Reform and the Bloc Québécois. How could the problem of Liberal dominance be fixed? The article is one long shrug. Harper and Flanagan doubted it could, because fixing it would require that the Liberals consent to give up the advantages that kept getting them elected.

The *Next City* article was reprinted widely in newspapers. It earned Harper and Flanagan a lot of criticism. Conservatives thought it was defeatist and whiny. Liberals, and others, thought it was pretty hilarious that two guys in the Alberta of Peter Lougheed and Don Getty and Ralph Klein were complaining about one-party rule anywhere, including Ottawa.

Harper wasn't close to forty yet and already he was turning into a bit of a pill. But that was about to change.

⇧

In the spring of 1998, Daniel Johnson, dignified and dedicated and thuddingly boring, resigned as leader of Quebec's provincial Liberal Party. Desperate to stop Lucien Bouchard's PQ government, Quebec's moneyed federalist elite more or less dragged Jean Charest from his position as federal Progressive Conservative leader to replace Johnson. Charest really didn't want to go; he left fingernail marks along Highway 417 halfway to Montreal.

Back in Ottawa the PC caucus, one-third the size of Reform's, was leaderless. Manning had already been looking for a way to broaden Reform's appeal. Now he launched a "United Alternative" to bring Reformers and other like-minded Canadians into a bigger, broader coalition. In concrete terms this meant an endless succession of meetings. But few Progressive Conservatives paid Manning much heed. Most could still delude themselves that Reform, or whatever it became, would soon shrivel up and blow away. Tory candidates to replace Charest who showed any interest in co-operating with Reform – Brian Pallister, a Manitoba provincial cabinet minister, and Michael Fortier, an unshaven Montreal corporate lawyer – got nowhere. The job went to Joe Clark.

In 1976, Clark had become PC leader because he happened to be standing around after the Tories had eliminated everybody they didn't like. In 1979, he became prime minister in the same way. It took him less than a year to demonstrate to an astonished nation that it was actually possible for a man to be more annoying than Pierre Trudeau. Now, and for as long as

Clark remained its leader, the PC Party would resolutely stand around, waiting for Canadians to decide that theirs was the least objectionable party on offer. What it sure as hell would not do would be to play footsie with Preston Manning and his reckless lot.

But amid all the excitement, something interesting happened. It didn't get much notice at the time. A few Ontario Tories knocked on Harper's door and asked whether he would run to replace Charest. Perhaps, they figured, this most urbane Reformer could haul the two parties together. Harper heard them out and turned them down. In turning them down he delivered a speech – to the Mortgage Loans Association of Alberta, because sometimes you just have to say your piece to whoever will give you a podium.

Typically, Harper's 1998 speech explained in detail how conservatives were getting it wrong. Quite atypically, it began to explore how they could get it right.

Harper lauded Manning for trying to broaden the tent. "However, with all due respect, it seems to me that the United Alternative effort is seriously flawed." Launched by Manning and pursued with the full institutional weight of the now-decade-old Reform Party, the process looked like a takeover of the Tories. What was needed instead was a negotiated merger of equals. Both sides had to want it. And each side had to begin by acknowledging its needs and the other side's qualities. And then Stephen Harper, champeen pointer-outer of everyone else's flaws and weaknesses, started practising what he preached.

It was all very good for Reform to be principled, said the vigilant guardian of Reform's principles. "However, I have also concluded that a strong sense of political principle is not sufficient to govern people. And this is where I turn to the strengths of the Progressive Conservative Party."

He explicitly was not merely coveting the seats the Tories held in regions where Reform was weak. He was applauding *cultural* strengths. "Governing requires a conservative tempera- ment. This temperament includes a respect for tradition, a pen- chant for incremental change, and a strong sense of honourable compromise." Those were Tory strengths, not Reform's.

Even some of the weaknesses of a reborn conservative coali- tion could be translated into an asset – and here, if Harper sounded like a bit of a loopy optimist, at least that had the virtue of novelty coming from such a dogged sourpuss. "First, the divisions into which conservatives have fallen for much of this century mirror the fundamental constitutional divisions of the country." Canadian conservatism had a Tory strain in the east, a populist strain in the west, and an autonomist strain in Quebec. The Liberals might know how to exploit those divi- sions, but it was Conservatives who had overcome them to build the Confederation bargain.

Then there was Jean Charest himself, "an unconditional Canadian." If he could get himself elected in Quebec City, it might "bring a level of comfort and trust to discussions between the different parts of the country."

And to think that some people in Harper's audience had expected a talk about mortgage loans. You can draw a straight line from that speech forward half a decade. A formal two- party merger designed to avoid the appearance of a takeover. A party that would display Tory caution while advancing principles Reformers held dear. A party that would work with Jean Charest to recast the relationship between Ottawa and Quebec, and reach out to three distinct traditions as it sought to govern the whole country. This wasn't sniping from the sidelines. This was a project.

What brought it on? In the speech itself, Harper said he started thinking along these lines just after his son, Benjamin, was born in 1996. He took a few weeks off to enjoy fatherhood. He had written a newspaper article in his grand prosecutorial style, arguing that Reform was getting ready to roll right over the Progressive Conservatives. But as he relaxed at home with baby Ben, enjoying his "detachment from partisan politics," Harper decided he didn't believe his own argument. He decided not to publish his triumphalist article. And he started thinking about how to reconcile with fellow conservatives instead of beating them.

But the speech to the mortgage-loans group was more foreshadowing than action. Harper wasn't yet ready to act. Manning was still in charge and was bound to be seen as a takeover artist, not as one party to a genuine merger. So, Harper told his audience, "a credible challenge to the Liberals is a long way off, and certainly will not occur in the next election."

⇧

Staying on the sidelines, Harper skipped the United Alternative conferences Manning organized in 1999. His friend Weissenberger went instead to take notes, without stirring up the fuss that Harper's presence might have caused. "I think he would have been interested to go and see what was going on, but he had no desire to give any indication that he was in the wings at all," Weissenberger says. And when the United Alternative turned into a lopsided, Reform-heavy Canadian Alliance, leavened with the addition of a few hopeful provincial Tories from Ontario and elsewhere, Harper sat it out. A few reporters wondered whether he would run for the leadership of the new party; he told them this was Manning's party and Manning would be making sure he became its first leader. He was genuinely surprised when Stockwell Day won.

Then just about everyone was surprised when Day turned out to be such a train wreck. Chrétien ran rings around him in the 2000 election. Harper had predicted that the new party, badly built, couldn't win. And yet when it didn't, he was unaccountably furious. He wrote an article for the *National Post* that was shocking in its bitter, sustained anger.

"The latest dribblings from the mouth of Canada's Prime Minister," Harper began, "suggest Alberta's wealth can be attributed to the federal government." There was an "implied threat" here: "If Ottawa giveth, then Ottawa can taketh away."

This was "just one more reason" why Westerners, especially Albertans, "should decide that it is time to seek a new relationship with Canada." What brought this on? The "rejection" of the Reform movement "by the very electorate that, in creating the Canadian Alliance, it had twisted itself into a pretzel to please."

The Alliance was brought down, not by its own weak campaigning, but "by a shrewd and sinister Liberal attack plan . . . to pull up every prejudice about the West and every myth about Alberta that could be dredged." Since that pitch had worked, it must enjoy "an enormous market" outside Alberta. Which meant Alberta and the rest of Canada were just irreconcilably different places.

"Having hit a wall, the next logical step is not to bang our heads against it," Harper wrote. "It is to take the bricks and begin building another home – a stronger and much more autonomous Alberta." How autonomous? "It is time to look at Quebec and learn." *That* autonomous? Actually, no: "We should not mimic Quebec by lunging from rejection into the arms of an argument about separation." Well, that's a relief. Unless it wasn't: "Separation will become a real issue the day the federal government decides to make it one."

Harper's article was wildly overheated and at times barely coherent. But it was more than just a rant. It was the penultimate expression of his belief that if people who thought like him couldn't win, the system must be stacked, dammit, and therefore illegitimate. The ultimate expression of that philosophy would come a month later with the "firewall letter," addressed to Alberta premier Ralph Klein and signed by Harper and five other prominent Alberta conservatives, including Flanagan and Ken Boessenkool, a brilliant young former advisor to Stockwell Day. Its real title was "The Alberta Agenda." Its logic flowed directly from Harper's post-election rant in the *National Post*, and proposed a more autonomous Alberta.

"We believe the time has come for Albertans to take greater charge of our own future," Harper and the others wrote. "This means resuming control of the powers that we possess under the Constitution of Canada but that we have allowed the federal government to exercise." In concrete terms, Alberta should withdraw from the Canada Pension Plan and the Canada Health Act; replace the RCMP in Alberta with an Alberta provincial police force; and collect personal income tax instead of letting Ottawa collect it. "It is imperative to take the initiative, to build firewalls around Alberta, to limit the extent to which an aggressive and hostile federal government can encroach upon legitimate provincial jurisdiction," they wrote.

So by the beginning of 2001, Harper had broken with Preston Manning, left Reform, given up on the United Alternative, and all but started building bomb shelters in the basement to prepare against the infamous Liberal attack on everything Alberta held dear. He had moved just about as far from an active and constructive role in federal politics as it was possible for a thoughtful, engaged citizen to get. The only thing that could jolt him out of this defensive crouch was an existential threat to the political movement he had spent his adult life trying to help build. Obligingly, the existential threat showed up just in time.

⇧

It turned out that losing an election didn't begin to exhaust Stockwell Day's capacity for trouble, disappointment, and chaos. From early 2001 on, barely a week went by without devastating news for the Alliance leader. The biggest was the Goddard affair. Before leaving Alberta politics, Day had written a letter to the *Red Deer Advocate* tearing a strip off a local lawyer and school board trustee, Lorne Goddard, for defending a man charged with possessing child pornography. Day wrote that Goddard "must also believe it is fine for a teacher to possess child porn." Goddard sued for libel. Day stoutly defended the case – on the Alberta taxpayer's dime. He refused to settle until the Alberta government threatened to stick him with the bill, which ran to $792,064.40. Then Day mortgaged his house so he could pay $60,000 of the mammoth bill. It was for moments like this that columnists kept the phrase "too little, too late" handy.

There was more. Two Alliance MPs, Darrel Stinson and Myron Thompson, hired a private investigator to dig up dirt on the Liberals. Day said he'd met the man, then said he hadn't. A Vancouver radio station aired an "interview" with Rahim Jaffer, a young Alliance MP, that turned out to be an interview with a member of Jaffer's office staff pretending to be the boss. On and on it went. Between the blunders, recriminations, mad schemes, implausible denials, catastrophic news conferences, and all the rest, it became pretty clear that Day wasn't the guy to run this party. MPs started bailing out en masse.

Harper's first instinct was to try to help Day. In April 2001, Day and his wife went to the house of Ted Morton, a University of Calgary political scientist who had signed the firewall letter. Most of the signatories were there, including Harper. So was Weissenberger. "We realized there was a very bad problem. How could we help?" Weissenberger recalls. "We didn't realize we were at the edge of a precipice and it just kept getting worse."

By July, Day had been forced to promise a new leadership race to stop the caucus rebellion. The group around Harper was terrified that Day would win the leadership again and the Alliance's collapse would continue. Most of the MPs would join Joe Clark's Progressive Conservatives. The rest would just go home. There would be nothing to show for a decade's work.

By August, Harper was confiding to his friends that he was ready to run for the Alliance leadership. "It really was a rescue operation," a friend recalls. "He wasn't saying, 'I'm going to become prime minister on this horse.'" On September 8, Harper went to the policy meeting near the Vancouver airport to tip his hand. On December 2, he launched his campaign formally.

On March 20, 2002, a tiny group of Canadian Alliance members gathered in Calgary to hear the results of the party's one-member, one-vote leadership election. Harper won easily, with 55 per cent of the vote. Day was well behind. The two other candidates, Diane Ablonczy and Grant Hill, had argued for co-operation with the Tories. But they couldn't even stop fighting with each other. They mustered less than 10 per cent of the vote between them.

Stephen Harper had indulged the luxury of critique and withdrawal for most of his adult life. But in the crunch, when he could no longer afford that luxury, he had chosen to act. What he would do now with this moribund party, and whether anyone would notice, was anyone's guess. He was nobody's idea of a charismatic leader.

After the results were in, Harper's supporters and a few journalists gathered at the James Joyce Pub on 8th Avenue for a few celebratory pints. I nursed a beer in a corner of the room, people-watching. I bumped into somebody and turned distractedly to apologize. It was Stephen Harper. I had been standing next to him for ten minutes. I hadn't noticed he was there.

2

COUP DE GRACELESS

⇧

I've always felt a little guilty about making that lady scream on the airplane. But it wasn't me, really; it was the times. Our tale begins on Friday afternoon, May 31, 2002. In another airport strip hotel, oddly enough. This one was the fabled Regal Constellation, a sullen, chalk-white behemoth down the road from Toronto's Pearson International Airport. Airport hotels are like catnip for political parties because they're roomy, cheap, and easy to get to if everyone's converging from out of town. So the Progressive Conservatives had had their share of meetings at the Regal Constellation, and the Canadian Alliance, and Paul Martin's leadership-campaign-in-denial. Over the years, more politics got done in that hotel's suites than in half the committee rooms on Parliament Hill. Also sometimes not politics, if you take my meaning. The Regal Constellation eventually closed, and when it did I thought the doorman should be asked to lie in state for a few days in the Centre Block rotunda.

Anyway. This meeting of Ontario's provincial Liberal wing had drawn more reporters from Ottawa than usual. Very few of us were actually interested in the weekend's agenda of business, or even in the scheduled Friday-evening showstopper, a speech by Jean Chrétien. Instead the buzz was about a competing event halfway across the Greater Toronto Area, in a union hall where Paul Martin was to address a fundraiser for a provincial Liberal candidate, Nellie Pedro.

Prime minister in one hall. Finance minister – and eternal partner/dauphin/rival – in another. Simultaneous speeches: it would have been delicious enough in an ordinary week, but this week was already way past ordinary. On Thursday, in Ottawa, Chrétien had stormed into a meeting of his cabinet and announced that he was going to govern for the rest of his four-year mandate, rather than stepping down anytime soon. Leadership campaigns were distracting attention from the government's business, he said. All aspirants to the crown must down tools or get out of cabinet.

During the meeting Chrétien's chief of staff, Percy Downe, was called out of the cabinet room. "I got a note sent to me by the press office saying the media were calling, that Mr. Martin was speaking the same evening as the prime minister in Toronto," Downe recalls. "And had I approved this? What did I know about it?

"So I called my office and I said, 'Send over the correspondence between Martin's office and myself.' And they had listed all the things they wanted to do [on Martin's scheduled three-day Ontario trip]. I have a copy of that letter somewhere in my file. But there was no mention of that speaking engagement. So I went out and called Murphy" – Tim Murphy, Martin's executive assistant, the senior staffer in the minister's political office – "and said, 'Is your boss speaking the same night as Mr. Chrétien in Toronto?' And he said he didn't know."

Percy Downe is a quietly amiable Prince Edward Islander with whom one would not normally fear a confrontation. "I always try never to lose my temper," he says now. But even as he says it, his voice takes on a tone of quite surprising menace. "But I got *extremely annoyed*. And I said, 'You're the EA to the minister and you don't know what he's doing?' Like, I didn't fall off the turnip truck yesterday. I have the letter in front of me."

Susan Delacourt's indispensable chronicle of the Chrétien– Martin wars, *Juggernaut: Paul Martin's Campaign for Chrétien's Crown*, tells what happened next better than I could. Rereading her account now, I'm struck by what once seemed a trivial detail. It's this: shaken and upset by Chrétien's demand that all leadership campaigns must end – and, later, that Martin cancel his Friday fundraising tub-thumper and amend a more serious speech on urban policy the next day – Martin and his entourage cast about for clues of what to do next.

What stimulus could inform the wisdom of the Martin men as their champion reached the fateful crossroads? The lessons of history? The counsel of a wise elder advisor? An inspired passage from someone's dog-eared copy of Rousseau's *Émile*? Uh, no. As Delacourt puts it: "The news coverage that night would settle the question."

So the gang gathered at the apartment of David Herle, one of Martin's most trusted strategists, to watch the evening's CTV news. And there was Craig Oliver, peering in the approximate direction of the camera to tell a worried nation: "Mr. Martin now has to make a difficult decision . . . whether to take his future and his ambitions into his own hands and do something decisive, which might include having to quit and fight

Chrétien from the outside in the way John Turner did to Trudeau and then Chrétien, by the way, did to John Turner."

Well then. The man on the TV wanted a decision. Who were they to let him down? By Friday afternoon, reporters arriving at the Regal Constellation were hearing from Martin's camp that the finance minister would have something big to say at the union hall. I hurried to catch a cab. On the way out of the hotel, I passed a line of Ontario Liberal MPs waiting to file onto the stage of their party function. The last of them was a Quebecker.

Jean Chrétien smiled. "Bonjour, Paul."

"Prime Minister, I can't stay for your speech," I said. "Paul Martin is giving a speech somewhere else at the same time."

Chrétien's smile tightened but didn't quite disappear. He looked away, into the middle distance, and in my memory he doesn't look defiant or angry, just a little sad. "I know."

At the union hall we gathered in the basement while Martin addressed the fundraiser upstairs and then huddled endlessly with his advisors. Martin helpers swarmed all over the venue. Brian Guest, his communications director. Melanie Gruer, his press secretary. Tim Murphy, his chief of staff, who apparently had managed to nail down the boss's whereabouts since his Thursday chat with Percy Downe. Mike Klander, a campaign organizer who'd jumped ship only a few months ago from Brian Tobin's abortive leadership campaign. Tony Dionisio, ditto. Pretty fancy crowd for a speech that hadn't been on the minister's official agenda eighteen hours earlier. Finally the sea of advisors parted, and Martin made his way to a makeshift podium.

Chrétien once said it was "fine for people to organize for the leadership," Martin told us. "In fact, he even encouraged *some* candidates" – a tilt of the head, a meaningful pause – "to present their candidature." Now Chrétien had pulled that rug from under everyone's feet. "That's his prerogative. I just really don't know how this is going to work. I don't know what it means."

When you and I don't know what something means at work, do we call the boss and ask? Do we send an email? Do we have our secretary call the boss's secretary and ask? By God, we don't! When you and I are confused by something the boss says at work and we really don't know how it's going to work and we are *earnest about wanting to find out*, we hold a news conference, live on all-news TV, from the basement of a union hall. Just as Paul Martin was doing now. "Let me just say that I'm obviously going to have to reflect on my options."

What, just because Chrétien had given him a wedgie? Nothing so petty. "There's something far more important at issue here. That's the government and the country . . . I have to reflect, given the events of the last couple of days, on my capacity as a member of cabinet, as a member of the government, to have an impact on those decisions."

Let's see. Chrétien had demanded that ministers stick to the business of ministers, and this made Martin wonder whether he could do his job as a minister. There is said to be a planet orbiting Sirius where that kind of logic makes sense. At least he was saying it was time for a decision, just as Craig Oliver had demanded. (Not that he was actually *making* a decision. In the end, as usual, that would be Chrétien's job.)

Now came the time for questions. Inevitably, the local broadcast reporters, with their gleaming on-air voices, were first and loudest with the least useful questions. "Does this mean you're thinking of resigning from cabinet?" one asked. Yessiree, Einstein. That's *precisely* what it means. That's what he just *said* with his *mouth*, so you already have a freaking *clip*, and we're wasting everyone's *time*, and he's *going to get away* . . .

After stammering something unhelpful, Martin spun on his heels and made a break for the exit. "Have you discussed this with the prime minister?" I shouted at his rapidly receding butt. But there would be no answer tonight from any part of the Martin anatomy.

Well.

Susan Delacourt and I hitched a ride back to the Regal Constellation with Tony Ianno, the local Liberal MP, who was playing hooky from the Chrétien event in the manner of a guy who has figured out on which side his bread will henceforth be buttered. At the Regal Constellation David Smith, the fireplug-shaped Toronto lawyer who was one of Jean Chrétien's closest advisors, was already huddling gravely in the lobby café with Richard Mahoney, a lawyer at Smith's firm and one of Martin's closest advisors. Upstairs, in a dozen suites, a dozen youngish Liberals had filled the bathtubs with ice and beer, and a dozen Liberal suite parties were rocketing into high gear. Two years earlier at the Liberals' biennial national convention in Ottawa, Liberals of all stripes had been made to chant, some through clenched teeth, a hymn in homage to Chrétien's invincibility: "Four more years! Four more years!" Now the slogan had been transformed into the war cry of a conquering army, and it rattled the walls of the Regal Constellation long past midnight: "No more years! No more years!"

The next night most of the reporters and MPs at the LPCO conference flew back to Ottawa for the Press Gallery Dinner, an annual display of forced bonhomie and creepy hack-and-flack insiderism. I stayed on the airport strip for another night of suite parties. More tubs of beer, more young Liberal war cries. No more years, no more years, nah-nah-nah-nah, hey-ey-ey, goodbye. Early Sunday afternoon I flew back to Ottawa.

As soon as the little Air Canada commuter jet landed in the capital, and everyone else on the plane was standing up to get their bags out of the overhead bins, I called my employers at the *National Post* for an update. My editor, Alison Uncles, said there would be a cabinet shuffle at Rideau Hall in twenty minutes. John Manley was the new finance minister.

I didn't realize I was repeating most of what Alison said out loud. "Cabinet shuffle. John Manley at Finance. Any other changes? OK." When I hung up every passenger on board was looking at me. Somehow it seemed appropriate to brief them. "Yeah," I said, "the prime minister just fired Paul Martin from cabinet."

That's when the lady standing in the aisle screamed.

Well, it wasn't a *scream*, precisely. More of an astonished, shuddering half-sigh, half-wail: "Ah-wo-wo-woaahh." The kind of sound she might make if she had, say, turned around to discover that an eighteen-wheel tractor-trailer were somehow barrelling down the aisle of that particular Air Canada Jazz flight toward her.

So if you're out there, lady, I'm sorry about that. But it was the times, wasn't it? On Sunday, June 2, 2002, it was possible to believe – no, it was an *automatic reaction* – that the departure of the Minister of Finance from his seat at the cabinet table was such a threat to the nation's proper governance that it constituted immediate personal peril to anyone learning the news. We would all learn soon enough that it wasn't that big a deal. The biggest challenge, after normalcy returns, is remembering how weird things got when they got weird.

⇧

That *frisson* of terror that many felt when they heard that Paul Martin was no longer guarding the nation's chequebook did not mark the summit of his career, but it meant the summit was in sight. From fearing that Martin was indispensable, it was a short step for his party, and much of the country, to decide that Chrétien wasn't. On the day he lost his cabinet job, the dauphin was already only a short climb away from the job he had wanted for decades.

In fact, if there is a constant in this fickle and flighty nation, it is the political ambition of guys named Paul Martin. There had been a Paul Martin running for the job of prime minister since before the dawn of medicare or of the Parti Québécois – indeed, since before Newfoundland joined Confederation.

Paul Martin Sr. was an old-school Ontario constituency MP and social reformer, born to francophone parents in 1903. Over the course of his forty-year career in politics, the elder Martin became a candidate for the leadership of the Liberal Party of Canada every time the job came open. It happened first in 1948, when William Lyon Mackenzie King finally gave up his seemingly endless reign as Liberal leader. But Martin had no chance to mount a serious candidacy. There were few things in Liberal Ottawa that King didn't control, including the elevation of his successor, the courtly Quebec City lawyer Louis St. Laurent.

But even knowing that the fix was in, Martin couldn't bring himself to simply let another man walk into the job. In *Maclean's* in 1948, Blair Fraser described a bizarre scene at the Ottawa convention that served as St. Laurent's coronation. A "draft Paul Martin" movement, whose spontaneity was open to debate, had sprung up across Ottawa while the convention was going on. Probably the little adventure could have been better executed. Hundreds of boisterous Martin supporters followed a bagpiper into the hall – and barged right into King's farewell speech. Martin insisted he'd done nothing to encourage the rebels. Fine, Fraser wrote, but Martin's colleagues thought he hadn't done enough to discourage them either. "They think he stood too long under the mistletoe, for a girl who was supposed to be engaged."

By 1958, the father had hit his prime. He'd been health minister, with a decade's reforms under his belt. He was as road-tested and wily a man as any the Liberals had. But three months before the Liberals were to choose St. Laurent's successor, Lester B. Pearson won the Nobel Peace Prize for helping to defuse the Suez crisis. There would be no arguing with the Swedish judges. Martin's time had gone again.

He served Pearson well until, another decade later, the top job came open once again. This time Trudeaumania put paid to the Martin family ambitions. The elder Martin accepted a Senate seat and abandoned his dream. It hurt. Getting his walking papers from a parvenu like Trudeau hurt worse. "I've been fighting for the Liberal Party for forty years," he told a friend later, "and the other day a man who only three years ago was fighting for the NDP, against the Liberal Party, sat across the table from me and told me I couldn't handle Canada's external affairs."

Yet before too many years had gone by, a second Paul Martin developed enough ambition to match and exceed the first's. In 1977, the father wrote in his diary about a chat with his son Paul, who had made a pretty good go of things in business in Montreal. Now he wanted to run for Parliament. "He has the bug, I'm afraid," the father wrote.

In 1979, the subject arose again. "Last night he said, 'Dad, I want to have a talk with you soon. Now is the time to get my feet wet,'" Martin Sr. wrote. "He even went further and said,

'Now is the time for me to begin to become a candidate for the prime ministership.' Shades of the father!"

Paul Martin Jr. never hesitated to name his father as his greatest influence in politics. But it would be too simple to say the son imitated the father. Like a very different political heir, George W. Bush, Paul Martin Jr. sought to learn from his father's mistakes as well as his successes.

Paul Martin Sr. had failed to get the caucus on his side. Paul Martin Jr. wouldn't. The same would go for the father's failure to build a serious political organization. "My dad did not prepare for the leadership," Martin told reporter Graham Fraser in 2002. "He did fundraisers, he spoke to people, but he did not put in place a political organization. Paul Hellyer had a political organization that was immensely superior to anybody's. And my dad was the most popular politician in Canada. But he had no organization at all. Paul Hellyer did."

One more difference. Christina McCall once wrote that naked ambition had helped sink the father in 1958. "He *wanted* power, curious creature, and he let people see this base desire." Lesson learned. The son would do his best to hide the desire that drove him. In fact, he would wipe any memory of that desire from his head.

In 1983, the memory wipe hadn't taken place. In that year he told the *Toronto Star* that he and his father were regularly arguing about his ambition. "When I tell him the time has come, I'm going for it, he throws up his hands in horror," Martin Jr. said then. But by 2002 he was insisting to the same paper that he had not considered entering politics before 1988, the year he captured Montreal's LaSalle-Émard riding. It takes real effort to deny the published record. Not for the last time, Martin was up to the task.

The life in politics, once it finally got underway, went pretty damned well, actually. There was a first run for the leadership, which probably went about as well as it was going to go. Jean Chrétien had a quarter-century head start. So the outcome of the 1990 leadership race was never in doubt. But Chrétien held Martin close afterward, letting him co-write the 1993 election platform and making him finance minister – over Martin's initial objections – when the Liberals won. You wouldn't have wanted Finance either; the country was in hock up to its elbows. Pundits lined up to pat the shovel on Martin's face before he'd even begun. "Be ready for disappointment on Budget Night," David Frum wrote in a 1995 *Saturday Night* cover profile of Martin, "and darkening economic vistas beyond it."

Yeah, whoops, that one kind of missed the mark. Martin – or Chrétien and Martin; they'll be arguing over that one until the last dog dies – reversed twenty years of escalating fiscal disaster without really even breaking a sweat. The Liberals benefited from constant pressure from Reform deficit hawks in the opposition benches, and from a hemispheric economic expansion that actually made it possible to clean up public finances in the United States, in France (briefly!), and elsewhere. In Canada, a generation of finance ministers, far from seeing their careers flame out, became shoo-ins for leadership posts: Jim Dinning and Stockwell Day in Alberta, Ernie Eves in Ontario, Bernard Landry in Quebec. Paul Martin in Ottawa. The lot of them (except Dinning, if he manages to duck the jinx) would learn that running a budget cycle was a walk in the park compared to running a party. But that part comes later.

While he was building his reputation as deficit-slayer, Martin became the most doggedly likeable man in Canadian politics. Chrétien's MPs liked to complain, cheerfully at first and then with increasing dismay, about the "wall of words" the boss would toss up whenever somebody tried to broach a serious topic with him. A chat with Chrétien was Chrétien's word, Chrétien's way, Chrétien's stale anecdotes about Joey Smallwood or Pierre Mendès-France or, more often than not, Jean Chrétien.

But *Martin* – well, any conversation with anybody Paul Martin met was about *that person*, in all his or her rich and fascinating human complexity. Not about Paul Martin. Paul Martin made sure of it. Say you were Mark Eyking, the Nova Scotia farmer turned Liberal MP. Martin would want to hear how your livestock were taking to their feed this season. Or maybe you were John Godfrey and you were writing a book on early childhood development. You'd mail a chapter to half the cabinet. But the hell of it was, only Martin would call back to talk about it. So you sent him a second chapter. He'd call back – on Christmas Eve! – to talk about that one too.

Even if you were Jim Abbott, the towering Canadian Alliance MP, Paul Martin would come vaulting across an airport departure lounge every once in a while, shouting, "Jim! How's your family? How are those seven grandchildren?" He never forgot there were seven of them. He might not be entirely clear on the size of the budget surplus but by God, he was not going to forget that Jim Abbott had seven grandchildren.

Pretty soon a minister who slays fiscal dragons *and* never forgets a birthday starts to go from looking good to looking like an heir apparent, to looking indispensable, to looking like the guy who has to get in there right away, even if it means turfing the incumbent. It was somewhere near the beginning of that decade-long transformation that I applied to work for Paul Martin.

It seemed to make sense at the time. By early 1996, support for Quebec sovereignty had gusted way past the 49.4 per cent the option had won in the referendum of October 30, 1995. In some polls the same question was commanding a 55 per cent majority. Chrétien seemed so rattled by the emergency that Preston Manning publicly petitioned the Governor General to fire the prime minister. (In his autobiography Manning admits he felt sheepish about the stunt later.) The country seemed headed for more danger, not less. As a reporter for the Montreal *Gazette*, I had a front-row seat to all of this. But I wasn't sure I could stand being a mere spectator. In 1994, Jean-François Lisée, one of Quebec's best reporters, had abandoned that career to become an advisor to Jacques Parizeau. I was no Lisée, but to me there seemed something noble in his gesture. For all you knew, you might have only one shot to win a country. Or to save the one you had.

⇧

Paul Martin was the most prominent and powerful federal minister from Quebec. In the national confrontation that seemed inevitable, it was impossible to believe he wouldn't be front and centre. When one of his advisors, Michèle Cadario, left the minister's office to work for a few years in the private sector, I told Martin's press secretary, Nathalie Gauthier, I'd be willing to work for him if anyone thought I might be useful on the Quebec file. Martin's executive assistant, Terrie O'Leary, called and arranged lunch. Then she cancelled. We rescheduled and she cancelled again. I sensed a pattern. I let the whole idea go. I never heard about it from Martin's entourage again.

No big deal: by the end of 1997 I was a columnist for *The Gazette*, and a year later for the shiny new *National Post*. Meanwhile Justice Minister Allan Rock and the owlish rookie Intergovernmental Affairs Minister Stéphane Dion had begun applying a judicial and rhetorical sledgehammer to the separatists' more facile assumptions. The country would survive without my help, and my career without Paul Martin's. I dredge this all up for one reason. Later, when I was almost alone in the Press Gallery in predicting that a Paul Martin government would be a shambles, I would catch wind of rumours to the effect that there was an element of sour grapes in my analysis. It's only fair to explain why that might be so. But I don't believe it is so. I didn't turn into a Martin skeptic in 1996, or 1997 or 1998. It was the last half of 1999 before the finance minister's behaviour became so disingenuous and shaky that I finally had to bail out of the Ottawa consensus that he was a great leader made to wait too long.

First, in an interview with Southam News and then again at a Liberal caucus retreat in Halifax, Martin played semantic games with questions about his own political future. More than two years had passed since the 1997 election. Would he run in the next? It wasn't a random question. There were strong rumours that he was so fed up with waiting for Chrétien to resign that he was preparing to quit himself. He responded with boilerplate. "We have a very strong team. And I think we want to keep that team together." Further questions bounced off the minister's rapidly receding butt.

Then he played semantic games with questions about Canada's political future. Dion was preparing to introduce the Clarity Bill, which would forbid Parliament from negotiating secession unless it found that a clear majority had voted for a clear question. The overwhelming consensus of elite opinion held that this was reckless brinksmanship and would play into the separatists' hands. (Not for the first time, the overwhelming consensus of elite opinion was utterly wrong.) In Quebec City, Lucien Bouchard called on reasonable federalists to stop these madmen, Chrétien and Dion. Then he called on Paul Martin to stop Chrétien and Dion. By name, which was interesting. Why would he do that? In Ottawa, why would Dennis Dawson, a Quebec City PR man with close ties to the Martin camp, be shuttling from one Liberal MP's office to the next, explaining to them that Dion's bill was folly?

This made the finance minister a story. But for days on end, any question about whether he supported his government's policy on the crucial question of national unity met with silence from the fleeing minister.

Finally there was the great Regal Constellation meeting of March 2000. Days before a national Liberal policy convention, dozens of Liberal MPs met secretly with Martin's senior advisors at the fabled airport-strip hotel to plot strategy. The message was that this convention wasn't the time to force a confrontation with Chrétien because the Martin loyalists had no mechanism for bringing the old man down. Unfortunately the message wasn't entirely clear. That was partly because, as Susan Delacourt has written, David Herle, the Martin camp's pollster and ranking strategist, showed the MPs a PowerPoint presentation whose theme fell a little short of Rally Round the Flag, Boys.

First Herle told the MPs not to be misled by polls showing the Liberals leading comfortably. The real numbers were far weaker, he said. Then he said Jane Stewart, who was facing a scandal over a nasty audit at Human Resources Development, could chip away at general trust in the Liberal government. Then he showed data suggesting that Paul Martin was beloved by millions. Then he told them not to do anything about all of this at the convention. There was "no advantage in a blow that only wounds." The only advantage could come from that *other* kind of blow, when the time came. Meanwhile? "Position Paul, not just as the heir apparent, but as the preferred option now."

In hindsight, it's striking how cloudy Herle's crystal ball was. His charts and graphs seemed to demonstrate that the Liberals were likely to lose their majority over Jane Stewart's audit scandal. Eight months later Chrétien increased his majority and Stewart increased her plurality in her Brampton, Ontario riding. But that's only in hindsight. What was striking at the time, when news of the Regal Constellation meeting leaked, was that a cabal of Liberal MPs had gathered for the purpose of deciding against striking a blow that would only wound, while they struggled to position their man as the preferred option now. You will be amazed to learn that Chrétien's people sensed infidelity when they heard about all this. Three reporters from different newspapers were promptly summoned to Chrétien's side, where they were told that he would certainly lead the party into the next election.

Which takes us directly to the Mother of All Butt Scrums. On March 16, 2000, after the Regal Constellation confab had received twenty hours of saturation coverage, Martin left a meeting of the National Liberal Women's Commission at the Ottawa Westin Hotel, one of the preliminary rounds before the full biennial party convention. A couple of dozen reporters circled him and asked about the secret meeting. He said it was a meeting to discuss the budget. Then he said he didn't know what the meeting was about. Then he said he didn't know whether he had known the meeting was even happening. Then he fled down three flights of escalators, scribes in hot pursuit.

I went back to the *National Post*'s offices at the Promenade Building on Sparks Street and spent the rest of the afternoon watching video of the minister's catastrophic little show. My column in the next day's paper began: "In theory, a political party that replaces its leader wants to trade up. You're looking for someone who can outperform the fellow who holds the job now." So what to do if you were a Liberal who was sick of Chrétien?

"Judging by yesterday's events, if you're looking for more agility, better preparation, better crisis management, and better communications strategies devised by a more reliable entourage, then you might as well look right past Paul Martin."

⇧

Eppur si muove. And yet, despite ominous early hints of fallibility, Martin moved into Chrétien's office. Despite Chrétien's best efforts to choose his own timing. The explanation for that lies in the aftermath of the 2000 election. And much of the fault cannot be placed anywhere but at Chrétien's own door.

For sheer effectiveness the 2000 election campaign has to be counted as Chrétien's master stroke. Throughout the summer of 2000 many Liberals – and certainly most of the group around Martin – saw in Stockwell Day a fresh, modern young leader who would make short work of Chrétien. But the Liberal leader watched the Alliance rookie across the floor of the Commons for a few weeks and decided Day was overrated. The campaign began in late October; by the time it was over the Liberals had increased their majority and Day's leadership had begun its death spiral. Chrétien liked to say that the best politician is the one who wins. By that cold standard this was excellent politics.

But he hadn't pitched the election as a test of tactics. He had framed it as a referendum: the minimalist government of Day's Alliance against the activist government of Chrétien's Liberals. "There are very important choices to make for the future as we enter an age of large budget surpluses," he said on the campaign's first day. But when the election was won, he didn't deliver anything resembling activist government.

In fact, it was kind of hard to find a pulse. There was no post-election shakeup; Chrétien shuffled his cabinet only enough to plug two holes that had been opened by the defeat of minor Liberal ministers. There was no spring budget. Before the election Chrétien had made Martin lard the fall 2000 economic update with tax cuts to steal the Alliance's thunder. But everyone had insisted the package wasn't a real budget. Now they said it was so much of a real budget that they didn't have to bring one down in the spring.

The Privy Council Office in Ottawa keeps an online archive of news releases from Chrétien's Prime Minister's Office. To read that archive today is to relive one of the most insipid spells of government in recent history. April 2001: "Prime Minister Announces Formation of Task Force on Modernizing Human Resources Management in the Public Service," April 3. "Prime Minister Announces Commission on the Future of Health Care in Canada," April 4. Well, that was Roy Romanow's task force. Not insipid, perhaps, but Romanow went off to work as soon as he was appointed. He didn't make Chrétien any busier or more purposeful. "Prime Minister Announces State Visit of President of Mexico," April 12. "Statement by the Prime Minister (National Volunteer Week)," April 26. And so on.

With no changes to his team or his economic plan, Chrétien sat sullenly in the Commons day after day. The opposition battered him with questions about the so-called Shawinigate affair, the appearance of impropriety in Chrétien's intervention to line up government support for a real-estate developer in his riding. "He was angry," a friend says now. "He'd run a third time to cut off Martin. He'd run early to cut off Day. But he didn't have any plan or direction. He won three majorities. He didn't see why that wasn't enough."

Any hope Chrétien might have had of getting some mojo back into his game in the autumn vanished on the morning of September 11, 2001, with the attacks against New York and Washington. In hindsight, the truly weird bout of national self-flagellation that overcame Canada after 9/11 now looks like a symptom of the general purposelessness that seemed to affect everything Chrétien touched at that time.

He didn't actually do anything wrong, but to many shocked and terrorized Canadians he looked like a spent force. In England, Tony Blair recalled Parliament on September 14. Chrétien waited until September 17. The difference between a Friday and a Monday. Also the difference between Britain and a country forty-one times as large, whose airports had been commandeered to accommodate the emergency landings of hundreds of American jetliners. By September 18, incidentally, Britain's Parliament was dark and empty again, while Canada's continued to sit. But in Canada newspaper columnists lined up to announce that Chrétien's lethargy made them feel ashamed.

As 2001's lethargy gave way to shock and trauma after 9/11, the appeal of a man who spoke a language of national possibility, and who didn't carry around ethical questions like a ball and chain, grew almost by the week. If Martin's job was to look like the preferred option now, then Chrétien was doing much of Martin's work for him. The finance minister's minions quietly firmed up their control over every branch of the Liberal Party's organization. In January 2002, Brian Tobin became the first of Martin's rivals to bow to the inevitable and quit the still-unannounced leadership race.

By now even Chrétien had decided treading water was no longer good enough. Budget deficits were a thing of the past. The steely response to al-Qaeda – border security, Canadian snipers patrolling the hills of Afghanistan – might be necessary, but it didn't leave him feeling much like a Liberal. He wanted to be an activist again.

Twice Chrétien had travelled to meetings of the Progressive Governance Network, a loose affiliation of centre-left heads of government launched by Tony Blair and Bill Clinton. Before both summits, at Stockholm in 2000 and Berlin in early 2002, so-called sherpas – senior bureaucrats from every country – held preparatory meetings before the main events. Canada's sherpa was Alex Himelfarb. Himelfarb was the slouching, chain-smoking deputy minister of Canadian Heritage. Whip-smart, quick to laugh, disinclined to stand on ceremony, he was one of the few senior bureaucrats with an unabashed lefty streak. Chrétien wanted to bolster his liberal credentials with a compact series of activist, progressive accomplishments. He figured he had a little less than two years to get it done. (Nobody around Chrétien expected him to finish his third mandate. Percy Downe had sold his Ottawa house and was spending weekends at home in Charlottetown during what he presumed were the twilight years of the Chrétien era.)

The Clerk of the Privy Council, Mel Cappe, was a stickler for due process and proper channels, precisely the kind of man Chrétien had needed to manage the civil service when he was running a government of routine. But in his conversations with Himelfarb at two heady global confabs of leaders who flattered themselves on their ability to get things done, Chrétien began to imagine the outlines of a legacy agenda. And here was a man who could help him deliver. On April 30,

Chrétien sent Cappe off to become Canada's High Commissioner in London. Alex Himelfarb, whom nobody had seen coming, was the new Clerk. Chrétien was finally ready to swing back into action.

It was too late. A month after he appointed Himelfarb, Chrétien told his ministers to stop campaigning to replace him and get back to work. Two days later Paul Martin was a martyred ex-minister. The Liberal Party apparatus, which Martin's people had infiltrated with a thoroughness even Paul Hellyer could never have imagined, prepared for the unsavoury task of cashiering the party's three-majority leader. The execution date was set for February 2003, at a party convention whose centrepiece would be an obligatory vote on Chrétien's fitness to continue as leader.

Chrétien took a while to realize his party had been stolen from under his nose – or, more galling still, that thousands of Liberals had walked away from him of their own accord. In mid-June, reporters at a garden party at 24 Sussex Drive asked their host whether he could win in a confrontation with Martin. "Of course I'm going to win," Chrétien said, amazed at the question. How did he know? "Because I know the Liberal Party, sir."

Not as well as he thought. There was no way to organize his way out of a party revolt. Before the end of the summer, Chrétien was forced to admit defeat. The party he had led since 1990 would have to soldier on without him as of 2004. It was a longer wait than Martin wanted, but it would do. Paul Martin and his father had been seeking this job for half a century. Now it would be his.

3

HOPELESS PLUS HOPELESS

⇧

The odd thing about Stephen Harper's early days as leader of the Canadian Alliance is this. Here's a guy who campaigned hard against the idea of any merger with Joe Clark's Progressive Conservatives, rolling right over the explicitly pro-merger candidates for the Alliance leadership. In his victory speech, on the night he won, he called the Alliance "a permanent institution that is here to stay." But apparently that was all pretty much for show. Because it turned out that Harper's first order of business was a serious attempt to reach out to Clark's PCs.

He becomes Alliance leader on March 20, 2002. Not quite three weeks later, on April 9, he's sitting down with Clark himself to talk co-operation between the Alliance and Tories. It's a short meeting, a spectacular failure, and actually rather funny – we'll get back to it – but it is not enough to dissuade Harper. Three weeks after the fruitless meeting with Clark,

Harper writes an op-ed article urging Progressive Conservatives to reconsider. And three weeks after *that* he's up in the House of Commons giving his maiden speech as Alliance leader. And what's the speech about? In large measure, it's all about what a swell guy Brian Mulroney was.

Clearly the party Stephen Harper resigned from in 1987 was much on his mind, fifteen years later. But then, the written record shows that it had been for a while.

When he won the Alliance leadership, Harper said he didn't expect the party would keep him around long unless he could get it to a place where it could "contend realistically for power." And a consistent theme of his writings in exile was that Reform-style populist conservatism couldn't realistically contend for power on its own. Which meant that reaching out to Progressive Conservatives, one way or another, would be inevitable. And not only to them.

"Along the Trans-Canada Highway from Calgary to Banff lies a prominent mountain called the Three Sisters," Harper and Tom Flanagan had written in their 1997 *Next City* article. "Legend has it that an Indian chief placed each of his three daughters on a separate peak to keep them away from unworthy suitors. The strategy succeeded so well that the three daughters died up there."

To Harper and Flanagan, Canadian conservatism was also a tale of three sisters: prairie populism; the more urbane Toryism of the Progressive Conservatives; and the *bleu* strain of Quebec nationalism – which, "while not in itself a conservative movement, appeals to the kinds of voters who in other provinces support conservative parties." The mood of Harper and Flanagan being what it was in 1997, they found the prospects for getting conservatism's three sisters down from their assorted mountaintops "bleak at the moment," a Reform–PC merger "out of the question," a *rapprochement* with the Quebec sister even harder to contemplate.

But now Harper was full-time chaperon to one of the sisters. He had to give unity a try. His immediate problem was that the sister he coveted most, Toryism, was guarded day and night by Joe Clark, who viewed Harper as a most unworthy suitor.

"Joe Clark was not warm to the idea of joining the parties," Susan Elliott, who was national director of the Progressive Conservatives when Harper came back to Ottawa, said in an interview. "He did not see them as an inclusive party, whether that was Reform or the Alliance or, frankly, the party today." Preston Manning, Elliott recalls, used to talk about the need for "like-minded Canadians" to join forces. To Clark's ears, this was nefarious code talk. "Joe's view is, the country is not all like-minded and it's not reasonable to say that only like-minded people will have a role," said Elliott.

To guard himself against the curse of like minds, Clark had unfailingly dedicated his own second life in politics, after he replaced Jean Charest as Tory leader in 1998, to wooing unlike minds. The only MP he lured from another party before the 2000 election was Angela Vautour, a New Brunswick New Democrat and an unflagging advocate of robust pogey for the chronically seasonally unemployed. Clark made a great show of swanning around PC conventions in the company of David Orchard, the sworn enemy of Brian Mulroney's free-trade legacy. This sort of open-mindedness made Clark Toryism a very big tent, but unfortunately without any stakes to hold it up. In the 2000 election the tent collapsed. Clark drove his party to its lowest share of the popular vote since Confederation. His twelve-member caucus was precisely one defection away from losing its status and its operating budget as an official party in the Commons.

But then salvation, of a sort, came from the disarray of Stockwell Day. The implosion of the apostates' party must have looked, to Clark's eyes, the same as the 1929 stock-market crash did to early Marxist scholars: clear proof that an illegitimate system was collapsing under the weight of its own absurdity. Sure enough, here came a trickle – then a flood! – of old-time Reformers willing to sit with Joe and his Tories in Parliament. Chuck Strahl, Deb Grey, Gary Lunn, Jay Hill . . . ready to accept Joe as their leader! Justice was return-ing to the universe!

But then Stock Day agreed to give competitors a shot at his crown. Almost as swiftly as they had left the Alliance, a few of the rebels returned. When Harper won the Alliance leader-ship, the rest were in a bind. Their stated reason for leaving the Alliance caucus had been Stock's ineptitude. Now Stock wasn't running their party any more. How could they justify staying estranged?

At first, faced with the prospect of an Alliance whose leader was not Stockwell Day and, therefore, not actively chasing MPs into his arms, Clark tried to rush what he had hoped would be a long, natural process of osmosis. In September 2001, he sum-moned Gary Lunn and told him the time had come to take out a PC membership card. Six weeks later Lunn was back in the Alliance caucus. Now Clark stood to lose almost a third of his newly enlarged caucus unless he at least kept up the appear-ance of a willingness to co-operate. He called Harper and asked for a meeting.

The two leaders met on April 9, 2002. Each man played to type. Clark suggested a process. Harper suggested a solution. Clark lost. In the course of that ninety minutes in a Parliament Hill meeting room, his political career suffered its final blow.

Clark suggested that the two parties set up committees that

would meet for four months to discuss possible kinds of co-operation: working together in the Commons, joint policy development, some kind of electoral method to make sure the two parties didn't split the right-of-centre vote at the next election. What outcome did he expect from all this? To Clark it was an alien question. A well-designed process, by its nature, reaches proper outcomes. In the meantime everyone could trust-build. Clark was big on trust-building. And just in case trust was too slow to build, each would maintain "the option for both of us to continue to build our political parties." So Clark was offering a long process of unknowable outcome whose central feature was a lack of commitment on either partner's part.

Harper's counter-proposal was elegant. And a little vicious. He proposed that the two parties begin sitting together as a combined caucus immediately – as in, within the next couple of days. As for the forthcoming election, they should agree then and there not to run candidates against each other in any riding, then work backward from that goal to find a workable mechanism. Clark was appalled. If his twelve Tories sat with fifty-eight Alliance MPs and Chuck Strahl's hardy band of rebels, it was pretty damned clear who'd be in charge. Not Joe Clark, that's who. "I did not, naturally, find the suggestion . . . to be a serious proposal," he told reporters afterward.

Why not? Harper cooed that this little sidecar arrangement was precisely the sort of thing Clark had been leading in the Commons since the Alliance rebels joined him. Sure, now Clark would be the one climbing into the sidecar and someone else would become the driver. But if the *principle* made sense, why would that be a problem? Hmm?

For twenty-two years, ever since he lost the 1980 election, some corner of Clark's mind had harboured the hope, gusting to cheerful expectation, that the fates would blow him back into 24 Sussex again as they had the first time. Alone among former prime ministers, he had made no arrangements for an official House of Commons portrait. He finally had to let John Turner and Brian Mulroney and Kim Campbell move ahead of him in line. I will always maintain it was because he never believed his first term at 24 Sussex would make for the best portrait.

Now, as Clark announced the collapse of his talks with Harper, he had to know what would happen next. Five of the seven DRC rebels would return to the Alliance the next day. Inky Mark would be the only one of the original baker's dozen to take out his PC card. The remaining Tories would blame Clark for his flirtation with the rebels, once so promising, now so ruinous. Clark's career as leader would last another fourteen months. And yet today he looked so *cheerful*. Looking on the bright side can be such a burden. Now he didn't have to bother. "In a certain sense," he told us in the press theatre in the basement of the Centre Block, "we are free now." When three reporters raised their voices to ask the next question, he affected dismay. "Don't shout at me!" Then he left with a grin.

Which leaves a pretty big question hanging in the air: was Harper's overture to the Tory leader mere performance art? Or was he genuinely disappointed that it didn't work? "I'd say somewhere in between," John Weissenberger told me when I put that question to him early in 2006. "Had he got a decent deal with Joe, he would have been OK with that. But we were in an improving financial situation, an improving strategic situation, so to him, that it didn't happen was OK. Then you move on to do the best that you can, with the resources you have."

Except Harper didn't move on. The Tories were closing quickly on a summer policy convention. Harper gave the coalition idea one more big push, writing an op-ed article for the *National Post* that pitched the deal he'd offered Clark to rank-and-file Progressive Conservatives. This was an expression of a belief that supporters of Manning's United Alternative had cherished: that outside of "Joe Clark's palace guard," no conservative of any stripe in any party opposed closer co-operation. For a long time this had proven a seriously over optimistic assessment. For a long time the PC Party and Joe's palace guard had been pretty much the same thing. Now, though, with the collapse of the PC–DR (Democratic Reform) experiment, Clark's party might be willing to divorce him.

But time was wasting. "All the activities necessary to make this proposal operational – approval of our caucuses and parties, joint candidate protocols, joint platform development, the disposition of your indebtedness – require time, effort, and incentive," Harper wrote. "We cannot afford to leave this offer on the table beyond this summer."

He wouldn't have to. Clark, who was still the PC leader, dismissed Harper's reheated offer on the day the article appeared. Then in August, the PC membership did the same at their summer convention in Edmonton. Delegates there voted to endorse the so-called 301 rule: the Progressive Conservatives would field candidates in every federal riding at the next general election. When the Commons returned in September, Harper told a reporter the Tories had pretty much destroyed the whole idea of co-operation between their party and his. "The Tories decided to kill it at their convention," he said. "They rejected every single method of proceeding – local, national, any combination."

In hindsight, though, there's a genuine doggedness to Harper's attempts to find some accommodation with the Tories, even while Clark was still leading the party. You could hear it in his maiden speech to the Commons as Canadian Alliance leader, on May 28, after his private overtures to Clark and his public offer to the PC grassroots had already been rejected.

The occasion was an Alliance supply-day motion – a debate on a subject chosen not by the government but by the Opposition – attacking the Chrétien government's performance in trade disputes with the Americans over farm subsidies and softwood-lumber exports. Harper spent the first few minutes of his speech rehearsing a familiar complaint, that Chrétien hadn't bothered to build the sort of close personal relationship with George W. Bush that would give Canada any leverage at all. Then Harper took a surprising turn indeed. "Where do we go from here?" he asked. "On this I will make a very controversial observation. When it comes to United States–Canada relations, the government has much to learn from former prime minister Brian Mulroney."

The Alliance leader, the man who had quit Mulroney's party four years after Mulroney became its leader, made it clear he was offering only a partial endorsement. "I can critique his fiscal record, I can critique his social priorities, and I can critique his approach to government reform and national unity," he said. And yet. "Under Mr. Mulroney, Canada–United States relations were infinitely better than they are now."

Of course it was a toweringly self-serving argument. It neglected the obvious ingredient of party affiliation: Canada–U.S. relations had been quite good when Chrétien's friend Bill Clinton was present. Nor had the presence of a Conservative in the Prime Minister's Office done any good for Canada–U.S. relations when the Conservative was John Diefenbaker and the president he faced, John Kennedy, was a Democrat. But so what. Harper's goal was to smoke a peace pipe with Mulroney's party as much as it was to urge closer relations with the Bush

White House. "Frankly," he told *Maclean's* reporter John
Geddes afterward, "I'm making a political point."

And he found a taker. John Herron, the young PC MP for
Fundy-Royal, New Brunswick, jumped up to put a question to
Harper. "A very solid speech," Herron said. Would Harper be
willing to concede "that some of the vitriolic and visceral language utilized by members on that side against the Mulroney
administration . . . might have been just a little over the top?"

Harper didn't disagree. There were indeed things to like
about the Mulroney legacy. And then he perched Herron on
the horns of a dilemma. "I challenge the honourable member
to embrace this legacy by walking away from the party that has
now embraced David Orchard and the extreme anti–free trade
position. I challenge him to walk away from that kind of coalition and instead embrace our offer of a full coalition here."

It's worth remembering that this was May of 2002. The deal
with Orchard that would cement Peter MacKay's leadership of
the PCs was almost precisely a year in the future. So Harper was
rehearsing his ultimatum to the Tories – stick with Orchard or
stick with me – long before it made any real sense. You can see
this happening, later, in his overtures to Quebec voters. He
starts making his pitch so early that he looks a little silly. But
that means only that when the moment really comes, he has
already laid serious groundwork.

In the meantime, there was a caucus and a party to manage.
In this, Harper profited from a well-lubricated interregnum
between Stock Day's tenure and his own. John Reynolds is a
tall, silver-haired British Columbian whose long political
career has seen him serve as a provincial Socred, a federal Tory
and a Reformer. When Day finally left the Alliance leadership
in the fall of 2001, he made Reynolds the interim leader of the
party in Parliament. With the job came the keys to Stornoway,

the Opposition leader's residence. One of the keys, Reynolds began reminding Alliance MPs, opened the wine cellar.

I was reminded of all this when I visited Scott Reid last spring. There are two Scott Reids in this narrative. Sorry for the confusion, but we all had to deal with it for a decade in Ottawa. Sometimes one would get a phone call intended for the other. It's a wacky town. One Scott Reid was a blond, short-tempered Liberal who would be Paul Martin's communications director. The other is a prematurely patrician Reform–Alliance–Conservative with a neatly tended beard who has, on occasion, been one of Stephen Harper's closest allies from Ontario.

I was visiting this second Scott Reid because I wanted him to remind me of the uproarious caucus conditions Harper faced when he returned to Ottawa. But Reid said the atmosphere was already far calmer by the time Harper arrived. "John Reynolds established a reasonable, disciplined presence," Reid said, "largely because he wasn't a threat to anybody. He wasn't seen as a potential candidate. And he had gravitas and a physical presence and a great deal of self-confidence. So things really quieted down."

Reid pulled a photo from his bookcase to illustrate the rest of his point. "You'll notice everyone's got red wine in their hand," he said. "Everyone" in this instance was Reynolds and several Alliance MPs who'd stopped by Stornoway after a day's session in Parliament: Reid, Jason Kenney, Gary Lunn, Monte Solberg, Rahim Jaffer. In the photo, everyone is wearing the same slightly loopy smile. "It was like a frat party a lot of the time," Reid said.

"But if you actually look at it, that's quite clever. He was reconciling people from different groups. Getting us to spend some time together, drinking." Different groups indeed.

Kenney, a devout Roman Catholic and one of the party's brightest young strategic thinkers, had gone to the wall to defend Stock Day's leadership. Lunn had left the caucus with the DRC rebels. Solberg, a Preston Manning loyalist, had considered doing the same but had stayed, neglected and bitter, in the Alliance caucus. Reid had worked to get Harper elected leader. And Jaffer? "I think Rahim is there because Rahim was also the kind of guy who could get along with everybody, all the time," Reid said.

So you can give Harper a lot of credit for a lot of things, but when it came to pulling the party out of its self-destructive death spiral, much of the course correction had taken place without him. I did find one member of Harper's inner circle who says the new leader imposed order "only by virtue of absolutely bloody-minded, brutal tactics, exercising completely iron grip on the party's organization." How so? "You know, actually no one was going to be out policy-freelancing any more," this Harper ally recalls. "There was going to be a proper policy process inside the party and inside the caucus. There was also a proper shadow-cabinet system that would chew stuff over and come up with a policy position at the end of it. And you know, you would have your piece of the discussion while it was going on. But once the caucus had decided that X was going to be the direction, X was the fucking direction. If you didn't like X, you could shut the fuck up. But there was no other path forward."

But actually, nobody else I talked to from that time can remember any particular need for such iron-fisted tactics. "Certainly, he's a stickler for the message," another veteran from the early days in 2002 recalls. "But the biggest thing he had going for him, as far as discipline goes, is that everybody was just so tired of fighting. The party had just gone through a bitter civil war. By the end of it everybody was just so tired of fighting."

This person recounted how a caucus rendered docile by a combination of battlefield exhaustion and Stornoway wine came to know a Stephen Harper who had, himself, matured and mellowed during his five years away from Ottawa. "You know, a lot of people in that caucus were quite frankly expecting to see the Stephen Harper of the old Reform Party days. An aloof guy who didn't really have much time for anybody around him and was more committed to himself than the team. But he was very good when he took over. He definitely said all the right things, admitted that he had made some mistakes, that he was wrong in a number of views. And he went out of his way – not so much to cultivate the people who had voted for him, necessarily, the people who saw him as a Reformer – but he went out of his way to bring back the DRC."

The rebel Alliance MPs were already trickling back into the caucus before Harper became Alliance leader, but he spent a lot of time on the phone brokering their return. He urged the caucus, most of whom had stuck with Day at immeasurable cost to their own popularity, to show clemency when most of the remaining rebels abandoned Joe Clark in May 2002. And Harper deftly handled their slow reintegration back into the Alliance caucus, a process few outside observers paid much mind. When I covered an Alliance caucus retreat in Barrie, Ontario, in September of that year, the DRC apostates were still eating their meals at different restaurants from the rest of the caucus. And when Harper unveiled his shadow-cabinet assignments at that retreat, few of the ex-rebels had any substantive role. Sure, they were back. But they would have to sit in the penalty box for a while yet before their talents could be put to use again.

The mood at that late-summer retreat in the gateway to Ontario's cottage country was placid relief at surviving the party's internal wars. "It's like the whole party has taken a Valium," one MP said. "It's great." Harper announced that over the summer he'd retired the party's $2.5-million debt. (How? "We took it from the riding associations," one MP smirked, adding hastily: "They were happy to make the donation.") And if the party had actually dipped in the latest polls, down from a modest post-leadership bounce to 13 per cent in national voter intention? Harper was philosophical. "Our room to grow has risen."

And there the Alliance might have stayed, cheerful and ineffectual, if two catastrophes hadn't hit the next spring. One befell the Alliance. The second, the Progressive Conservatives. Each catastrophe would shatter a party's complacent illusions. Together they set the stage for the Tory-Alliance merger on which Harper had all but given up.

⇧

Perth-Middlesex was a sprawling riding that covered, a bit haphazardly, much of the farmland, industry-land, and Shakespeare-obsessed-small-town-land (that would be Stratford) between London and Kitchener in southwestern Ontario. Its Liberal MP, John Richardson, won handily in 1997 and 2000, largely because the Tories and Reform-Alliance split the non-Liberal vote. In the fall of 2002, Richardson's failing health made him resign the seat. The Liberals had neglected to inform voters that their man might not last. It made the party unpopular in the riding. Conservative and Alliance strategists started eyeing the riding with more than the usual amount of interest. This place might be a harbinger: whoever could win here could lay claim to credibility as the Liberals' Ontario giant-killers.

Jean Chrétien must have been getting discouraging numbers from Perth-Middlesex, too. When month after month went by without Chrétien calling a by-election, Joe Clark started asking questions about it in the Commons. Why were the Liberals depriving the good folk of Perth-Middlesex of a voice in Parliament? What was Chrétien afraid of? Finally Chrétien called the by-election for May 12.

The Alliance had sent an organizer to the riding to get a candidate nominated almost as soon as Richardson resigned the seat. But then nothing much happened. There was in-fighting in the riding association between Stock Day loyalists and DRC sympathizers. More volunteers were told they couldn't participate, because of this or that wildly arcane doctrinal dispute, than were welcomed into the campaign. By February, Harper was getting antsy about the whole thing. He called in Tom Flanagan, who by now was working as his chief of staff. Time to take over the Perth-Middlesex campaign, he said. Time to send in Doug Finley.

Doug Finley was a bearded, chain-smoking fifty-five-year-old Scot who got his start in politics campaigning for the first Scottish Nationalist ever elected to the British House of Commons. By the 1970s, he was running campaigns for federal Liberals in Montreal. By the 1980s, he'd given up on the Liberals. In 2002, he applied to be director of operations for the Alliance. Harper and Flanagan didn't hire him but they remembered his credentials as a tough riding-level organizer. So they reached out to him now, and he brought the news to the bewildered townies that they were no longer in charge. A bit like Alec Baldwin in *Glengarry Glen Ross* ("I'm here from Downtown. I'm here from Mitch and Murray"). He set up his phone banks and his riding maps and started knocking some sense into the whole business. Flanagan began sending a constant stream of Alliance MPs to the riding to knock on doors. Harper himself visited the riding at least five times. The whole Alliance caucus spent a weekend in the riding, fanning out to any community event that would let them come.

Somewhere in there, Finley met Ian Brodie, a young political scientist from the University of Western Ontario who was driving into Perth-Middlesex to help prop up the flagging Alliance campaign. Brodie, a slim and intense man with a close-cropped beard and a cheerful demeanour, had known Harper since Brodie landed at the University of Calgary to work on his M.A. in 1990. He started in March as the Alliance's executive director. From Perth-Middlesex onward, Brodie and Finley would be the most trusted fixers in Harper's entourage. Whenever something was really, seriously, badly broken, Harper would turn to one of them or the other. Usually to both.

But nobody can work miracles. "We never dared to total up the final cost. Nobody wanted to know," somebody who worked on Perth-Middlesex recalls. A normal by-election costs maybe $100,000. "My guess is we probably spent $750,000 in that by-election. And got smoked."

The Alliance candidate came in third. The entirely nondescript Tory, Gary Schellenberger, won, beating the Liberal by 1,000 votes. The Progressive Conservatives were weeks away from choosing a new leader. For Joe Clark, it was one last sweet vindication. For the Alliance it was shattering. They'd thrown everything they had at precisely the kind of small-town Ontario riding they needed to win if they were to have any hope of growth. And nothing. Jim Armour, Harper's communications director, summed up the predicament in an interview he gave to *National Post* columnist Don Martin: "This turd won't polish."

Martin ran the quote without attribution, but Harper recognized the speech patterns of the jovial Newfoundlander who worked for him. He phoned Armour from Paris: "That wouldn't be you calling our party a turd in public, would it?" Yet Harper couldn't be very angry. It wasn't, after all, as though this turd could be polished. Harper might have saved the Alliance from complete destruction, might have kept his caucus from slinking in ones and twos into Joe Clark's seductive embrace. But its momentum was stalled completely. The prairie-populist sister of Canadian conservatism had gone as far as spinsterhood would take her.

Fortunately the Tories' luck was about to run out, too. The campaign to replace Clark ground to a shambling halt at the party's leadership convention in Toronto on May 31. For a party that had come close to being wiped out for the second time in a decade at the 2000 elections, the Tories actually had some passable leadership candidates. There was Peter MacKay, a rangy Nova Scotia rugby player with immense hands, a ready smile, a smattering of the royal jelly – his father, Elmer, had been a Mulroney cabinet minister – and a prosecutorial style that made Liberals fear him in Question Period. Or Scott Brison, another Nova Scotian, gay if you must know but much more interested in talking about ideas for free-market reforms that would have curled Joe Clark's hair: flat taxes, private health care, abolishing regional-development pork agencies. And Jim Prentice, a Calgary businessman who'd abandoned his candidacy for Preston Manning's old seat in Calgary Southwest a year earlier so Harper could win the riding unopposed. Prentice was the tentative, baby-steps candidate of cooperation with the Alliance. And, finally, David Orchard, the

Saskatchewan farmer and anti-free-trade crusader. Anyone tempted to write Orchard off as a joke candidate did so at his peril: he was poised and articulate, if humourless. Worse, wherever he went he brought surprising numbers of poised, articulate, humourless supporters out of the woodwork.

So there they all were in Toronto, surrounded by hundreds of Tories in campaign scarves and funny hats. The voting went to a second ballot, then a third. MacKay, with his old-school credentials, his vigour, and his cheerful inability to say anything remotely surprising about any issue, was in front from the first ballot. But his support refused to grow. Meanwhile Brison threw his support to Prentice, who now had an outside shot at overtaking MacKay. Which is when MacKay got the boost he needed by signing away his credibility.

The groom at the shotgun wedding was David Orchard, who managed to get MacKay's signature on a makeshift contract Orchard had scrawled on a scrap of paper. "No merger, joint candidates with Alliance," the accord said. It also pledged the two men to set up a panel to review the North American Free Trade Agreement. That coalition with David Orchard that Harper had warned Tories about, a year earlier? Here it was.

"It's sort of hard for me to describe the scene," Jim Prentice recalls. "It was a very unusual, almost eerie end to the convention. There was a real sense of disquiet in the room. The Orchard delegates were in tears. The MacKay delegates were in tears."

⇧

So here was Canadian conservatism in the aftermath of the Perth-Middlesex by-election and the MacKay–Orchard deal: Alliance, hopeless. Tories, hopeless. Maybe hopeless plus hopeless could equal hope. Harper's talking point had been ready for a year. At Alliance fundraisers in Calgary on June 12 and Toronto on June 19, he asked whether Progressive Conservatives were actually so allergic to the Alliance that they saw Orchard as a better date. It was a much more effective line now than a year before. In mid-July, Jim Prentice ran into Peter MacKay at the Calgary Stampede. MacKay told him the two parties were in talks, but that it had to stay hush-hush.

By late summer, rumours of the negotiations had leaked to the newspapers. Geoff Norquay, a veteran PC strategist who worked for Mulroney, Kim Campbell, and Clark, couldn't believe what he read one morning. Merger talks? It was news to him. Norquay had a regular gig as a talking head on Don Newman's afternoon show *Politics* on CBC Newsworld. To his astonishment, Norquay got a call from Stephen Harper shortly before heading over to the CBC studio to shoot the pundit panel. Norquay barely knew Harper. He'd spent less than five minutes of his life talking to him at that point, mostly in elevators. Now he was saying: "Geoff. It's Stephen Harper. These rumours of negotiations? Please don't dismiss them out of hand." Uh, sure. Whatever. When Newman raised the question, Norquay ragged the puck for a few seconds but managed not to say anything conclusive.

In fact, the first discussions had progressed far more quickly than Harper and MacKay expected. Throughout the talks, the Alliance side would have the consistent impression that the Progressive Conservatives were making a point of asking too much. It would be a handy way, after all, to ensure that the talks would fail without the Tories shouldering the blame. But throughout the talks the Alliance team would amaze and unnerve their interlocutors by saying yes. The tone was set at the first meeting. Don Mazankowski, Brian Mulroney's former deputy prime minister and MacKay's lead emissary, suggested that the two sides dispense with rickety vote-splitting mechanisms and simply merge into a single party. As Harper biographer William Johnson has written, Harper was taken aback. But only for a few days. Then he realized that Mazankowski was offering what Harper had long thought was the ideal situation, but had never believed possible. If this was a bluff, he would call it. If it was a serious offer, he'd take it.

Just before Labour Day, Harper held a conference call with several Alliance staffers. "This was like, 'OK, we're going to do it. So strap yourselves in,'" one person on the call remembers. "'And let's just make sure that we're setting the agenda as far as the media goes.'"

What followed was an extended game of orchestrated media leaks, almost exclusively from Harper's team, designed to hold the Progressive Conservatives to their word. An element of Harper's negotiating style was becoming evident. He had picked a bottom line. Everything that could advance that bottom-line requirement was negotiable. Nothing was sacred if pitching it overboard would help advance the basic goal. Harper had road-tested the approach during his failed 2002 meeting with Joe Clark: if the goal was to run one candidate at the next election, why not simply *decide* to run one candidate at the next election and settle the details accordingly? The approach failed then because Clark could still cling to false pride, could still pretend that his party didn't need Harper's. Now, after Perth-Middlesex and MacKay–Orchard, neither side had that luxury. They both needed a deal to survive.

This was far more obvious to the Alliance than to their skittish dance partners. "Harper in a lot of ways was playing catch-up to the caucus," a former staffer says. "The majority of the caucus had already gone through this once with the Canadian

Alliance. So there were a lot of people in the caucus who wanted to make some sort of a deal. In a lot of ways, they were way more bullish on a deal than Harper was. So they would have voted for *any* deal."

Nowhere was this more obvious than in Stockwell Day's behaviour. The deposed Alliance leader was still in caucus and he remained the de facto leader of the party's most socially conservative faction. If anyone was going to complain about getting into bed with the heirs of Joe Clark, or put value conditions on the terms of a merger, it would be Stock. And my colleagues in the Press Gallery knew it. "We were getting calls from a lot of media seeing if we were going to come out and do that," recalls Pierre Poilièvre, who sits today as a Conservative MP but was working then as Day's legislative assistant. "'We can't give up on this issue and that issue' – that could have been fatal. The fact that Harper did not have to deal with that gave him a real free hand in moving forward."

MacKay had far less leverage. He was an untested leader. He'd won the job in a seriously weird way with the Orchard deal. His caucus and party membership were about one-fifth the size of Harper's, his party's debt hole, far deeper. And he had a veritable Greek chorus of prominent Tories publicly second-guessing his work. "This does not even deserve to be called opportunism," Senator Lowell Murray wrote in the *Globe and Mail* when Harper first came courting MacKay in June. "It's political fantasy."

And surely by now Lowell Murray must be some kind of an expert on fantasy. He had orchestrated Joe Clark's 1980 defeat in Parliament, believing that Clark would win the ensuing election. Murray was the salesman who made the Meech Lake and Charlottetown accords what they are today. He had worked hard to make the doomed PC-DRC partnership work.

If ever there was anyone in Canadian politics less able to spot a winner than Lowell Murray, that person probably choked on his own tongue long ago. But Murray wasn't letting that stop him. "Reform conservatism, which is what the Alliance practices, relies on people's fear of moral and economic decline combined with nostalgia for a Canada that no longer exists." A Canada governed by people like Lowell Murray, you mean? No, actually: "Tories are more realistic and, yes, more compassionate." All MacKay had to do was resist the "merger/acquisition mentality that Alliance Reformers bring to the discussion of the country's current – and temporarily – fractured politics," and put "this respected old party . . . back into contention for government."

With Murray's and similar appeals to realism ringing in his ears, MacKay was a difficult negotiating partner. So Harper herded him, with the help of a few border collies in the Parliamentary Press Gallery. Just as Harper had once used leaks to newspapers to make clear his distance from Preston Manning, now he used them to strengthen his bargaining hand with the MacKay Tories.

"The point all the way along was to hold them to it," someone who was involved in the negotiations for the Alliance said. "To avoid backsliding. Or to force them to take a position that they thought we would never accept." So if the Conservative negotiating team edged closer to a deal in a closed-door session, or hinted at a principle that might make bargaining easier, they'd read about it, to their astonishment, in the *Globe* or the *Post* a few days later. "It's sort of the way that Stephen generally operates. So he would muse a little bit about how one-person, one-vote was important to him, and it was a hallmark of the Reform Party, and everything else he stood for." That position would promptly appear in a newspaper or television report.

"So then the Tories would go, 'No no, we absolutely insist on some sort of regional vote.' And he'd go, 'Yeah, OK, fine, I'm good with that.' And trap them, right?

"So we would either leak something to hold them to it, or Stephen would float an idea that they would try and hold him to. But part of his strategy was, they would come back and say, 'Well, it'll have to be this,' thinking he would never accept it. Which of course he would. Because the caucus quite frankly would accept anything."

It almost failed a dozen times before it succeeded. In October, the talks nearly collapsed over the toughest issue: how to choose the new party's leader. In the Reform-Alliance tradition it was assumed that each party member should have a vote. That would have meant the much larger Alliance membership could have chosen a leader over the objections of every single former Tory. MacKay wanted each riding to send an equal number of delegates, so Tories could leverage their organizational edge in the Atlantic provinces and Quebec. There was deadlock. Harper suggested they take Thanksgiving weekend off. Then he leaked a memo to the media complaining of MacKay's "lack of any spirit of compromise." MacKay promptly heard from another wing of his party – the wing that included Mulroney and wanted him to do a deal – urging him to get back to the table and be serious about it this time. On October 16, the two leaders announced they'd made a deal. Five years after Harper had mused about merging the parties, it was going to happen.

Of course not everyone was happy. Joe Clark said he would sit out his career as an independent rather than join this makeshift new contraption. In the Senate, Lowell Murray reached a similar conclusion. André Bachand, a Quebec PC MP, said he wouldn't be a candidate for the party in the next election. Why bother? This new crew didn't understand Quebec. Scott Brison and John Herron, two of the most prominent younger members of the PC caucus, jumped to the Liberals.

More important, the new party seemed unable to find anyone willing to run it. Mike Harris, the former Ontario premier, stayed out of the race. So did Bernard Lord, the effortlessly bilingual young New Brunswick premier who was many Conservatives' dream candidate. The provincial power-houses of Canadian conservatism had been urging their federal cousins to get their act together for a decade. Now that it was done, no new champion emerged.

Why? Because there was a juggernaut coming. We're getting near the end of 2003 here. On December 12, Paul Martin would be sworn in as Canada's new prime minister. The polls were giving him somewhere in the neighbourhood of 220 seats in a 301-seat house. And Martin's advisors were saying he wouldn't wait long to go to the people in a spring election. John Weissenberger recalls: "Some of the bigger names, Harris and Lord, decided, why not let whoever gets elected (as the leader of the new Conservative Party) get slaughtered by Martin? And then we'll come in and pick up the chips later."

The heavyweights, the guys with something to lose, decided not to risk it. So Stephen Harper became a candidate. Later, so did Tony Clement, one of the group of young Ontario Conservatives who had helped make Mike Harris premier, served well as the province's health minister, and been swept out of office when Dalton McGuinty's Liberals won the October 2003 election. Belinda Stronach, a car-parts heiress (daughter of Frank) who had made phone calls and hosted meetings to urge the Harper–MacKay negotiations toward success, became the third candidate. Stronach was rich, blonde, rich, young, rich, and entirely unknown to most Canadians. She promptly attracted some of the most powerful political strategists in Canada, many from the Ontario Conservatives, to her campaign. Guy Giorno and Jaime Watt, former Mike Harris advisors, joined Stronach's campaign. Mark Entwistle, a former Mulroney communications director, was on board, as was Geoff Norquay, the veteran aide-de-camp and spokesman.

Harper, meanwhile, had the same crew he'd been deploying, in different ways, for a few years now. Tom Flanagan took a break from running the Office of the Leader of the Opposition to run the leadership campaign. Ken Boessenkool did policy and messaging. Ian Brodie ran the campaign tour. What did he know about running a leadership campaign tour? Nothing. He'd pick it up as he went along.

Today Stephen Harper is the prime minister of Canada, and it's hard to make people remember that he once seemed a long shot to beat Tony Clement and Belinda Stronach in Ontario. Four years earlier, Preston Manning had not been able to overcome the widespread assumption that a new party needed a new leader. Now the same logic played against Harper. But he was more experienced, more confident, and much more versed in the issues of national politics than the two Ontarians. In the end it wasn't even close. Stronach's canny campaign team, along with a substantial dose of her family fortune, had gained her control of a disproportionate number of ridings in Quebec and Atlantic Canada, where just a few newly minted Conservative members were enough to take over a riding association. But Harper held his advantage in Western Canada – and rolled right over the Ontarians in their home province.

On March 20, 2004, Harper won the leadership of the shiny new Conservative Party of Canada with 55.0 per cent of the leadership votes nationwide, compared to 35.0 per cent for Stronach and 9.5 per cent for Clement. In Ontario, he had 56.9 per cent of the vote, solidly more than Stronach and Clement combined.

Five years after he had outlined a merger of conservative parties to the Alberta Mortgage Loans Association, Harper had made it happen. And now he was in charge. His little band of Calgary policy wonks had accompanied him through two leadership campaigns and two years leading the Opposition in Parliament. They were starting to get the hang of practical politics. But they were also exhausted, and it is an understatement to say the hard part still lay ahead. Paul Martin was now the prime minister of Canada. And for all the people around Harper knew, a federal election might be only weeks away.

4

DOIN' THE HIGHLY CHARACTERISTIC SHUFFLE

⇧

For lo, the night had come when Paul Martin became the leader of the party to which he had given his life. Liberals from across the country repaired to the Air Canada Centre in downtown Toronto for the great moment. "Over the years, in various leadership conventions, a small number of Canadians have stood on a stage like this," Martin said from the floor of the hockey arena on the evening of November 14, 2003.

"In the past while, I have thought about them. And wondered just how I would feel as I stood before you at this moment. And what I would say and what I would do.

"As it turns out, it is deeply moving – and much more difficult than I thought."

What a touching admission of vulnerability at the moment of triumph. Also: what transparent dime-store fiction. Even as Martin was confiding to a few thousand of his closest friends that this was harder than he had thought it would be, dozens of reporters, loosely herded in a bullpen on the floor of the arena in front of the new leader, were reading along with the prepared text, which Martin's legions of helpers had handed to us before he began speaking. Sure enough, there it was, a third of the way down Page 1: *Much . . . more . . . difficult . . . than . . . I . . . thought.*

Earlier that afternoon Martin had read the speech (". . . much more difficult than I thought . . .") at that same podium, in a dress rehearsal. Alexander Panetta, a young reporter from the Canadian Press Ottawa news bureau, lingering just outside the hall, heard an audio feed of the performance, took notes, and sent out a summary of the speech to CP member organizations across the nation, four hours before Martin began delivering the speech for real. This affront against the fragile crafts of stage management would briefly earn Panetta a stint in the Martin press shop's chilly little doghouse. Not for long, though, because pretty soon Alex Panetta's insistence on doing his job would be the least of anyone's problems.

Which means that among the small number of Canadians who had stood on stages like this, before Paul Martin did, was . . . himself. Paul Martin. *De deux choses l'une,* as we say: either this deeply moving experience was *precisely* as difficult now as it had been during months of draft speech rewrites, meetings, and conference calls, as well as at the big dress rehearsal this afternoon – or it was *even more* difficult now than then, in which case Martin and his communications team had *factored in* the requisite increment of difficulty, aiming ahead of the hurtling clay pigeon like so many ace skeet shooters, and included their eerily prescient hunch about that supplementary burden in the text of the big guy's acceptance speech.

You're right. Probably I'm overcomplicating things. Probably it was just a fib. The simplest explanation is that Paul Martin was walking into the job of his life in character. There was an irreducible quantum of artifice about the whole affair, as though he had decided to give the speech in Groucho glasses and a bushy moustache, or to deliver it, without explanation, in a heavy Swedish accent.

The role he had chosen to play, in the end, was that of a humbled ex-finance minister named Paul Martin who lands on a stage of the sort only a small number of Canadians has ever occupied, and who finds it more difficult than he thought. The role is not without challenges. Should the voice catch at that moment? The eyes mist over? The posture crumple slightly to reflect the surprising burden? No wonder he had rehearsed. But the unassuming central character of this one-act play was out of step with its theme. The advance copies handed out to reporters carried the title *Making History*. And it fell to this abashed and tentative character to proclaim himself the herald of a new epoch. "We stand together on the edge of historic possibility," this Paul Martin announced. "It is a moment when destiny is ours to hold . . . It is a time to turn an historic circumstance into transformative change – to summon a new national will."

It's easy to snicker now. But one must guard against the false lessons of hindsight: on the night this all happened, there wasn't a lot of snickering going on. As he spoke, Paul Martin enjoyed the strongest mandate of any Liberal leader in at least half a century. He had won 3,242 of 3,453 eligible delegate votes, so many that the organizers of the convention had briefly debated the most decent way of announcing the result without unduly embarrassing his only surviving rival, Sheila

Copps. (In the end they announced only his total, leaving arithmetically inclined Liberals with a mean disposition to deduce hers.)

Two months earlier, Martin had travelled to Quebec's Charlevoix region for the weekend-long housewarming party at Sagard, the sprawling new retreat of Power Corporation kingpin Paul Desmarais. Martin joined a golf foursome with Brian Mulroney, George Bush Sr., and Paul Desmarais Jr. At one point during the round, Martin mentioned to his golf companions that he was on the way to a 200-seat majority in a 308-seat Parliament. Nobody thought he was bragging. No serious analyst was predicting any different result. Across the aisle, Progressive Conservatives and Canadian Alliance members had united their parties in a spirit of *sauver les meubles*; the best guess the new party's strategists could concoct was that they might save between 65 and 75 seats in the face of the Martin onslaught.

But here at the Air Canada Centre, it was hardly clear what, specifically, Martin was offering that would stimulate such massive voter excitement. Oh, sure, the excitement was there. There were lights. There were pins and buttons. There was an endless supply of thunder sticks, cigar-shaped inflatable balloons that Liberals were asked to slam together to produce a deafening and meaningless noise. But what project was all this ruckus meant to celebrate? What was historic about this circumstance? Why had destiny chosen this moment to become portable? What was the new national will being summoned to *do*?

Martin made a show of being in too much of a hurry to give specific answers. "As a people, we know what we can do, we know how to do it, and we just want to get on with it." And what did "we" want to get on with? Well, Martin called for Canada's place in the world to be "one of influence and pride." He wanted "a twenty-first century economy in Canada for Canadians," which he defined, among other ways, as "a government that treats taxpayers' money like it is your money." You mean because it is? "Because it is."

This all received the applause that boilerplate generally does at political conventions. But a few observers noticed that the night was oddly flat compared to the previous evening's intermittently tacky and stirring farewell to Jean Chrétien. Paul Anka, singing "My Way," with the lyrics specially mangled for the occasion, had provided the tack. Chrétien had brought the roof down with three thunderous standing ovations as he rhymed off his accomplishments: the Clarity Act on Quebec secession; the decision to stay out of the Iraq War; and a bill to legalize gay marriage.

None of those applause lines was in Martin's speech. In fact, Martin was famously uncomfortable with every one of the decisions that had made his predecessor most popular *among Liberals*. And Martin's speechwriters could think of nothing specific that would stir this crowd in the same way Chrétien had done.

In a way, they weren't even trying.

The goal of the Martin transition, members of his entourage admitted much later, was not to excite Liberals, but to confirm Canadians, even Canadians who hadn't voted Liberal for a long time, in their growing comfort with the idea of voting for Paul Martin. To broaden the tent. To create and deliver the record-breaking coalition of voters that Martin's pollsters – everyone's pollsters – had predicted for him. All Jean Chrétien had ever given Liberals was a bird in the hand. Paul Martin brought the promise of two in the bush.

John Duffy is a Toronto political consultant, a lifelong Liberal, a Martin loyalist since the late 1980s, and the Martin entourage's in-house amateur historian. Long after the Martin project had gone rather resoundingly off the rails, Duffy had lunch with me in a more or less convincing French bistro in Toronto to piece together how it was all supposed to work out. "Martin was about, in political terms, expanding the coalition into two zones where we weren't. Regionally, Western Canada and francophone Quebec. And demographically, consolidating a beachhead among men over forty-five.

"His time in politics up until 2004 had been oriented toward talking to those people. And saying, 'You can be a Liberal.' Paul Martin's mission in life, at times, appeared to be to make people realize they didn't know how Liberal they could be. All they needed was the Liberal Party to stop doing the things that *annoyed* them, like horrible misspending under Trudeau. And wrecking the economy. And taking the economy into honorary third-world status. And the NEP" – the National Energy Plan, by which Western oil was basically expropriated by an Eastern Liberal government in the early 1980s – "and all that other stuff. And then a lot of Canadians could gravitate back toward the natural Liberalism that was available to them."

The goal of the new Martin regime, then, was to be all things to all people. Or more things to more people. Well, let's be honest: to *not be one guy in particular* to a very large number of people. Which guy? Oh, you know. Dennis Dawson, the Martin camp's ranking Quebec strategist, recalls that at the time of the Air Canada Centre acceptance speech, "we were basically hitting the roof as far as polling was concerned. And it wasn't based on Paul being Paul. It was based on Paul being anybody but Chrétien."

Now here's the problem. Again it looks pretty obvious in hindsight, but at the end of 2003 you couldn't find three people in Ottawa willing to pause long enough to consider it.

If "being anybody but Chrétien" was all you needed to take the Liberals from 173 Commons seats to 200 or more, then probably somebody else would have managed it already. After all, Kim Campbell, Preston Manning, Joe Clark, Jean Charest, and Stockwell Day weren't Jean Chrétien either. Every one of them, incidentally, had come to the party, or thought they did, with better credentials than Chrétien's among Western Canadians, francophone Quebeckers, and men over forty-five. But they spent the dying years of the twentieth century getting their teeth handed to them by Jean Chrétien. To say this is not to argue that he was a genius, although clearly he knew a thing or two that his detractors didn't. It's simply to say that "being anybody but Chrétien" had historically been a rickety ladder to power.

We can state this more broadly. Massive majorities simply don't happen in Canadian federal politics unless rare circumstances are met. Even then, as a rule, they don't last. My authority for this is Tom Flanagan, Stephen Harper's long-time organizer. But Flanagan was wearing his political scientist's hat, and he wasn't even talking about Paul Martin, when he pointed out the rarity and fragility of really big parliamentary majorities.

In 1998, Flanagan published *Game Theory and Canadian Politics*, an introductory university textbook on the application of basic economic theory to political choice. One of the ideas Flanagan introduces early in the book is the notion of the "minimum winning coalition" – the idea that it's better if a prize is shared among the smallest possible number of winners. First, because each player takes home a bigger share of the prize and has a greater stake in success. Second, because a small coalition is less prone to fracture than a large one. This turns out to be true in Canadian politics, too. Flanagan showed that governing majorities much larger than half the seats in the House of Commons are rare. They hardly ever happen unless a serious crisis, such as war or recession, pushes strange bedfellows together. And they tend to collapse into faction and squabbling as soon as the crisis passes, or sooner. "Of the four largest parliamentary majorities in Canadian history," Flanagan writes, "two fell apart spectacularly within one or two subsequent elections."

Political theory isn't physics. Martin's two-hundred-seat coalition wasn't doomed from the start, just because Tom Flanagan wrote a book. But Flanagan helps us understand why the Martin project was shaky from the outset. There was no great crisis pushing Canadians of radically divergent opinion to Martin. Nor was there a galvanizing project to unite them. All the Martin team could come up with was the notion that Paul Martin represented "change." As early as December of 2000, three years before Martin became prime minister, his strategists were rehearsing their argument. The goal, one of them told Robert Fife of the *National Post*, was to "make sure that Paul . . . leads a renewed and refreshed new party that makes people think that they are changing the government by electing him."

How important was change? "It was everything!" John Duffy says. "It was everything. It was always at the heart of what I saw our challenge as, and what a lot of people agreed was our challenge, which was to be the agent of positive, manageable, safe change. That was Paul's cachet."

Here again there was a theory. It was widely shared – I heard it in separate interviews with three different members of Martin's entourage – but the first one to write it down was John Duffy. He didn't air it in public until March 31, 2004, in an article for the *Globe and Mail*, but it drove a lot of the entourage's decisions during the transition from Chrétien's government to Martin's.

Martin's arrival, Duffy wrote, corresponded to a historic type: a party in power changing leaders and hoping to retain power. "There have been nine previous such attempts at the federal level, seven of which ended in failure," Duffy wrote. The most recent failures had been the Liberals' in-office replacement of Pierre Trudeau with John Turner, and the Progressive Conservatives' subsequent replacement of Brian Mulroney with Kim Campbell. Chrétien–Martin would be the tenth transfer of leadership by a party in power in Ottawa since Confederation.

Now. If you and I were students of political success, and we knew that an operation had failed nine times and succeeded twice, we might want to look very closely at the two success stories. For the record, those two successes were Pierre Trudeau, who took over the Liberals from Lester Pearson in 1968; and Louis St. Laurent, who succeeded William Lyon Mackenzie King in 1948.

In his *Globe* article, Duffy pays no attention to Trudeau and St. Laurent. He hangs out his shingle as an expert in winning and proceeds to ignore the winners. Instead he indulges in some guesswork about what scuppered two of the nine losers, Turner and Campbell. In each case, the new leader was too timid about appearing before the electors as an agent of change. Duffy's thesis, then, is that Turner and Campbell didn't run away from their predecessors' legacy fast enough.

If that was the mistake, the Martin strategists were adamant that this time they wouldn't make the same one. "Liberals in the past couple of years," Duffy wrote, "have been understandably anxious at the prospect of seeking a fourth mandate in the face of a wave of political change that has now defeated five provincial governments from B.C. to Newfoundland and Labrador."

Well, close. Four provincial governments had indeed been defeated in the most recent round of elections: Ujjal Dosanjh in British Columbia, Ernie Eves in Ontario, Bernard Landry in Quebec, Roger Grimes in Newfoundland and Labrador. But six more had been re-elected: Ralph Klein in Alberta, Gary Doer in Manitoba, Pat Binns on Prince Edward Island, Lorne Calvert in Saskatchewan, John Hamm in Nova Scotia, and Bernard Lord, just barely, in New Brunswick.

As waves of change go, this one was pretty gentle. Six of ten provincial governments had won re-election. In the absence of a fancy theory about "change," you might say the ones that survived were *popular*, and the ones that didn't were *less popular*. Pat Binns's island was right out there in the Atlantic Ocean, but no wave of change could touch it. Neither was change sweeping Klein's Alberta or Calvert's Saskatchewan – even though Calvert's provincial NDP had hung on to power through a change in leadership.

And yet nobody could have argued that Calvert had survived by sweeping aside the legacy of the Roy Romanow years. The same is broadly true of the two federal success stories Duffy so conspicuously ignored. Pierre Trudeau was *sui generis*, of course. In his person, he represented something close to a revolution after the Pearson years. But not in his manner or his billing. Trudeau's first cabinet had only three ministers who hadn't been in Pearson's last cabinet. And when Trudeau almost lost his second election in 1972, he brought back the fixers and schemers – Jim Coutts, Keith Davey – whose presence in the Pearson government Trudeau had once found so distasteful.

And St. Laurent? Grandpa Louis? Agent of change? Puh-lease. One could argue, in fact, that "from 1948 under St. Laurent, the Liberals had continued to successfully apply King's formula for holding power." One could even argue that "on a good day – and the period from 1945 to 1957 was mostly a very long, good day – the entire King–St. Laurent system of politics and government worked beautifully." In fact, one has argued all of that. The one who's made these arguments is John Duffy, in his wonderful book of Canadian electoral history, *Fights of Our Lives.*

One more thing. Take a look at those four provincial governments that went down to defeat in 2003 and 2004. Dosanjh, Eves, Landry, Grimes. What did they have in common besides unpopularity? That's right: each had succeeded a leader in power. So if you combine the federal and provincial cases, Duffy's data set isn't just seven failures in nine tries: it's eleven failures in fourteen tries (Calvert in Saskatchewan being the only successful provincial hand-off). That's a 79 per cent failure rate for parties that replace their leader while in power.

The clear-eyed lesson that *could* have been drawn from the cases Duffy selected is that it's really reckless to replace your leader. Not that anyone should have expected the people around Paul Martin to see that. Northrop Frye once wrote about advertising and propaganda that they "are designed deliberately to create an illusion. . . . When such oratory pretends to be, or thinks it is, rational, it adopts a highly characteristic shuffle derived from a desire to reach certain conclusions in advance, whatever the evidence suggests." The goal here wasn't to learn history's lessons. The goal was to rummage through the rattle bag of history to find some rationale for acting the way Paul Martin and his entourage wanted to act. And at the end of 2003, just about the entire Liberal Party, including 93 per cent of the delegates at the Air Canada Centre, were dancing the Highly Characteristic Shuffle.

⇧

Rewind six months, to the late spring of 2003. In office buildings across downtown Ottawa, at Paul Martin's farm in Quebec's Eastern Townships, and in conference calls across the country, the group around Martin was preparing to make him prime minister.

The core of the transition team was Mike Robinson. In 1990, he had managed Martin's campaign for the Liberal leadership. Now he was a principal at Earnscliffe Strategy Group, the Ottawa PR firm that had long served as the home-away-from-government for several of Martin's closest associates – David Herle, Elly Alboim, and for a time Scott Reid. Robinson's group was assigned to set up the management structure of a Martin government, including the cabinet and Prime Minister's Office. Jack Austin, a Trudeau-appointed senator from British Columbia, was in Robinson's group. So was Arthur Kroeger, a senior civil servant throughout the 1970s and 1980s who had become, since his retirement, one of Ottawa's leading authorities on the public service. Kroeger was not a Martin loyalist, just an expert happy to help.

A much larger group handled policy, campaign strategy, and everything else. For the most part, this was the group that would become famous as "The Board": the emotionally tight-knit but organizationally amorphous band of loyalists who would accompany Martin for every moment of his time in power. This included Herle, chief pollster and strategist; Scott Reid, principal spokesman, and his close second, Brian Guest;

Alboim, a veteran television journalist turned Earnscliffe principal; and the three people who had acted as chief of staff during the decade Martin was finance minister: Terrie O'Leary, Ruth Thorkelson, and Tim Murphy. Michèle Cadario had spent most of the 1990s working in Martin's ministerial office. John Duffy had stayed in Toronto but was never out of touch.

For a group whose campaign pitch in 1990 had been that their man understood Quebec better than Jean Chrétien did, the Martin Board was chronically thin on Quebec muscle. Dennis Dawson, a Trudeau-era Liberal MP from Quebec City, was Martin's lead Quebec man, as he had been since 1990. Paul Corriveau, a young Montreal lawyer who had worked for three years in Chrétien's PMO, was brought on board belatedly when the group's meagre francophone representation bought it some nasty headlines in the Quebec newspapers.

Duffy helped launch a massive policy-generation exercise, featuring as many as twenty-two virtual "round tables" divided by area of interest. So there was a foreign-policy round table, an economy round table, a cities-and-communities round table. Each with a website where members – experts, MPs, friends, friends of friends, people who wanted to feel useful, people who sometimes actually were – could post papers and debate ideas.

Frankly, much of the round-table work was designed to keep people busy, to reduce the number of idle hands in the extended Martin entourage. Very little from the round tables ever made it back to the core campaign team. "Some of the tables produced good, sound, inventive ideas," a transition-team member recalls. "Some of the tables produced pablum. Some produced worse than pablum."

"There were a lot of ideas," another transition-team member says, "but you start to cross them off. You say, 'Let's think about this a little more. Yeah, China's really neat. So what? What does it mean? What do you *do*?'"

As the transition team, which was mostly the 2002–3 campaign team, which was mostly the 1990 campaign team, gathered at intervals through the summer, it started to become apparent to some participants that a revolution in Canadian governance wasn't exactly around the corner. "It had the feeling of a bunch of university students sort of vaguely aware that they had an exam in a few months, you know?" one participant said. "And sort of finding this all quite funny and getting sort of punchy about it. And I never had any sense in the process of where Paul's head was at. There was never any kind of filter that, 'The leader will want . . . *this*.'"

This person "kept waiting for the Holy Shit moment . . . and it never, that I saw, really happened." What would a Holy Shit moment look like during a summer-long policy brainstorming session? "The night before your stats exam and you realize you don't know anything about stats. And you've sort of been winging it. And you wind up there in the exam room and you can't bring your textbook. And your study partners can't be there. That would have been the moment. Somebody saying, 'We actually need some comprehensive and consistent policy on this.' And instead, the process was really much more speech-driven. It was much more, you know, 'If we have something to say about this on this file, then we're sort of okay for the moment.'"

John Duffy offers a partial explanation for this vagueness of the Martin policy apparatus. He recalled a meeting from long before the summer of transition – at least a year earlier, when Martin was officially no more than an apostate ex-minister. "It was a group meeting with a lot of stakeholders – not stakeholders, big thinkers. Big, important thinkers who were brought in for, you know, four hours of just the biggest-picture, blue-sky, what's facing the country and what needs to be done." Duffy declines to identify the group, except to say with a chuckle that it was "just Paul and a bunch of friends who happened to be Companions of the Order of Canada, except for me and Elly [Alboim] and David [Herle] and one or two others."

The big thinkers were all hot on "deep integration," the post-9/11 idea that Canada had to get inside a security and customs perimeter with the United States because the alternative was to be stuck outside it. They also had a lot to say about productivity, using technological innovation to squeeze more value out of every Canadian worker.

"And then Elly Alboim, who's been patiently listening, says, 'That's nice. Nobody in the public understands any of this,'" Duffy recalls. "'Here's what the public wants, and it's overwhelmingly clear from any poll that anyone has taken in the past, you know, five years. They are desperate about the health-care system, they are completely losing faith in it. They are feeling very squeezed, particularly the middle class, with regard to education costs. And they are really noticing that everything around them, physically, is crumbling. The roads are full of potholes, the subways are crowded, the bridges are shaky.'"

This all stuck in Duffy's memory because it helps explain why there was no whiz-bang unified field theory that would explain the Martin prime ministership. The heir apparent agreed with much of what the smart guys with the Order of Canada pins were saying – after all, he'd invited them. But his own campaign staff couldn't reconcile that stuff with what they perceived to be the imperatives of retail politics.

"As a result, what came out of that mill was not so much priorities as three buckets: building a twenty-first-century

Canadian economy, securing the social foundations of Canadian life, and a place of pride and influence in the world. You know, those were buckets. It was understood that they weren't rifle-shot deliverables, they were conceptual buckets. And the inadequacies of that from a messaging perspective were well understood."

Translated from jargon, Duffy was saying you couldn't boil the Martin mission down to a bumper sticker. "You were bound to have an approach that was going to necessarily come across as fairly bureaucratic. Of course back then, we were in a political position where we were looking at having so much support that we would have the leeway to be able to work with very fuzzy messaging nonetheless. So it didn't seem like the end of the world." Translated again, Duffy was saying that since Martin was on his way to two hundred seats, he didn't need to explain clearly what he planned to do with them.

If change isn't inherent in the mission, where is it? In the people. The change-agent narrative that dominated the Martin transition, one senior Board member said, is about offering enough change to satisfy – while still portraying the other parties as too much change. "That, actually, is the sweet spot," this Board member said. "And you try to do everything to hit that sweet spot. Including cabinet."

Cabinet! The little group around Robinson had looked at the question and decided that too many ministers meant trouble. With twenty-five ministers, you'd have less conflict, disagreement, incoherence. With more, you'd have more. It was a variation on Tom Flanagan's notion of the "minimum winning coalition." What about the idea of an inner and outer cabinet? A ring of ministers with real clout, and a periphery of secretaries with more limited responsibilities? Robinson's group studied the British cabinet, which is built along those lines. "We found that, of course, all these second- and third-tier ministers want to become first-tier ministers," a member of the transition team said. "So they're all competing with one another. So they're all aggressively promoting departmental interests and not behaving very collegially. It was not a model that looked all that attractive."

In the end it was the model Martin used. The cabinet he unveiled on December 12, 2003, was among the largest any new prime minister has had, with thirty-eight ministers. Around them were a group of parliamentary secretaries – junior ministers who would, for the first time, be sworn into the Privy Council and invited to a cabinet meeting if their specific responsibilities were to be discussed. Martin himself had three such helpers. He would need them. The maze of new cabinet committees threatened to keep him infernally busy, especially since he was to chair a bunch of them personally: Priorities and Planning, Global Affairs, Canada–U.S., Aboriginal Affairs.

The new government would do almost nothing one way if it could find a way to do it three different and competing ways. So there would be a new Minister of Public Safety and Emergency Preparedness, Anne McLellan. But also a National Security Advisor to the Prime Minister; a Cabinet Committee on Security; and a National Security Standing Committee of the Commons. Martin's foreign minister would have to compete for his ear with a parliamentary secretary for Canada–U.S. relations, a new Canada–U.S. secretariat in the Privy Council Office, and a new Canada–U.S. parliamentary-relations office in Washington.

With all those jobs, there still weren't enough for everyone who'd worked in Jean Chrétien's cabinet. A few of them, like deputy prime minister John Manley, saw what was coming and announced they were leaving politics rather than be pushed.

Others waited to be pushed, and were. Stéphane Dion, Bob Nault, Jane Stewart, Sheila Copps, Don Boudria, Maurizio Bevilacqua, and others would have no place in the new cabinet. Martin offered to make Dion the ambassador to Spain if he would only agree not to run for re-election. Dion preferred to stay and fight.

For Dennis Dawson, who was part of the cabinet-building team, the only problem was that more Chrétien ministers, especially in Quebec, couldn't be given the heave-ho. "You build your cabinet with the wood that is given you. You've got wide planks, you've got new wood, you've got ticks and you've got termites. But you can't make your cabinet with wood that's not there. In Quebec, you finished off with a Martin cabinet that was Chrétien-plus. Most of them were Chrétien ministers and they carried their Chrétien baggage and they carried their Chrétien attitude. And they were dedicated to Chrétien, the party, and then to Paul. So that doesn't make for a close-knit team . . . We had to have ministers who would either second-guess everything Paul or Paul's people were saying, or would in certain cases just object to it completely. So you can imagine that it was not the ideal scenario."

I asked Dawson whether the goal was a change of faces or a change in ideas about Quebec's place in Canada. "It was a lot of change in attitude, certainly. No – start by being very frank. Change for change."

One member of the transition team recalls: "I'm pretty certain that no one around that table sat back and said, 'Maybe there's change that matters and change that doesn't matter. And the Paul Martin that's prime minister now is the most significant change of optic we could have, since we're all Liberals.' And whether you're throwing out Allan Rock and

John Manley or adding Joe Volpe and Tony Ianno it's change, but I'm not sure it matters to anyone.

"And all this flurry of machinery changes? My sense of the group as a collective is that they wouldn't have thought, you know – caution would not be tolerated around that table. And [there would be] a default assumption, born more out of ignorance than anything else – this knee-jerk assumption that everything that was done before was not as good as it could be."

Now, it's possible to overstate this. The purge at cabinet level wasn't complete. Chrétien ministers who had refrained from direct confrontation with Martin or the Board were kept on, including Pierre Pettigrew, John McCallum (shuffled from Defence to the backwater of Veterans' Affairs), and the affectless, apparently indispensable Lucienne Robillard. Two close Martin allies from the Chrétien days, McLellan and Ralph Goodale, were kept and promoted, Goodale to Finance, McLellan to deputy prime minister. And at the staffing level, in ministers' offices, very few Chrétien-era employees found themselves hard up for a job.

Still, some trends were emerging. First, a preference for not doing whatever Chrétien had done. Second, a surprising but comprehensive lack of distinctive, or even coherent, new policies. Third, effective control by a loose network of Martin loyalists whose informal discussions tended to trump whatever formal structures were supposed to be in place. Those trends were entirely determinative when the Martin government faced its first crisis. Also its last crisis, and the only crisis that was needed, as things turned out, to finish the Martin government off: the sponsorship scandal.

5

GROUP THERAPY

⇧

Everyone on Paul Martin's team knew when he became prime minister that an audit into the federal government's sponsorship activities was on the way. Sheila Fraser, the Chrétien-appointed auditor general, had delivered a preliminary, nasty report on a small number of shady contracts in May 2002, and promptly announced she was going to study all of the federal government's sponsorship, polling, and other visibility efforts. The report was to be tabled in November of 2003. But Chrétien prorogued Parliament just before the target date – right after the November Liberal convention – to make way for Martin. Fraser, an officer of Parliament, temporarily had no Parliament to report to. (Some of the Martinites would forever blame Chrétien for failing to stick around long enough to jump on that particular grenade. So suddenly Paul Martin wanted Chrétien to stay *longer*?)

The Martin government knew the audit was coming, and that it would not be pretty. The scale of the trouble ahead sort of depended on whom you asked. "In the briefings we received, it was never presented as, 'This is going to be the biggest bomb that you're ever going to see,'" one Martin ally said. "It was never presented as, 'This is going to be a crisis.' It was simply on the list of things coming down."

When it came down, at first glance, it was breathtaking. Between 1997 and 2003, Fraser reported, $100 million had been paid in fees and commissions to Liberal-connected communications agencies. In many cases she could find no evidence that any serious work had been done to earn the money. The ostensible goal of these programs had been to make the Canadian government more prominent in Quebec in the aftermath of the 1995 secession referendum. Many observers were left with the impression that the real goal had been to line the pockets of friends of the regime.

But who was responsible? Fraser couldn't know: her job was to investigate administration, not political decisions. Where had the money gone? Again, not her problem. Once the money was paid by federal officials, it left her auditor's field of vision.

The Martin government had perhaps two weeks before the audit was to be made public on February 10, 2004, to decide how to respond. Senior staff discussed it in Martin's PMO. Cabinet's Operations committee, chaired by Anne McLellan, discussed it. "At the end of the day, the calculus was, are we going to be part of the problem or part of the solution?" a senior Martin staffer says. "And how do we show that?

"Some voices were arguing very strongly that we needed to take it seriously, do something big and real to show that we were upset. Others argued about what the cost would be, to us, for taking this action. That was the debate."

Something big and real would be a public commission of inquiry, chaired by a judge with broad terms of reference. He would go off and hold an endless series of public hearings, at which every shady character who'd benefited from Liberal bad faith or sloppy management would spend hours recounting the sordid details. People with long institutional memories weren't thrilled with this idea. Francis Fox, Martin's principal secretary, had been a cabinet minister in the Trudeau years. He knew the tendency for inquiry judges to empire-build, far overstepping their budgets and deadlines – and, more importantly, their original mandates. Without arguing strongly against the idea of a commission of inquiry, he made sure the rest of the Martin entourage knew about this history.

Others were more adamant in their opposition. All of the scheming and profiteering had been done in Quebec; the Quebeckers around the table were especially leery of airing all that dirty laundry in public. "I can't remember a parliamentarian from Quebec who wanted a public inquiry," recalls Steven MacKinnon, the Liberal Party's executive director and a member of the group that plotted strategy for the Fraser audit.

In the end, Martin threw everything he had behind the audit. Justice John Gomery, a Montreal judge four years away from retirement, was called on the morning of February 10 and asked to run the public inquiry. In addition Martin would name a "special counsel for financial recovery" to hunt down any sponsorship money that might have found its way back into Liberal Party coffers. The Fraser audit would also be referred to the Commons Public Accounts committee, a ramshackle assortment of more or less diligent MPs from every party who were, nonetheless, the designated parliamentary body for investigating shady or incompetent program delivery.

Martin's staff announced all of this on the very day Fraser's report was made public, February 10. Alfonso Gagliano, the former Chrétien public-works minister on whose watch this mess had been allowed to spread, was immediately fired from his cushy exile as Canada's ambassador to Denmark. Martin appeared before reporters in the lobby of the House of Commons and announced all these actions. He would get to the bottom of this mess, he said. But he insisted he had known nothing about any of this scandal while it was happening.

Trouble ensued.

The one thing almost everyone around Martin is now willing to admit is that announcing the Gomery commission on the day of the audit ensured that in the first instance, the remedy would be drowned out by the news of the scandal itself. What they didn't expect was that almost nobody in Canada would believe, on the face of it, that a finance minister from Quebec had been ignorant of a financing scandal in Quebec. Martin had to come back, on February 12, to hold a news conference with a new explanation. Sure, he said now, he knew something was amiss – after Fraser's first audit in March 2002. But before then, Chrétien had kept him in the dark about the sponsorship program because the two had "different views on Quebec."

What were Martin's views on Quebec, he was asked at that news conference. All he could say was that he had always believed that "the best way to ensure national unity was to accomplish great goals." Ah. King, Trudeau, and Chrétien had all governed through harrowing national-unity crises. King, meanwhile, was raising great armies to help defeat the Nazis. Trudeau repatriated the Constitution. Chrétien ended a generation of deficit spending. If they had only aimed high, Martin seemed to be saying, the nation would have been out of danger.

The early reviews were not glowing. One of David Herle's polls showed the Liberals losing seventeen points in forty-eight hours. "No one had seen a slide like that," Duffy says. "Ever."

Soon, everything the Martinites could throw at the audit would prove to be insufficient. More was needed. Jean Pelletier, the former Chrétien chief of staff, was fired from his job as chairman of Via Rail. Marc Lefrançois, the president of Via, the Crown corporation implicated for impropriety in the Fraser audit, lost his job too. (Both promptly sued.) And Martin left on an extended coast-to-coast media tour whose only purpose was to demonstrate that he was at least as angry about all this as anyone else.

Before the prime minister left on what would forever be remembered as the "Mad as Hell Tour," though, somebody close to Martin would do irreparable damage to the Liberals' fortunes in Quebec, using a technique of which the Martin crew was notoriously fond: the anonymous leak.

"Mr. Martin's own advisers were on the phone to reporters across Ottawa," John Ibbitson wrote in the *Globe and Mail* two days after the audit was released. "The real problem, they said on condition of anonymity, was the ancient and dishonourable tribalism of Quebec politics, in which friends do favours for friends, rules are made to be skirted, and the end justifies not inquiring too closely into the means. This was the political culture personified by Mr. Chrétien, they alleged, and the real purpose of a judicial inquiry would be to finally break the power of the corrupt old guard that Mr. Martin had fought for so many years."

I do wish I could tell you who Ibbitson's source was for that. Whoever it was, he or they had a busy day, because that day's newspapers were full of the same talking points. Jane Taber in the *Globe*: "Senior Martin advisers tried another tack, spending

Wednesday calling up journalists to 'spin' them on their version of events. . . . They described the way in which the Chrétienites played politics in Quebec as 'tribal.'"

Bob Fife in the *National Post*: "'. . . a certain approach to politics in Quebec that was negligent of rules and unconcerned with proper conduct,' said the senior official. . . . 'You have people who were deliberately running a program under what appears to be essentially criminal directives. . . . This is Jean Chrétien and his fundamental belief and those around him that the end justifies the means. . . .'"

One result of this day-long campaign to smear an entire province's political culture from behind a mask of anonymity was that Michel David, *Le Devoir*'s influential political columnist, wrote a bitter, brooding column in response to the Ibbitson column. David wrote that you might expect a hockey lout like Don Cherry to peddle theories like this. But "it is much more troubling to learn that the theory of the rotten apple" – that is, the theory that Quebec is Canada's rotten apple – "seems to be shared by the office of Prime Minister Paul Martin," David wrote. "Lord knows what miracle – perhaps his Ontario roots – kept Mr. Martin from being contaminated by this deplorable culture."

Another result is that Mario Laguë spent forty minutes, on the day Ibbitson's column appeared, wading through the press scrums after Question Period in a frantic exercise of damage control. Laguë was a rotund, bearded, laconic, and fearsomely intelligent career civil servant who had served in Quebec's provincial administration when Robert Bourassa was premier, before moving to Ottawa. He had been on his way from the Privy Council Office to a diplomatic posting when the Martin camp asked him to act as the prime minister's communications director until an election. To French-language reporters,

Laguë was of considerable help, because he spoke their language and knew Quebec. English-language reporters barely noticed he was there. Most simply ignored him and phoned Scott Reid or Brian Guest for the straight goods.

But on this day, Laguë was intent on telling any reporter who would listen that in fact, Paul Martin did not actually believe that Quebec was a hive of ancient and dishonourable tribalism run by a corrupt old guard. I had to ask: Was it a problem that people were peddling this analysis on the boss's behalf, if Martin's stance was that he didn't actually believe it? "Yes, it's a problem," Laguë said.

Then what was to be done about it? Laguë pondered, shrugged hopelessly. "That's for the prime minister to decide."

Today, nobody who supported the decision to call an inquiry will hear a word against the decision. "People will argue forever whether it was a smart or dumb political call," Duffy says. "I don't think you can argue the morality of it." But some of the people around Martin also admit that the decision was made easier by the knowledge that Chrétien would never have sicced an investigative magistrate with a wide-open mandate on his own party. The change narrative, remember, was everything. "In every way, we tried to say we were different," Duffy says, "including our approach to sponsorship – and I concur with you that some of what animated our approach was a need to show a difference."

Another Martin Board member agrees. "Was the decision to do the public inquiry made easier by the fact that there was a change imperative? Sure. If you're going to talk change, then you have to be prepared to do things differently."

Five days after the Fraser audit was released, David Herle appeared on Don Newman's *Politics* on CBC Newsworld. "Isn't this the perfect opportunity to demonstrate that you're an agent of change?" he asked. "Isn't this the perfect kind of issue on which to say, 'Here is something that happened in a previous government – under a different administration – and as soon as it's come out, here's the actions that I've taken.' To me that is an agent of change." And change was everything.

⇧

Here and there, a few lonely souls wondered whether the Martin Board was making the right call with the inquiry and the tour and the rest. Some, of course, were Liberals loyal to Chrétien, who smelled an orchestrated witch hunt. Others were non-combatants in the Chrétien–Martin wars who simply knew the file.

John Embury was the communications director to Ralph Goodale through every one of the Saskatchewan minister's incarnations over a decade, from agriculture minister to Natural Resources, to government House leader, to Public Works, and on to Finance. Goodale landed at Public Works in 2002, just as a nasty smell was beginning to emanate from the *Globe and Mail*'s coverage of the sponsorship program. It fell to him to figure out how the program had been administered, freeze the program while he got up to speed, then reinstate it after making massive administrative overhauls. The biggest was simply to cut out the ad firms that had pocketed the immense commissions for performing pointless and often fraudulent middle-man services between the government and the organizers of individual events.

The decision to restart the program in late 2002, Embury emphasizes, came not from Chrétien but from Goodale himself. "There's a number of small festivals that really need" federal funding, Embury argued. "And as a communications device – you can argue about whether it's really useful, but big companies sponsor things all the time. There's a use for it, a communications benefit." As for Fraser's audit, Embury recalls that when it came out, he was amazed, not by its revelations, but by how few revelations there actually were to anyone who'd been following the file.

Daniel Leblanc and Campbell Clark at the *Globe and Mail* had been covering the story since 1999; Joël-Denis Bellavance at *La Presse* had been quick to join the chase. A series of audits had preceded the big one from Fraser. Goodale's 2002 overhaul was only the latest in a series of reforms – instituted, to be sure, by a Chrétien government that had the Opposition and the Press Gallery hot on its heels, but instituted nonetheless. Don't take my word for it. At the risk of jumping ahead in our narrative, here's Judge Gomery, in the first of his two reports, tabled at the end of October 2005: "It is reasonable to assume that if the guidelines and procedures introduced in 2001 by Communication Canada to manage the Sponsorship Program had been in place from its inception, the mismanagement and abuses that occurred from 1996 to 2000 would not have been possible."

So here's John Embury, who'd been following the sponsorship file for three years instead of three weeks. "The thing that killed me was, I mean, the auditor general's report came out – and Daniel and Joël-Denis and Campbell had written every one of those stories. There wasn't one piece of new *anything* that came out of that [report]. But there was just this firestorm." I asked Embury whether the government could have simply ridden out the storm, letting the RCMP handle criminal abuse and explaining patiently what Martin's predecessor had done to fix the program's administration. Was that an option? "It could have been. I mean, Ralph had handled it up to that point. Could he have continued? Probably. But it just went in a different direction."

Now, that's just one guy's opinion. Almost nobody in the group around Martin is willing to consider the possibility that a public inquiry was an inappropriate response. They may well be right. The outrage over the sponsorship scandal was immense. The police would catch the people suspected of criminal wrongdoing – in fact, nobody but the police could ever have a mandate to do so – and the special counsel would trace the money, if anyone could. An inquiry, however, might give a clear-eyed explanation for what had happened at a political level. And besides, the Opposition would certainly have demanded one if Martin hadn't been so quick to set one up.

But once that inquiry was given its marching orders, what possible business was it of Paul Martin's to go on tour and promise that he, a senior minister in the government under investigation, would be the one to "get to the bottom" of the scandal? From any rational analysis of the proper role of the executive in a democracy, what was the Mad as Hell Tour about?

Steven MacKinnon, like most of the Martin entourage, continues to maintain that the Gomery inquiry was the appropriate response. But the garment-rending tour that followed? "That's another thing. In what world does it make any sense to have the guy who's going to deliver 220 seats go across the country and wear this? Makes absolutely no sense to me." Was this an argument that could get any traction at the time? "No. Because the decision was made. This was Mr. Fix-up, Mr. Change, Mr. Clean-up, Mr. Go Across the Country and Shoulder the Responsibility for Fixing This Up."

The decision was made? Who made it? MacKinnon pauses to consider. "Everyone."

⇧

And so we come back, inevitably, to the Board, the tightly knit, tightly wound group of 1990 leadership campaign veterans whose members would be at the centre of all Martin's big decisions. Who was on the Board? "The membership was not inscribed in a book somewhere," John Duffy says. "And it's fair to say that for a fair number of us, myself included, sometimes we were very, very involved, and then it would sort of trail off a bit, then it would start up again. It was pretty darned informal."

One definition of the Board, in fact, might be: that group around Paul Martin that others could work with, but never penetrate. "It's like an Irish family that's been around forever," says one former Martin staffer, who worked closely with the inner circle for months before leaving (that's another defining characteristic: if you left, then you had never really been a member). Says another: "You couldn't pierce the armour that was around that group of people. It was like a Spartan army."

For Robert Steiner, a Toronto business consultant who did a stint working on policy and writing speeches for Martin in 2002 and 2003, it wasn't quite that dramatic. Steiner worked well with the Board. "They opened up to me enormously. When they saw the product that I was producing for them and they liked it, they opened up to me like I never believed they would open up to me. . . . But what happened was, when you penetrate up to a certain point, you couldn't get much farther. It was a bit like a guerrilla group. You'll accept the new recruit but you'd better be bloody sure that they'll be there for you, and they're not just there to be opportunistic or to spy on you. So guerrilla groups grow, but you've got to be a convert to get in."

On his way in, Steiner was briefly amazed at what a close rapport he seemed to be striking with Martin. Writing a speech for Martin was famously an elaborate, iterative torment, with countless drafts going through endless overhauls by committee. But in 2003 Steiner had to write a speech alone, on short notice, for Martin's appearance at the inauguration of the Montreal Holocaust Memorial Centre. A week after the event, Steiner was in Ottawa. Martin said he'd loved the Holocaust museum speech and more work should follow. "I want to work very closely with you on a bunch of stuff," Steiner recalls Martin saying. "I want to work directly with you. I don't want a ton of other people in the room." Steiner was flattered, but out of courtesy he informed Tim Murphy of his new mano-a-mano working relationship with the big guy.

"And the reaction was along the lines of, 'Oh, you've had *that* conversation,'" Steiner says. "'This is the normal conversation that happens with all the newcomers when he tries to take them away. You can't do that. Obviously, talk to him every time he calls, and work for him and do all the things you need to do with him, but you can't cut us out of the loop.'"

"This sort of became a running theme," Steiner says. A few weeks later Martin called him at home to go over the notes of another speech. "And he started going over my notes and he said, 'And you're just going to work with me on this, right? From this point forward, you're not going to speak to anyone. You're just going to work with me.'" And once again, when Steiner called Murphy or Alboim to announce he would be flying solo, he was told no, that wasn't allowed.

This, too, is a running theme. The group around Martin defended its prerogatives and didn't let anyone have too much autonomy. Including Martin. They had been with him for two decades. They would stay with him. "There was a core group of the Board that had been tight-knit in the youth wing of the party, and had enemies, and those grudges carried forward for twenty years," Dennis Dawson recalls. "That probably turned into a little bit of arrogance. We were probably – not probably, we were *definitely* – too tightly knit.

"We had groupthink, we were the first guys on the Hill with BlackBerrys, we were up-to-date on spinning before spinning – you know. So there were advantages to being a small group. But one of the disadvantages was that we did become arrogant. And that made us not nice to caucus members, not nice to a bunch of people. And we paid for it in 2004, we paid for it in 2006, and God knows we're still paying for it today."

When I interviewed Dawson, late in the spring of 2006, my ears just about popped out of my head when he used that word. Groupthink. In day-to-day conversation, it just means a group whose members can't make a decision independently. But in social psychology it has a very specific, heavily documented meaning. I had already been reading heavily into small-group psychology to try to understand how the people around Martin acted – how the very structure and status of the Board influenced its decisions. I believe the way Paul Martin's government handled the sponsorship scandal is a classic case of groupthink.

The term was coined in 1972 by Irving L. Janis, a research psychologist at Yale University and the University of California at Berkeley. Janis's *Victims of Groupthink: A Psychological Study of Foreign Policy Decisions and Fiascoes* examined some of the red-letter cockups in the history of American public administration. The list included the preparedness of the U.S. Navy at Pearl

Harbor in late 1941; Eisenhower's decision to chase the defeated North Korean army on its home territory; Kennedy's Bay of Pigs invasion of Cuba; and Lyndon Johnson's escalation of the Vietnam War. Janis later, and most famously, applied the groupthink analysis to the group around Nixon during the Watergate crisis. In each case the key decisions had been made by a small, highly cohesive group around the main leader, usually the president.

In his first attempt at defining groupthink, Janis called it: "A mode of thinking that people engage in when they are deeply involved in a cohesive in-group, when the members' strivings for unanimity override their motivation to realistically appraise alternative courses of action." Generations of researchers have amended and deepened the definition since then, but the characteristics of groupthink – what makes it happen and what predictable flaws it produces – are consistent.

The first characteristic is cohesion. As Paul 't Hart, a research fellow at Leiden University in the Netherlands, points out in his 1990 book *Groupthink in Government: A Study of Small Groups and Policy Failure*, this simple idea is what makes groupthink so counterintuitive and therefore so much fun to study: "the realization that . . . harmonious, cooperative, team-like entities may be a liability rather than an asset in producing high-quality decisions. This is not what one would expect."

Second, what 't Hart calls a "provocative situational context." In other words, trouble. "The chances of groupthink markedly increase when decision makers are under stress, dealing with a crisis situation," 't Hart writes. "In these circumstances, decision makers may perceive threats to their self-esteem because of the tremendous burden of having to decide about impenetrable, morally complex issues."

Janis and his successors found several characteristics of groupthink processes and decisions. First, a tendency to overestimate the group, including a belief in its inherent morality. Second, a kind of closed-mindedness: a tendency to rationalize the group's decisions and to stereotype "out-groups," players from outside the main decision-making group. Third, pressures toward uniformity, including social ostracism of dissenters.

Significant failure doesn't necessarily rattle a group's cohesiveness. Indeed, it may make it grow. In 1961, two social psychologists, A.J. Lott and B.E. Lott, found that when members of a group believe that a failure is arbitrarily imposed on them by outside forces they can't control, their attraction to the group may become even greater.

One of the most intriguing findings of social psychologists is that groups are often more prone to take great risks than individuals in the same situation. Later research found that this "risky shift" isn't guaranteed. Sometimes groups are *less* reckless than individuals. The theory that eventually emerged is one of group polarization, or extremization: If a group's members are all initially inclined toward a certain mindset or ideology, its decisions will be more extremely oriented in that direction. So timid people make for really timid groups, conservative groups favour more right-wing policies than their individual members would – and, one can postulate, a change-obsessed group with Chrétien on the brain might find itself itching to show change from the Chrétien way of doing things at the moment of its first big decision.

What causes the risky shift and other kinds of extremization? 'T Hart points to overconfidence, and says this is likelier in some situations than others. One of the moments when groups are most over-optimistic, he writes, is "during the so-called 'honeymoon period' of newly-established regimes or governments." The classic ruined honeymoon is the Bay of Pigs episode, a plan to overthrow Castro that the Kennedy administration inherited when Kennedy arrived in the White House and failed to sufficiently consider before implementing.

Lord knows those guys were overconfident. 'T Hart quotes Arthur Schlesinger on the spirit of the moment: "The currents of vitality radiated out of the White House, flowed through the government and created a sense of vast possibility. The very idea of the new President taking command as tranquilly and naturally as if his whole life had prepared him for it could not but stimulate a flood of buoyant optimism. . . . Intelligence was at last being applied to public affairs."

You could almost say the Kennedy entourage thought this was a moment when destiny was theirs to hold.

⇧

Now, before we get too carried away with fancy theories, let's hold on just a minute. As Dennis Dawson's use of the term suggests, groupthink is an idea that gets tossed around pretty lightly in some circles. Indeed, 't Hart's book is in some ways an extended warning against applying the label where it shouldn't be applied.

First of all, groupthink is about decisions by small groups. "Most government decisions," 't Hart writes reasonably enough, "are taken by decisional units other than small groups." You're way more likely to see a minister making a decision alone, or a hierarchical bureaucracy manufacturing decisions in ways that destroy group chemistry.

Absolutely. But no recent Canadian government has privileged the small group as the decision-making forum more than Martin's. Martin was famous for revelling in the so-called

CMO (for Council of Minister and Others) process for budget-making, which was no more than an endless series of meetings at which ranks and titles were tossed out the window and the *group* – as an undifferentiated cluster of stem cells – hashed over every decision. The same processes continued in government. The bureaucracy was not immune, nor was cabinet. "One knew there were a hell of a lot of players out there with their spoon in the soup, causing trouble," a senior Martin minister told me.

The even more important caveat that 't Hart imposes against anyone who would toss around "groupthink" diagnoses too blithely is that groupthink cannot happen except in a highly cohesive group. Most groups in government aren't that cohesive. First, they don't have time to get to know one another. Second, they haven't bonded under fire. Third, cabinet-making is driven by considerations that hinder cohesiveness, like regional and ideological diversity within the governing party. You almost never get important decisions made by small groups that have been together forever, formed intense emotional bonds, and tend all to think similarly on big issues.

But then there's the Board.

There is no more fascinating chronicle of group cohesiveness in the birthing than a history of Paul Martin's first Liberal leadership bid written by its national youth campaign director, Charles Bird, less than a week after Chrétien beat Martin at Calgary in June of 1990. There's a copy of Bird's short memoir, *Just Do It: Reflections on the 1990 Liberal Leadership* at the Library of Parliament. But you can't take it out without permission from Bird, who was Ontario campaign director for Martin in 2006. That's understandable: in some stretches it chronicles the passions and enthusiasms of a student in his early twenties in ways that its author probably regrets. I got my

copy through other channels. Let us tactfully snip out the pas-
sages that smack too heavily of a Dobie Gillis confessional.
What remains is the birth of the Board.

As the memoir opens, young Bird is sitting in the remains of
the Martin campaign office, watching friends cart away their
personal goods. "At the end of the week, we'll say our last
tearful good-byes, and we'll part with the knowledge that one
day, we might just come together again and do it right," Bird
writes. "I truly hope that day comes."

It all began, we read in flashback, when Bird became part of
the group defending John Turner against a challenge to his
own leadership launched in 1986 on Chrétien's behalf. The
"dark side" of the anti-Turner forces, he recalls, "were sym-
bolized by certain lesser individuals, who are not worthy of
being named. . . . There are no individuals anywhere I despise
more – the individuals who used the legitimate opposition of
many to the Meech Lake Accord and bastardized it to the
point where the Liberal Party, and Canada, bled for their vindictiveness. I will never forgive them, and I will always wait for
them. They too will bleed one day."

Onward. Bird gets to know an Ontario Young Liberal executive "dominated by ruthless individuals whose sole purpose
was the furthering of their own, and Jean Chrétien's, respec-
tive causes." These people rub Bird the wrong way: "self-
serving, lazy, inconsiderate bastards."

He is much more impressed by the group forming around
Paul Martin, including a wise father figure named Mike
Robinson and a more youthful crew including David Herle
and Terrie O'Leary. "They all knew each other socially as well,
which facilitated the ease with which they communicated."

He's also fond of two "dear friends, Bruce Young . . . and John
Bethel," who sixteen years later would play leading Campaign

2006 roles for the Martin Liberals in British Columbia and Alberta. "To me these two epitomize the spirit and vitality of the Martin Youth Campaign, a sense that . . . the role we were playing was vitally important, to Paul, the Party, and maybe even to Canada."

The Martin campaign faces organizational setbacks, but they are dealt arbitrarily by forces beyond their control. "We knew instinctively that we were being cheated, but the Alberta Liberal Party was so biased in favour of Chrétien that we never did get close enough to figure out how."

The bitter winds of an unfair world only make the young Martin team huddle more closely together. At one crisis moment, Bird confides in Michèle Cadario. "I will always love her for being there when she was." He spars with, then grows to respect, an organizer named Karl Littler. "There are few Young Liberals I feel closer to than him." He shares moments with "Paul's speech writer, my old and dear friend John Duffy." He swears that he "will always have a kind word for Scott Reid, a Martin youth from Queen's University." When it all ends badly, he cries on David Herle's shoulder. "What he said to me then I won't repeat but I will always love him for it. I don't say that of many guys."

During the week-long Calgary convention, the Martin youth have a party. Usually a party is just a party. But "that Wednesday night at Winston's was a major turning point for our youth campaign . . . a degree of bonding took place among our young people, in a way which never happened, noticeably at least, among the Chrétien youth." The only shadow over the good times is the prospect of the Meech Lake constitutional amendments dying at the end of the week, as the three-year deadline for ratifying the changes runs out in Newfoundland and Manitoba. Young Bird feels "a dark sense of foreboding, at what would befall the Party and quite possibly the country in the next few hours, and in the days and weeks to come."

(As it happens, the decision to hold the Liberal leadership convention on the weekend of the Meech deadline was forced by Martin sympathizers on the Liberal national executive, who pushed for the convention to be held months later than Chrétien wanted it, in hopes of giving Martin time to catch up. Paul 't Hart notes that one characteristic of groupthink decisions is a "collapsed time-perspective," a refusal to consider the long-term consequences of decisions as a coping mechanism for dealing with the stress of the moment.)

In the end Paul Martin loses, Bird and Herle share a moment, and Chrétien and his self-serving bastards take over the party and quite possibly the country. While Bird waits for the moment when they too will bleed, he ends his chronicle with a note to the man he did it all for. "To Paul Martin: I and so many others will be there for you again. We have taken your dream of this nation to heart and it has changed us fundamentally for the better."

Thirteen and a half years later, Charles Bird was still working for Paul Martin, albeit at some distance in the Liberals' Ontario campaign organization. But Terrie and David and Mike and Scott and Karl and Michèle and Dennis, almost the whole old gang from 1990, were in the loop when an overconfident government in the first flush of its honeymoon applied its shared perspective and its predisposition to do whatever Chrétien wouldn't to its first tough decision. The group was confident of its morality, suspicious of out-groups, collapsed in its time-perspective, and unfettered by regional and ideological diversity. It worked out about as well as could be expected, given the circumstances.

6

FALSE STARTS OF OUR LIVES

⇧

Nobody was ready for the 2004 election. It's that simple. The Harper Conservatives had no time to prepare for a serious campaign. The Martin Liberals had had half a decade to prepare, but the campaign they were ready for – the campaign to grow the Liberal majority – was never going to happen.

By the end of March 2004, all the best strategists and organizers in the new Conservative Party were exhausted from the party's leadership campaign. And for all anyone knew there was very close to zero time to get ready for a national election. Martin had fast-tracked amendments to the Elections Act – designed among other things to increase the number of MPs from 301 to 308 – from August to the beginning of April. The Harper camp's planning assumption was that the new prime minister would drop the writ on April 4 for an election.

April 4 was two weeks away.

Harper dispatched Ian Brodie and Doug Finley to Conservative Party HQ to clean up the party organization. Brodie became executive director, Finley, director of political operations and campaign manager. The party was a mess. No field organization to speak of. No fundraising organization. No IT department. No planes and buses. Nobody who knew how to *get* planes and buses.

Harper's leadership team became the core of the party's campaign team. Not because these guys flattered themselves that they were the only talent in the party, but because there was no time to build working relationships with the *other* talent, which had spent the winter trying to stop Harper.

The party office in downtown Ottawa became a campaign war room. From there, Finley ran the field organization, which included figuring out who the party's candidates were supposed to be and inculcating them in the virtues of message discipline. Ken Boessenkool was assigned the task of preparing the campaign message. But since this party hadn't had time to decide where it stood on any major question, that was an even bigger task than it sounded. One Conservative described Boessenkool's to-do list: "The scripting plan. The communications plan. And the fucking *platform*." William Stairs, who had been Peter MacKay's communications director during MacKay's short interlude as Tory leader, would lend Boessenkool a hand, as would a young ex-Alliance spinner named Mike Storeshaw.

The versatile were routinely punished with new assignments. Tom Flanagan still liked to think of himself as a political scientist; his new job was to set up an advertising strategy and produce ad products. Brodie's wife, Vida, had to come up with buttons and posters and the other paraphernalia of a campaign. Somebody pointed at Dave Penner, another staffer at the party office, and told him he would be the wagonmaster for the leader's tour, rustling up food, filing facilities, and hotel rooms for a busload of grumpy reporters for five weeks.

Then there was Stephen Harper. His first job as leader of the united Conservative Party of Canada was to beg for mercy. To Harper's astonishment, Paul Martin gave him some.

Within days after the leadership vote, Harper was back in Ottawa demanding that the Liberals refrain from calling a snap election. He did his best to make it sound like a principled argument, but he was transparently trying to save his own skin. Before the merger talks had begun in earnest in the fall of 2003, Harper's Alliance had made real progress in election planning, right down to details like registering a more attractive new Alliance logo with Elections Canada. But the merger and the leadership campaign had done worse than stall that planning. It had rendered much of the plan obsolete. Finley, Brodie, Boessenkool, and the others were quick studies, but they were behind the eight ball. Harper, who had learned a thing or two about taking advantage of an opponent's weakness, expected Martin to do that to him now.

In the end, battered by the polls after the Fraser audit, Martin did delay – not from spring to autumn, but from early April to late May. To this day, Harper tells close associates that Martin's biggest tactical mistake was to give the Conservatives that time.

In the end Martin could delay only for weeks, not months. For one thing he was running out of people. Deposed Chrétien-era ministers and other have-nots of the dawning Martin era were already announcing their intention to retire from politics. They could be persuaded to keep their Commons seats until May, but not until, say, November. As they left, they would make the Martin government vulnerable to defeat in confidence votes.

Second, Martin was already running out of ideas. Despite all the policy round tables, the password-encoded Internet forums, the endless meetings, and more than a year's unanticipated preparation time, the Martin crew came to office with very few projects ready to deliver. The goal was to use the massive apparatus of the public service to cook up big projects for the autumn. That left a space that had to be filled, and nothing to fill it except elections. "It is clear that prolonging the House session will lead to more debates on bills," Dennis Dawson told *Le Devoir*. "If we delay, delay, delay, at some point we'll have to find things to debate."

That just wouldn't do. So on May 23 Martin called his election for June 28. The extra weeks before that writ drop gave both leaders just enough time to show themselves in the worst possible light. In what would quickly become a theme, Martin ran as hard as he could away from demonstrable fact. And Harper gave vent, at least once, to a truly epic display of temper.

Martin first. On April 27, Pierre Pettigrew, the wavy-haired, dandyish health minister, appeared before the Commons Health Committee. He discussed the proper mix of private-sector and public-sector involvement in providing health services. Nothing he said was remotely novel or controversial.

"If some provinces want to experiment with the private-delivery option, my view is that as long as they respect the single-payer, public payer, we should be examining those efforts," Pettigrew told his colleagues. "And then compare notes between provinces whether . . . it doesn't work. If it doesn't work, they'll stop it. But if it works, we'll all learn something."

Nothing Pettigrew said was any different in substance from remarks a previous Liberal health minister, Anne McLellan, made in 2002. Here's what McLellan said: "Does corporate structure necessarily matter in terms of a hospital, as long as when I take my Alberta health card, they take that card and my stay in that hospital and the treatment therein is covered by a publicly funded, publicly administered health-care plan?"

Anne McLellan's reward for saying this was to be promoted to deputy prime minister as soon as Paul Martin could make the call. Pierre Pettigrew's reward for expressing the same sentiment was public humiliation.

"It was a furious Paul Martin at this week's caucus meeting," Jane Taber wrote in that weekend's *Globe*. "His face was red; he was gesticulating angrily; and some say he was shouting." The object of his wrath was the hapless Pierre Pettigrew. "Mr. Martin told his caucus that he had watched his father, Paul Sr., work hard to bring in medicare and wasn't prepared to stand by and watch it unravel." With that, Taber's sources told her, Martin announced that Pierre Pettigrew was just going to have to march out of caucus and read a clarification.

Minutes later Pettigrew did just that. His comments of the previous day "left the impression that I favour increased private delivery within the public health system," he told the TV cameras. "That was in no way my intent. Nor is it the intent of the government of Canada." This government would not "encourage private delivery, even within the terms of the Canada Health Act."

How would a Liberal government roll back private delivery? It couldn't. The Canada Health Act gives the feds no tools to restrict private delivery as long as it is publicly funded. Martin had sent his minister to the scrum mic to express a preference, a druther, a fond wish. As if he had announced that the government of Paul Martin would prefer that next Tuesday be sunshiny instead of grey.

What had caused this astonishing display of disingenuousness? Two things: an electoral strategy based on demonstrating that Stephen Harper stood for darkness and the Liberals for light, even if this meant drawing distinctions between the two parties where none existed; and a single morning's embarrassing headlines. The banner headline in the morning's *Ottawa Citizen*, for instance, was "The New Liberal Agenda: Paul Martin Steals a Page From the Conservatives in Run-up to Election . . . Provinces Free to 'Experiment' With Private Delivery of Health Care."

The Liberals could simply have explained that there was no news, nor any theft of Conservative pages, in what their minister had said. But that would have taken an allegiance to plain truth, a measure of immunity from panic, and a stock of patience measured in some scale higher than hours. For Paul Martin, none of those traits could be taken for granted.

The Martin government's disingenuous stance on private health-care delivery would be the gift that kept on giving. On May 4, the *Globe*'s Richard Mackie had a new wrinkle: "Prime Minister Paul Martin warned against 'chequebook' health-care . . . at a campaign-style event in a Toronto hospital that offers basic health procedures after hours paid for under private contracts outside the Ontario Health Insurance Plan."

Hoo boy. Could it possibly get worse? Sure. Here's Glen McGregor in the *Ottawa Citizen* on May 7: "Prime Minister Paul Martin receives medical treatment from a family doctor who operates a chain of private MRI clinics."

⇧

Let us leave Paul Martin wrestling with the ghost of his father and the incoherence of his health-care policy and check in on Harper. The Conservative leader was welcomed to his new post by a series of Liberal attack ads based on the most piquant statements from Harper's public record. A series of pre-election television spots quoted Harper saying something out-rageous or simply a little weird. Then a man's voice told us what, in the minds of the Martin campaign staff, Harper *really* meant. Then viewers were sent to a website, www.stephen-harpersaid.ca, for more choice quotations.

One ad showed a still photo of Harper while a voice read an excerpt from a Harper interview with the *Alberta Report* magazine. "Stephen Harper says, quote, 'West of Winnipeg the ridings the Liberals hold are dominated by people who are either recent Asian immigrants or recent migrants from Eastern Canada. People who live in ghettos and who are not integrated into Western Canadian society.'

"What's Harper saying?" the voice-over man asks, before suggesting an answer. "New Canadians shouldn't be allowed to vote."

The Conservatives quickly responded, in news-release rebuttals, that the voice-over guy was full of it. Harper had never argued and never believed that new Canadian citizens shouldn't be allowed to vote. There was enough of a creepy Jacques Parizeau referendum-night "money and ethnics" tone to his on-the-record comments that the extra Liberal spin amounted to counterproductive overreach. But another Liberal ad would prove harder to rebut.

This ad asserted that, "If Stephen Harper was prime minis-ter last year," – in 2003 –. "Canadians would be in Iraq this year," in 2004. The "reality," the Conservatives asserted, was that "Stephen Harper believes Canada should have morally supported our allies." In scrums and interviews, Harper hotly claimed he'd never called for real live Canadian soldiers to be sent, in any quantity, to fight in Iraq. All he'd ever asked for was "moral support" – and besides, the Liberals had left Canada's army in no shape to fight a shooting war in Iraq.

So on May 13, when Tonda MacCharles showed up to compare Harper's claims with the record, he took it badly.

Harper was doing a series of pre-election interviews. MacCharles, the *Toronto Star* reporter whose beat assignment was to cover the Conservatives, showed him a press release from January 28, 2003, on the letterhead of the Office of the Leader of the Opposition. The release was from Stock Day, the party's foreign-affairs critic. Its title read, "Canadian Troops Must Join Allies in the Gulf." The text made no reference to moral support. "More Canadian troops should now head to region to help enforce U.N. resolution, disarm Saddam."

When faced with the evidence, MacCharles wrote, "Harper became visibly angry, and insisted he did not have to 'revisit' these questions. 'If it was so important, you should have asked me about it at the time,' Harper said, refusing to look at the release."

At the time? Nobody would have thought to ask Harper "at the time" whether he really wanted Canadian troops sent to Iraq to disarm Saddam Hussein because "at the time," Harper was leaving no room for doubt on the matter. As his biographer William Johnson has pointed out, Harper spoke in the Commons on Iraq thirty-seven times between October 1, 2002 and May 5, 2003. He maintained that his Canadian Alliance would "urge the necessary military preparations that make the avoidance of war possible" – a line of argument that was being pursued, at the time, by George W. Bush and Tony Blair. He predicted that the *Liberals* under Jean Chrétien would "eventually join with the allied coalition if war on Iraq comes to pass" – but that Chrétien's government would be ill-prepared for war, whereas an Alliance government would be well prepared.

When Chrétien finally did decide not to send Canadian troops in any significant number to Iraq, Harper openly mourned what he saw as Chrétien's failure. "Reading only the polls and indulging in juvenile and insecure anti-Americanism, the government has, for the first time in our history, left us outside our British and American allies in their time of need," Harper said.

Harper would argue, ex post facto and with an admirably straight face, that he had mourned only a lack of "moral support," that in his mind – "at the time" – Canada could have lived up to its historic obligations to its British and American allies by offering them a hearty clap on the back as they filed on to the troop ships. Could, in fact, have offered no more because the Grits had let our armies rot. But there was the small matter of the press release from Stockwell Day. And thirty-seven interventions in the House during which Harper failed to make the distinction he would claim, in 2004, to have made so clearly. And the small matter of a vote in the Commons on March 20, 2003, on a supply-day motion from Bloc Québécois leader Gilles Duceppe:

"That this House call upon the government not to participate in the military intervention initiated by the United States in Iraq."

The fifty MPs who voted Nay included every Alliance MP who voted that day, except Keith Martin. Stephen Harper was one of the fifty. If Tonda MacCharles had asked him on that day whether he really meant what he was saying, it is reasonable to suspect he would have become even more "visibly angry" than he did, thirteen months later, when she asked why his story had changed.

As always, hindsight is imperfect counsel. In 2003, a *lot* of people wanted Canada to participate in the military intervention in Iraq. They included Brian Mulroney; Joe Clark, who voted with Harper on the Bloc supply motion; Ralph Klein; Ernie Eves; David Pratt, who would become Paul Martin's first defence minister; almost every editorialist in the country who didn't work for the *Toronto Star*; and, in private conversations, at least some of Martin's most senior advisors. But by 2004, Iraq was clearly a lethal mess. Harper's stance had become inconvenient. He did everything he could to cram the toothpaste back into the tube. And when a reporter busted him, he became furious.

Again, we see themes emerging. With Paul Martin, the theme is a doe-eyed disingenuous streak a mile wide. With Stephen Harper, it's that temper. There would be many more examples.

⇧

Out in front of Rideau Hall, Paul Martin told Canadians they would vote on June 28. It took a while. He was nervous. In announcing the date, he stumbled three times. He took only four questions before leaving to begin his campaign tour.

He had a lot to be nervous about. The broad outlines of the Liberal campaign were based on assumptions that had already become ludicrous. "I remember the assumptions going in," Steve MacKinnon, the Liberals' executive director, recalls, "planning to sweep the country. I don't think we ever got out of that mindset, right up to and including the election. 'We can win seats in Alberta.' At a certain point the evidence in favour of that was pretty overwhelmingly" – MacKinnon paused here, searched for the appropriate word – "gone. But we were still built to win 220 seats, as opposed to built to win 135, which is what we won."

Nowhere was this more obvious than in Quebec. Jean Lapierre had been a key Board member since before 1990. He had quit the Liberals on the day Chrétien became Liberal leader, gone on to form the Bloc Québécois with Lucien Bouchard, bad-mouthed the very idea of Canada in Parliament for two years, then quit to spend a decade as the most cheerfully glib of the empty-calorie battalions who manned the microphones of Montreal's talk-radio stations. Who could ask for more, really. So Lapierre became Martin's chief Quebec organizer. He would be the senior Quebec minister after the election. Because he was just so freaking *great*.

Painted in the most charitable light, Lapierre's ascension was all about the difference between a campaign designed to grow the majority – the fantasy campaign the Martin legions never got to fight – and a campaign designed to salvage the Liberal base. "We weren't built for the first twenty seats in Quebec. They were ours and expected and deserved," MacKinnon recalls. "The next forty" – out of seventy-five federal seats in the province – "were to be Lapierre's job."

You see, Jean Chrétien had won the *easy* seats. It would fall to the pros to take the rest. "On paper, we were going to win sixty-five seats in Quebec," MacKinnon says. "On paper, Jean Lapierre was the best-known, most talented federalist not currently on the ballot. And he was seen to be a symbol of a soft nationalist seeing that his aspirations could be fulfilled in the Paul Martin government. Not flawed judgment, in my view. Again, fell down in the execution."

To John Duffy, Martin's forced abandonment of his ambition to grow the party helps explain why some people finally decided the Liberal leader wasn't a straight shooter. "What happened, once sponsorship hit, was Martin was forced into defending the Liberal base. A more narrow base than Chrétien had had. What it takes to turn on that base is some pretty different stuff than what you use to expand on that base.

"So here's a guy who for many years had been talking to Albertans about how he felt the NEP was a terrible thing. And now he's turning around and saying to Quebeckers on the West Island how much he loves Kyoto. In effect he was pointed in one direction and he was forced by circumstance to point in the other direction. And it showed. And it produced an effect where a lot of people said, 'Is this guy still the same guy who I originally saw?'"

If the Liberals had to throw out much of their campaign plan, the Conservatives were spared any such trouble: they didn't *have* a campaign plan. Or rather they had about half a plan. A modern leader's tour is mostly about "scripting." This is the combination of geographical location, visual backdrop, props, talking points, news releases, and announceable policy that add up to the succession of "earned media" moments over the five weeks of a campaign. ("Earned media" is the charming term all political professionals use for the decisions journalists make about what to cover in a campaign. It's a complement to "paid media," that is, television and newspaper ads. Earned media and paid media are supposed to complement each other.)

Scripting takes time. You need an electoral map of Canada, a stack of polls, a speechwriting staff, a props department, some press secretaries with marching orders, and, you know, ideally, a platform. At that point all Ken Boessenkool had was wit and industry. He managed to get about half the scripting done before the campaign started. It was just a nasty coincidence that Harper and the campaign ran out of things to say at the three-week mark – what Conservatives now call, with pained expressions, "child-porn day."

In the English-language leaders' debate, Martin had taken a run at Harper for refusing to say he would never use the Constitution's "notwithstanding" clause to override the Charter of Rights and Freedoms. Harper came right back, saying he'd be glad to use the controversial clause to bring back the child pornography legislation the Liberals had declined to defend against free-speech challenges in the courts. "That was a good, winning moment," the Conservative insider said. "All of the focus groups showed that was a great moment in the debate." In the sudden absence of any scripted campaign message, "the view was that we would come back to child porn for a day and try to hammer home this message. And, uh, it was just miserably badly executed."

In the Conservative campaign headquarters, three people were supposed to triple-check news releases. Yaroslav Baran, a young Alliance staffer whose strong organizational skills usually made up for a bit of a smart lip, was running the war room. Geoff Norquay, a veteran of the Mulroney and Clark years, was the wise elder. William Stairs, Peter MacKay's former communications director, was the third pair of eyes.

In theory. But everyone was overloaded and Baran couldn't find anyone to proofread the child-pornography news release. So out it went, where the whole world could read its first sentences. "Martin says he's against child pornography, but his voting record proves otherwise." "Otherwise" would suggest he was *for* child pornography. "Proves" suggests an elevated level of certainty. Just in case anyone couldn't make that leap, the release's title was helpful: "Martin Supports Child Pornography?"

Martin was quick to respond that, in fact, he didn't. So were the New Democrats, who had been the targets of a similar Conservative news release under the title, "The NDP Caucus Supports Child Pornography?"

An hour after they sent it out, the Conservatives recalled the release. But you actually can't recall a news release. It was out. People had read it. You couldn't make them forget reading it. So Harper had to decide whether to apologize or stick with his damaging message. This should have been a no-brainer. Cheerfully accusing people of supporting child pornography was one of the Stockwell Day mistakes that made a Stephen Harper comeback necessary in the first place.

But the reason the word *no-brainer* exists is that sometimes people have no brains. During a quick conference call from Harper's campaign bus, the entire senior Conservative staff urged Harper not to apologize. The only dissenters were Jim Armour, the Reform veteran on the campaign bus, and William Stairs, the former Progressive Conservative back at campaign HQ. (Eventually, for reasons not directly related to the topic at hand, Harper would have occasion to fire both men.) Two more of Harper's instincts were kicking in: that temper, and a disinclination to do whatever a pack of reporters wanted. Out Harper went to scrum. Wasn't the child-porn release distasteful? "What's distasteful is the Liberals' position on child pornography," he said.

With that, a Conservative polling lead that had caught the Harper campaign by surprise melted away and ceased to bother them. The Liberal comeback of '04 was improvised, Duffy allows, but it was easy enough to describe in retrospect: "Staggeringly good negative advertising combines with effectively delivered negative messaging from the prime minister, and Harper errors, to create that earned-media/bought-media creative frame that moves votes." The Liberals had known they might find themselves behind. "We knew that our ace in the hole was always going to be the negatives associated with Harper," Duffy says. "So we used them."

The home stretch of the '04 campaign was all about Harper finding himself fresh out of positive stories to tell about a Conservative government, while the Liberals told their dark stories about him. He was furious about it. At one point, in Quebec City, he just snapped. "I can't fucking believe there's no fucking script for tomorrow," he shouted at his staff. "I want some fucking answers! And I want a fucking script!" Then he stopped and pondered for a moment. "I also want to know why nothing ever happens unless I use the word *fuck!*"

⇧

With no positive Conservative story to tell, reporters and the Martin campaign – the earned media/bought-media creative frame – were free to concentrate on a series of Conservative MP eruptions. Early in the campaign Scott Reid, the Conservative official-languages critic, had resigned the post after casting doubt on official bilingualism. Cheryl Gallant compared abortion to beheading. An old video surfaced in which Randy White heaped scorn on the courts' interpretation of gay rights.

Paul Martin does indignation well, and at last the Conservatives were giving him a lot of fodder. Then in the campaign's last days, he started urging NDP voters to back the Liberals as the best way to stop Harper. "If you are thinking of voting NDP," he said in one B.C. campaign office, "I ask you to think about the implications of your vote. In a race as close as this, you may well help Stephen Harper become prime minister." (In the event, the NDP vote in that riding, New Westminster–Coquitlam, collapsed – allowing the Conservative, Paul Forseth, to squeak out a 114-vote victory over the NDP candidate. The Liberal finished third. By warning voters there about the dangers of conservatism, Martin had saved the seat for a Conservative.)

Where was the debate over the future of the country? It barely happened. Harper released his platform on a Saturday, ensuring it would receive no serious coverage. Martin released his in Windsor, then killed any chance that it would get any coverage by scrumming in Montreal on the same day about what he imagined Harper's position on abortion might be. To the extent the Liberals *did* try to talk about ideas for government, Duffy says, they shouldn't have. "We . . . wasted $4 million advertising our platform. We ran television spots on windpower. Buh-bye! Might as well have given the money to charity. The whole first three weeks we were doing platform rollout events, television advertising on it, blah blah blah, auxiliary tour . . . It didn't work."

Urging Harper along while he self-destructed did work, if just enough to save the Liberals from collapse. Martin salvaged 135 seats, to 99 for the Conservatives and only 19 for Layton's NDP. In Quebec, the Bloc Québécois took 54 of 75 seats. For the first time since 1980, Canada's governing party would control only a minority in the House of Commons.

⇧

The day after the election Martin held a news conference in the National Press Theatre in Ottawa. He'd gone from 168 seats to 135. Ten days earlier he'd looked like the first Liberal loser since 1988. Would he make any changes to his staff or his approach?

"No," the prime minister said curtly. "I'm not planning any changes at all."

Whether he made any, in fact, seems to be open to interpretation. I asked Dennis Dawson, who ran and lost in a riding outside Quebec City, what post-mortem analysis the Liberals carried out after the 2004 election. "We didn't. We didn't," Dawson said. "The biggest mistake of 2004, we made believe we'd won. We'd won the election but we'd actually lost the campaign. Since we didn't do a post-mortem – and we *didn't* do a post-mortem – we repeated the same campaign [in 2006]."

Dawson may have been too busy recovering from personal defeat to pay close attention, because in fact the Martin entourage did carry out a detailed post-election analysis, beginning within days of the 2004 election. Scott Reid told me about some of it.

"I think that there are two levels to approach it on," Reid said, "strategic and tactical." The tactical stuff, the daily grind, was not particularly romantic. The Martinites decided they needed a greater emphasis on visuals at their campaign events. They debated balancing Paul Martin's time between the national press heavyweights on the campaign bus and regional broadcasts Martin could reach by satellite. Small stuff, but worth doing, especially since they'd just come out of a campaign they'd won by inches.

"But strategically, I think, a couple of things," Reid said. "We firmly identified some problems we had. We had to concentrate on our knitting in Quebec: solidify our base and then grow it, rather than start with growth and count on our base." A complete turnaround from the philosophy that had just bought them losses in Quebec. Second, the Martinites wanted to capitalize on polling that showed Martin's personal numbers consistently stronger than Harper's. If anything, in the next campaign even more than in the last, they wanted to turn differences on issues into heads-on confrontations between Paul Martin and Stephen Harper. "So when there were points of differentiation on key issues, make certain that we seized those moments and dealt with them."

What else? "We were always bothered by, you know, the notion that we were just troglodytes that wanted to take over the party so we could just wage internal warfare with anyone who ever worked for Jean Chrétien," Reid said. "That's a vulgar misreading of us and our intentions. A very vulgar misreading. It will bother me for the rest of my life." But the Martin entourage decided they had reinforced that impression by pushing a few key legacy Liberals, especially Sheila Copps, aside as they installed their own players.

"And so we made a strategic decision that we wanted to try and make sure that we would not have the kind of nomination fights and arguments that we had had in the past. And that we didn't put ourselves in a position where we could be accused of being abusive. So we protected nominations." Next time, incumbent MPs would be assured that they would be the nominee in their ridings, without facing competition from newcomers.

One more conclusion. As their numbers tumbled downward, the Martin campaign had faced criticism from party elders and panicky candidates who said Martin was too reluctant to run on the Liberals' sterling economic record. Deficits to surpluses, tax hikes to tax cuts, plummeting unemployment, low interest rates, billions to universities – why not talk about that?

"We decided that in the next campaign we would make a far more aggressive effort to run on the record," Reid said, "and that we would try to be more creative in trying to sell the record." Not that many Board members had overwhelming faith in their ability to make that sale. "Because as a government, you can't just get up on a Monday morning in the middle of the writ period and say, 'Now I'd like to talk to you about some of the swell things I did with our economy.' Because (people will say), 'You actually aren't responsible for the economy. So don't take credit for it.'"

But the period between the 2004 election and the next one, whenever it might come, gave Martin time to sink that legacy. The prime minister had made a number of high-profile commitments during the election. The two biggest were a plan to set up a national daycare system, after decades of unfulfilled promises, and a plan to, in typical understated Martin prose, "fix health care for a generation." The Martin campaign team decided its job would be easier next time, Reid said, if Martin moved smartly to fulfill those promises.

But when Martin told reporters he wasn't contemplating changes, in many ways he was telling it to us straight. He made few personnel changes at the Prime Minister's Office, and the changes he did make had the effect of reinforcing his permanent campaign team's hold on the PMO. Board members moved closer to the centre. Karl Littler and Michèle Cadario came into the PMO as deputy chiefs of staff. And the ranks of non-Board members in the PMO shrank. Francis Fox, Martin's principal secretary and a former Trudeau-era cabinet minister with a wide range of experience, went home to Montreal. His replacement was Hélène Scherrer, a defeated one-term Quebec City MP who had close to no knowledge of Ottawa backrooms or of the country outside Quebec. Mario Laguë left as communications director, taking the diplomatic posting in Costa Rica that had been waiting for him since he joined Martin's PMO.

In hindsight, some of the people around Martin say the harshness of the post-game analysis wasn't commensurate with the drubbing the party had just taken. "There was certainly a post-mortem," one senior Board member recalls. "There was certainly a what-went-wrong. There was certainly a what-can-we-do-to-be-better-prepared-next-time. And as part of that post-mortem, there was a recognition that there were flaws in that campaign.

"But it was drowned out by a profound sense of relief that the government had survived. The fact that we had a reasonably healthy working minority was such a relief that it drowned out the other reflections. I thought that the prime minister would reflect more on the message that was being sent, and make more profound changes in the things he did and the people around him than he did. You know, in spite of the post-mortem, in spite of the near-death experience, there didn't seem to be very much that changed as a consequence, in terms of either personnel, style, priorities. It looked a lot just like business as usual."

Why? This Martin stalwart offers one explanation. "There was frankly still a very strong belief that Mr. Harper was our greatest asset."

Another explanation comes from another senior campaign official: "Loyalty. Even those making the harsh critiques weren't willing to go the next logical step, which is to make the harsh decisions. And the secondary argument was 'Give us time. No new government gets its traction immediately. Give us time. We'll get our traction.'"

7

LUCK BE A RICH LADY WHO CROSSES THE FLOOR

⇧

P aul Martin would have almost a year to get some traction before Stephen Harper made his first serious
attempt to defeat the Liberal prime minister in the
Commons. When that confrontation came, Martin won, thanks
to one televised speech and one newly minted Liberal.

At the time, the defeated no-confidence motion of May 19,
2005, seemed a humiliating defeat for Harper. Later it would
become clear that losing the vote saved Harper from an election he was not ready for, and would have lost. When Martin
finally lost the confidence of the House in November of 2005,
seventeen months had elapsed since the 2004 election. As it
turned out, Harper needed almost every week of those seventeen months to finish transforming himself from Martin's
greatest asset into the instrument of his downfall.

First, he had to cope with his own defeat. The Conservatives
hadn't expected to win more than eighty seats until halfway

through the 2004 campaign. Nothing in their plan was meant
to put them ahead by the halfway point. When that's where
they found themselves, they decided they liked the prospect of
victory, however unexpected. Defeat, when it came, shouldn't
have come as any surprise. But one of Harper's characteristics
is that he has always taken defeat badly. Another is that, before
long, he sets to work figuring out how to do better.

"Stephen was disappointed, initially," one friend says. "Very
disappointed. He was pretty quiet. He was not hugely involved
in trying to plan for Parliament that fall. Ordinarily he would
be." Harper even said publicly that he would consider whether
he had a future in politics. Coming from a guy who'd united
two parties, won the leadership only months earlier, and added
thirty seats to their parliamentary score, it was a surprising
statement. Even people close to Harper had a hard time
gauging how serious the idea of resigning was. Probably not
very. And in any case the thought didn't last long.

"He went out and did a pile of events, which nobody ever
covered, and therefore [the press] said he went to ground for
the summer," an advisor says. "Actually not true. Actually he
went all over the goddamned place. And got pretty good
crowds, actually quite good crowds. Which is what convinced
him that the party was still alive and that he was still in a position to carry on as leader."

And as he sometimes does when he is trying to wrap his
head around a new situation, Harper turned to his pollsters.
There's a dose of irony here. It was Paul Martin who became
famous, and indeed drew derision in some quarters, for his
close association with pollsters, particularly David Herle. But
Harper and Tom Flanagan have long been advocates of polling
to identify the key voter blocs that might listen to Conservative
appeals and the policies that might catch their ear.

Way back in his 1995 Preston Manning book, *Waiting for the Wave*, Flanagan complains that Manning "showed no interest in using [polling] data to identify and target the geographic, demographic, and psychographic groups that might be expected to respond to our policies." And Flanagan quotes with approval "the conventional wisdom of contemporary politics," as expressed in the "Ten Commandments for campaign managers" by John Laschinger, the dean of Canadian political organizers, the man who would manage Joe Clark's last national campaign in 2000 and David Miller's upset victory in the Toronto mayoral race a few years later: "Always choose a pollster who gives advice. . . . Use the numbers to drive the strategy. . . . Always poll, even when broke."

Harper's Conservatives weren't broke in July of 2004, but he polled anyway. "He commissioned a pile of polling," a close associate says. "He had a thousand questions he wanted answered. He had a huge, massive amount of polling done to see where things had gone wrong. How badly the party's brand name had been beaten up in the campaign. How much *his* name had been beaten up. Is the party still viable? Is the leader? A kind of internal retrospection.

"At what point in the election campaign did you make up your mind? How many of the Liberal ads did you see? How many of our ads did you see? Do you think the Conservative Party's too extreme? Which party do you think most represents Canada?"

Most of that polling was carried out by Dimitri Pantazopoulos, the Conservatives' party pollster. There is no public record of the answers Harper received to all his questions, but the data Pantazopoulos gathered fed into a rolling, improvised, but extraordinarily thorough election analysis that occupied most of the Conservatives' time through the summer of 2004.

The Conservative post-mortem exercise was different from the Martin camp's brief bout of introspection in just about every way. It was more delegated – few people knew what files others were working on, and few except Harper, Brodie, and Flanagan had any sense of the whole process. It took much longer. And it led to deeper reforms in organization and strategy. This was still a new party, after all. In a way it was doing what any new party has to do: decide how to advance its ideas via the ungainly mechanism of an election campaign. Viewed from that perspective, the near-miss 2004 campaign was a kind of gift, because it removed these obligatory calculations from the realm of the theoretical. After only three months as leader of a new party, Harper had already lived through a point-by-point case study in how not to win a national election.

Harper's staff worked with the sting of defeat fresh in their memory, spurred on by the sure knowledge that in a minority Parliament, they might not have much time to apply the lessons they'd learned. Within days after the election Ken Boessenkool wrote a long memo about the mistakes he'd made in producing the campaign message and the mistakes everyone else had made in getting it out. Two of his subordinates, Mark Cameron and Patrick Muttart, worked together on a memo of their own. That analysis and Boessenkool's went to Tom Flanagan, the campaign manager, who had returned to his family and his academic career in Calgary. But when Boessenkool saw the memo that Cameron and Muttart had written – brutal in its honesty, coolly analytical in its application of lessons learned – he also sent a copy directly to Harper.

If there was a single big take-away from the 2004 campaign, it was that these academics and policy wonks around Harper had become pretty good at the things they'd had to learn to do during two leadership campaigns. And *not* very good at the things they *hadn't* had to learn to do. A leadership campaign is a hermetic little operation that flies, whether its managers like it or not, way below the media radar. You're mostly talking to party members singly and in small groups. So leadership campaigns depend on direct targeting: telemarketing, direct-mail, and a lot of time in community-hall basements shaking hands. Every once in a while a reporter might drop by, but the earned-media campaign of news coverage isn't a big part of the game plan. Neither is the paid-media campaign of print and broadcast advertisements. Within the confines of a leadership race, talking to reporters and buying ads would waste far too many scarce resources on people who won't be voting.

So the Harper people were disappointed, if not particularly surprised, to conclude that when they finally needed to, they had run a lousy ad campaign and a lousy media strategy. On paper, Boessenkool's plan to release a chapter of the platform every day looked kind of majestic, leading up to the big Saturday release of the whole platform. Except no national newspaper publishes on Sunday and no network newscast makes its star anchorman work on Saturday night. So, short of FedExing the platform to Bratislava, unveiling it on Saturday was pretty nearly the worst way to get any coverage. And once the Conservatives had announced everything, they couldn't get a single reporter to pay attention, for the rest of the campaign, when they tried to re-announce something. This problem led directly to Harper's Quebec City fuck-fuck tantrum, and to worse.

The heart of the communications problem, then, was that Harper had been made to carry too much of the message by himself, without help from the ad campaign or even from the way the campaign's broad themes evolved over five weeks. The first week had been about "making the case for change," which meant chronicling Liberal failings, mostly the ad scandal. Fairly mild compared to the mudslinging to follow, but it didn't put a strong face forward for the Conservatives. It was the sort of message that would take points off the Liberals without giving anyone any reason to vote for Harper's party. The second week was strong-face-forward on traditional conservative ideas like law and order. By the third week, which was supposed to be "broadening the conservative family" – explaining why you should vote Conservative if you never had before, which is sort of the point of winning an election – Harper had run out of script, and out of luck.

While Harper huddled with his communications people after the election to come up with something better, Flanagan offered to come up with better advertising. "Even if we'd been smart enough to know that we were getting our heads kicked in on advertising," Harper told his staff at one point, "I don't think we had the wit to fix it. Or the capability in our ad firm."

There was nothing wrong with the boutique Calgary ad firm the Conservatives had used, Watermark, except the scale of the challenge it had been asked to tackle. National parties typically go into elections with dozens of ads in the can, many of which will never air. Then they turn around even more ads as the events of the campaign warrant, sometimes shooting, editing, and placing them within a day or two. The Conservatives had produced only a few ads in advance. And they weren't able to adjust them, either in content or in the mix of broadcast markets where they played, as the campaign evolved.

Watermark was thanked and dismissed, and Flanagan proceeded to swipe a page from the Liberal playbook. Liberal English-language campaign advertising is done, every time out, by a Toronto-based consortium called Red Leaf Communications. Composition changes with party leadership, but the idea remains the same. Get a seasoned ad pro to build a team using the best people he can lure from various agencies.

Flanagan called Perry Miele. Miele is a former Progressive Conservative Parliament Hill staffer who left politics and moved to Toronto to found a fabulously lucrative ad firm called Gingko. He sold it out for millions and set up some capital funds to invest the returns. "He's the kind of guy who knew the business and could go to all the hot companies and say, 'Come on along,'" Geoff Norquay says. "Just like Red Leaf does." The Conservatives also set up a similar consortium in Montreal to produce French-language ads. Just like the Liberals.

So those are all examples of the ways in which Harper made early and substantial changes to his strategy. But at least in the immediate aftermath of the election, he didn't make many more changes to his team than Martin did. The Conservative leader did move Jim Armour, his main press spokesman, from direct contact with reporters to a less prominent organizational role. It was clearly a demotion. But it made sense from a tent-broadening perspective, even to Armour, because it allowed Harper to bring in Geoff Norquay, who came from the Progressive Conservative loyalist camp, and who had worked on the Belinda Stronach campaign against Harper.

While Tom Flanagan had been the campaign manager in '04, he had given up his old post as Harper's chief of staff in June of 2003. His deputy, Phil Murphy, continued as the new chief of staff. Murphy had spent a decade in the Reform and Alliance House Leader's office. He was good at keeping track of parliamentary committees and following bills through the legislative process, but he wasn't there to be a chief of staff in the traditional, voice-of-God, brook-no-opposition sense. In that sense, Harper was his own leading strategist and enforcer.

Ian Brodie stayed on as executive director of the party, with two mandates. One was to make sure the Conservatives had enough money to run a national campaign – and *soon*. This was a challenge. Canadian politics is wired so it takes most of the four-year gap between elections to raise enough money for a campaign. This time they would have perhaps a year.

Brodie's other big job was to organize the Conservative Party of Canada's first national policy convention. Nobody bothered to hide the goal of this project. If the Liberals had stopped Conservative momentum in mid-campaign by peddling scary tales about what Conservative policy might be on hot-button issues, they mustn't get a chance to do that again. "It was a giant PR exercise," one convention organizer admits. "The goal was to go into the convention, come out of the convention, not fuck up, and come up with moderate centre-right policies and show the public that we were not a scary prospect."

The MP eruptions of Campaign '04 – Cheryl Gallant comparing abortion to the beheading of hostages in Iraq, Randy White chuckling "to heck with the courts" – were certainly the product of a Conservative policy vacuum and arguably the product of a journalistic double standard. Any reporter in the Parliamentary Press Gallery could rattle off the list of Liberal MPs who were indefatigable anti-abortion crusaders, such as Paul Szabo or Tom Wappel; or entrenched and sometimes loopy theorists about "judicial activism" as it related to gay marriage, led by Roger Gallaway and Joe Volpe. Yet even after Paul Martin elevated Gallaway to a junior cabinet post and made Volpe his lead political minister for Ontario, the Liberals had never been subjected to any particular journalistic scrutiny for harbouring hard-liners on these files. (It helped, of course, that Volpe was only too happy to discard his previous convictions on gay marriage as soon as he snagged a cabinet post.)

But the press corps, whether friend or foe, is fickle. The policy vacuum was the real problem. If a party doesn't give us news, we'll find some of our own. As a stop-gap upon uniting the Alliance and Progressive Conservatives, Harper had assigned Peter MacKay to go through the two parties' platforms and find common ground. There was a lot. Everyone was big on lower taxes, for instance, and both parties wanted at least the long-gun registry abolished. But the gaps were bigger than the common ground, and it was all too easy for a freelancing candidate to stride blithely into some of those gaps, making up policy as he went along. The time had come to fill the gaps.

⇧

The convention was set for March 2005 in Montreal. The choice of location, while hardly revolutionary, was part of a growing Harper charm offensive aimed at Quebec voters. Harper had made the unusual choice of naming Josée Verner, a failed Quebec City Conservative candidate, to his Opposition shadow cabinet even though she'd failed to get elected as an MP. He was spending more and more time in Quebec, to the vexation of such ordinarily sympathetic observers as the editorial board at the *National Post*, which argued that he was wasting his time chasing pipe dreams in Quebec instead of nailing down winnable votes in Ontario.

Just as the Montreal locale fit into a broader strategy to get the Conservatives noticed in Quebec, the topics of the convention debates were chosen as part of a broader strategy to cool the party down in the minds of easily alarmed swing voters. On a few issues, Harper and his staff decided that not only could the party survive some good honest debates, but that holding the debates was the best way to get some closure. One objective, a Conservative strategist recalls, "was to confront abortion head-on, and let the generally pro-choice forces of the party win. Because the grassroots of the party *are* generally pro-choice." The pro-life component tends to be louder and often better organized. But here was one issue that could actually be left to the silent majority. Same thing with official bilingualism. Those who didn't like it really, really didn't like it. But they'd be outnumbered, especially if the price of voting was that you had to get all the way to Montreal. The whole process leading up to the campaign was tightly centrally controlled, an emerging hallmark of any process run by Ian Brodie. But the goal was less to constrain debate than to limit the number of topics debated.

All along, from shadow-cabinet committees to full caucus discussions to regional policy conferences to the big show in Montreal, the instincts of Conservatives were similar: hug the political centre. Don't let the Liberals paint the party as extremist. Harper gave a speech at one regional policy meeting in Vancouver. When he left, Geoff Norquay stayed to listen to the debates. "It was people at the microphones, arguing about policy," he recalls. "And it was people saying, to anyone who got too far out, 'Hey asshole, I think I'd like us to be government. Why don't you just take that and stuff it?'"

Harper and Tom Flanagan might choose more delicate phrasing but they shared the sentiment. "Politics is not a seminar, winning power is not the same as making debating points, and half a loaf is better than no bread at all," Flanagan wrote in the *National Post* at one point. "Activists and thinkers in the conservative movement should work to ensure that the Conservative Party is positioned to the right of the Liberals on major issues, but they must remember that staying reasonably close to the median voter is essential for winning elections."

In the end the convention went off without a hitch. Well, almost. There was the small matter of Peter MacKay threatening to tear the new party back apart.

The crisis was provoked by one of those seemingly arid little procedural debates that actually strikes at the heart of an organization's self-image. When Harper and MacKay negotiated the union of their parties, Harper took pains to concede lots of ground to MacKay, who was weaker, led a smaller party, and had to herd a more skittish caucus and membership. One concession was the manner of choosing delegates to Conservative conventions. Reform and the Alliance were big advocates of representation by population. By contrast, the Progressive Conservative tradition in recent years had been to give each riding an equal number of delegates. (Neither system is transparently superior. It depends what value or group you're trying to protect. The Liberals, for instance, send the same number of delegates from every riding to their conventions. Reform, on the other hand, was created in part as an advocate for equal Senate representation from every province, which, when you stop to think about it, flies in the face of representation by population.)

MacKay wanted the equal-riding system to be reflected in the new party's rules. It was an obvious way to protect Progressive Conservative traditions, political reflexes, and, yes, influence. MacKay's party had far fewer members than the Alliance in 2003, but Tories at least outnumbered Alliance members in corners of Central and Eastern Canada. Harper relented, but only for the party's first leadership convention and its first policy convention. It would be up to members at the Montreal convention to suggest and debate a different delegate-selection process for the future if they wanted.

And one did. Scott Reid the MP, a former staffer in Harper's office during Harper's first term as a Reform MP, put forward a motion that would have sent fewer delegates from electoral districts whose riding associations had fewer than 91 members. It was a pretty mild compromise. An Alberta riding with 16,000 active members and a New Brunswick riding with 140 would both send the same number of delegates to a convention. Reid's motion would simply have reduced the clout of the most pathetic rotten boroughs. That way you couldn't buy influence at a national convention by giving away memberships to 20 people in some far-flung corner of Quebec where nobody had ever even heard of the Conservative Party. This happens to be the technique Belinda Stronach had used to run up her representation from Quebec in the first Conservative leadership campaign. Stronach was now dating Peter MacKay.

MacKay took Reid's suggested amendment as a betrayal of old Tory values. He stormed out of the workshop where Reid's resolution was being debated and made straight for the nearest cluster of television news cameras. If he'd known this sort of change was coming, "there would not have been a merger," he told reporters. And if the amendment passed, "This party is in real jeopardy, in my view."

Sometimes tantrums work. Reid's motion was defeated at the next day's plenary, as MacKay wanted. Delegates also defeated a pro-life motion on abortion and passed a motion in support of official bilingualism. On same-sex marriage, it was the social conservatives who won at least a face-saving victory. A new Harper government would put gay marriage to a free vote in Parliament. It wasn't clear what Harper would do if the vote to undo gay marriage passed. Unmarry the thousands of

gay and lesbian couples who were already getting married? Use
the Constitution's "notwithstanding" clause to remove a right
the courts had recognized? Clarification would have to wait.
For now, each of the party's factions could point to victory on
one file or another. As a bonus, the convention actually made
money for the party.

All that remained now was to bite Peter MacKay's head off.
Stronach's too. The car-parts heiress had resisted the temptation
to actually defend the rotten-borough delegate process in front
of the cameras. But she had complained enough about Scott
Reid's motion in private that everyone knew where she stood.

The convention wrapped on Sunday morning. Early in the
next parliamentary week, Harper had MacKay and Stronach
visit him separately in the Opposition leader's office on the
fourth floor of Parliament's Centre Block. The message, delivered in salty language and at high volume, was: *Don't pull a
stunt like this again. You nearly ruined a crucial convention. If you
wanted to debate Scott Reid on the floor of the policy workshop or the
plenary, fine. But you don't take it outside, and you sure don't make
your membership in the party conditional on the outcome of a single
debate. You're in or you're out.*

MacKay's bravado collapsed. You're right, he told his leader.
I'm in, not out. This was not worth a big fight. But Stronach
equivocated. I'm uncomfortable with your approach, she told
Harper. If you're going to speak to me this way. . . . She left the
threat hanging, unfinished.

"From that point it was just a matter of time until she was
gone," one Conservative says.

Oh, come on. You saw Stronach's defection coming? "No,
it's not like the Jo-Jo Psychic Hotline," another Harper veteran
allows. "He just made the assessment that she wasn't with him
and that she was going to try and undermine him." In fact, this

Conservative says, Harper's vague insight may have hurt any chance of a rapprochement, or at least of a less spectacular departure. "He tends to be too strategic for his own good," this person says. "He made the assessment that she was going to betray him. And rightly so. But instead of using that knowledge to sort of jolly her along and make sure her departure was on his terms and his timing, he just cut her off. And of course she just left at the worst possible time."

That's the way it felt when she left, anyway. But within days Belinda Stronach's defection would seem like a gift from Conservative-loving gods.

⇧

Serious trouble arrived for the Liberals on April 7, when John Gomery removed a publication ban on former Quebec adman Jean Brault's testimony before Gomery's commission of inquiry. Brault was facing a criminal trial for fraud. Gomery wanted to make sure that nothing said before him would prejudice that proceeding. As soon as he was satisfied that it wouldn't, Gomery allowed most of it to be published. Reporters who had spent days listening to Brault's testimony instantly published their summaries on their organizations' Internet websites or broadcast their pre-taped updates on the television news channels. The nasty claims they documented were all the more powerful because they had been pent up for a week.

Brault described a kickback scheme designed to funnel some of the sponsorship program's misspent tens of millions back into Liberal Party of Canada coffers. His tales of clandestine meetings in Italian restaurants where satchels of cash changed hands seemed to confirm Canadians' worst fears. The Liberals' poll numbers, which had stabilized ahead of the Conservatives', dipped again. Harper decided the days of letting the Liberals survive were over. It was time to bring them down.

But could he? If every opposition party voted against them, the Liberals couldn't survive. Even with Layton's little NDP caucus on Martin's side, Conservatives plus Bloc Québécois plus independents would probably be enough to bring Martin down. The Bloc, consistently high in Quebec polls, was happy to go to the voters any time. Jack Layton, his voters spooked by the merest possibility of a Harper government, was reluctant. It was up to Harper to decide whether to attempt a confidence vote.

Ian Brodie had everything on the Conservative Party side ready for an election: money, field organization, central organization. Not many candidates nominated, though. Harper sent orders to have 308 candidates nominated within five weeks, a formidable demand. Doug Finley went out to round up candidates and organize the candidate-selection assemblies in each riding.

His numbers dropping, his shaky alliances in the House of Commons collapsing, Paul Martin decided to address the nation on the topic that seemed consistently to inspire his boldest moves: his own survival. The prime minister told the television networks he would be speaking on the evening of April 23. It wasn't quite an emergency address. He didn't invoke the Broadcasting Act, which would have forced the networks to carry his statement. He didn't have to. What were they going to do, not carry his statement? Here was a prime minister in crisis, pleading for his political life. As pure television, this was going to be better than *Da Vinci's Inquest*.

As politics, it was consistent. At every turn, Martin had avoided the grand gesture and the direct appeal to voters whenever it came to defending his ideas for government. There would be no great speech to the people about ballistic-missile defence or global warming or the Darfur slaughters. There would be no whistle-stop tour through Quebec to explain his ideas about federalism or through Alberta to discuss his vision for natural resources. The most powerful techniques of public pedagogy were reserved for one objective: to save his own political hide.

The deal Martin offered Canadians was simple enough: let him keep governing while Gomery kept working. He would begin an election campaign within thirty days of the judge's report. In effect he was pleading for a stay of political execution that would last until early 2006.

One measure of the fearsome momentum toward catastrophe that had forced Martin's desperation play was how hard it was to find anyone, immediately after the prime minister spoke, who thought his gambit would work. Harper sure didn't: responding to Martin's statement minutes later in the foyer of the House of Commons, the Conservative leader left no doubt that he would press without delay toward a confidence vote.

And yet the principle Martin had appealed to was simple enough, likely to command broad support, and truly hard to rebut: Let's give a judge time to finish his work. You try winning an argument in Canada by suggesting that a judge's deliberations be interrupted. Martin's plea was pathetic and sad, but that did not make it less effective. A few columnists argued, with Martin, that nobody wanted an election just yet. In the days ahead, Geoff Norquay and other Harper surrogates would argue gamely that, sure, nobody wanted an election. But neither does anyone like to visit the dentist, and you still have to go. The comparison showed how completely Harper had failed to understand how Martin had changed the frame of the debate. The Gomery inquiry, mightily flawed though it might be as an instrument of public investigation, was like a set of dental X-rays sent off to a lab. Martin argued that the nation should wait until the lab sent back a report before deciding whether a root canal was necessary. Harper preferred to fire up the dental drill and bore in, sight unseen.

For once, it was Jack Layton of the NDP who showed the keenest strategic sense. In the 2004 election, Martin had made last-inning gains by portraying a vote for the New Democrats as a wasted vote that could have been used to help a good Liberal stop Harper's hordes. Layton could not afford to go into the next election without being able to demonstrate that a vote for the NDP could have practical value. So alone among the leaders responding to Martin, he barely mentioned Liberal corruption and parliamentary process, instead inviting Martin to "work together" to solve ordinary Canadians' problems.

Layton's hint could hardly have been more obvious, and in the circumstances, Martin had no real alternative. The next day, Liberal and NDP officials were negotiating a package of amendments to the Liberal budget that would reflect NDP campaign priorities. On April 26, they announced the results: $4.6 billion in new spending over two years on affordable housing, post-secondary education, the environment, pension protection, and foreign aid. Layton's support was now ensured for any confidence vote. But the combined opposition of the Conservatives and Bloc meant there would be a vote anyway. And together the Liberals and New Democrats were still just short of a majority.

As the confrontation neared, the House was so divided that a single vote either way might make the difference in the Martin government's survival. Which is how things stood when Stronach followed Martin into the National Press Theatre on May 23.

To this day, Martin's staff swears that Stronach approached them with her offer to turn Liberal. "This thing rolled down the street and hit us," Scott Reid recalls. Why would Stronach jump ship? Partly because the Conservative Party was becoming a less congenial home by the day. Stronach had blown tens of thousands of dollars on a swanky cocktail reception at the Conservative convention, but her colleagues still didn't seem to be taking her seriously. Shortly after Harper tore a strip off her for sowing division in the party, she had tried to rally MPs to her side of another argument at a meeting of the party's Ontario caucus. "I've had enough of this shit," one MP said, theatrically getting up and leaving in the middle of Stronach's spiel.

Paul Martin, on the other hand, was all ears. He had long admired this bright young MP, he told a pack of agog reporters as he announced her defection to his party at the National Press Theatre. In fact, making Stronach the minister for human resources and democratic reform was about improving the quality of the Liberal government. It had nothing to do with the fast-approaching confidence vote, he said.

Whereupon a room full of reporters laughed long and hard at the prime minister. Eight months later, the *National Post* columnist Andrew Coyne would call this Martin's "Ceausescu moment . . . the instant it was clear the jig was well and truly up." For years reporters had kept a straight face while Martin claimed to have no opinion on the question of who should be Liberal leader. They had heard him deny knowledge of meetings attended by all his supporters and his entire staff. They had watched him punish one health minister for saying what another health minister had said years earlier, seen him pledge to save health care for a generation, suck and blow on any number of files. His insistence on denying the obvious had seemed trivial at first, then odd, then annoying. Now it was just funny.

In the end, the reporters' math would be better than Martin's. Stronach made all the difference, and just barely enough: the confidence vote Harper had initiated and expected to win led to a tie in the Commons. Stronach gave the Liberals one more vote, and the Conservatives one fewer, than if she had stayed put. Chuck Cadman, the ailing independent MP, made it a tie by voting with the government. Peter Milliken, the jolly little Commons Speaker, voted to break the tie by letting the government survive. But it wasn't just reporters who had, at some level, hung up on Paul Martin. In early May, the Strategic Counsel polling firm investigated Canadians' attitudes toward political leaders for CTV News. When asked to name which leader was most dishonest, 63 per cent named Martin, compared to 20 per cent who named Harper. Sixty-one per cent said they believed he would lie if it would help him politically. Fifty-four per cent called him hypocritical.

Over at the CBC, the weekly newsmagazine *CBC News: Sunday* tested public opinion a different way. A staffer held up a box of doughnuts for passersby on a street corner somewhere, who were asked to select the pastry that best represented each of the party leaders. For Harper, the doughnut-poll respondents selected the blandest possible treats on offer: no icing, no filling. But to represent Martin, they consistently and spontaneously selected crème-filled and jelly-filled doughnuts. Why? Because, respondents explained, Martin always winds up tasting different from what you thought you could expect.

⇧

In the run-up to an election, for any national party, it's all hands on deck. The party apparatus gears up a continent-wide war machine with components in every riding. Meanwhile the leader's office or its delegates work on strategy, message, and above all, the proper use of the leader's time. At Conservative Party headquarters, in the days before the confidence vote, Ian Brodie felt pretty confident. He had a war room rented with dozens of staffers in it. He had phones, computers, networks, buses, planes, ad time booked on TV stations, $17 million in the bank, all ready to go.

On the day of the vote, he checked with Phil Murphy, Harper's chief of staff, on the chores that had been delegated to the leader's office: Tour plan, strategic message, ad themes. The plumbing of a campaign – the hardware – was ready. How was the software coming?

There was none. Or nothing useable. The platform? "It was like an eighty-five-page bible, no form, no nothing, just a compendium of everything the party had ever said about every subject under the sun," one insider recalls. "It was appalling." The campaign theme? "We still didn't have the message planned for what the campaign was going to be about. Except Liberal corruption." With the Gomery revelations fresh in the public mind, a campaign of woe and scandal would have been effective for a while before it began to seem arid and vindictive. But for five weeks? No chance.

There was nothing Brodie and Harper could do immediately about the disarray and lack of preparation in the party office. Parliament sat for another month and a half after Harper's failed no-confidence motion; the election team had to stick around, on standby, in case some surprise or mishap brought the Martin government down. Finally the House rose in mid-June. There being no way to defeat Martin in a House that wasn't sitting,

Harper had one last chance to clean his own house. He brought Doug Finley in from the Conservative Party office to investigate the operations of the Office of the Leader of the Opposition.

Finley spent six weeks studying Harper's shop. Though he never put it in these words, he decided it looked too much like Martin's government: long on staffing and structure, short on purpose. There were way too many people whose job nobody could define. And of the genuinely valuable staffers, too many had started to leave, especially from Harper's embattled communications shop. After the most stressful springtime some of them had ever seen, Geoff Norquay and Jim Armour and Mike Storeshaw and a few others left for the private sector. The research department was hemorrhaging, too. Stephen Harper had been leader of the Conservatives for barely a year and already his office was succumbing to simultaneous attacks of bloat and vitamin deficiency.

The leader was taking this new defeat in the House as badly as he had taken the election loss a year earlier. "His lows are pretty low," Norquay says. "And by the time I left, he was really, really worn down and angry and bitter. And I didn't think he could pull out of it."

Doug Finley and Ian Brodie watched it all and wondered whether there was much point in carrying on. Since Perth-Middlesex, two years earlier, the dour Scot and the scruffy academic had risen to become the two fixers Harper depended on for his toughest jobs. But they had come within a hair of a second national election, only to discover they were barely more prepared than when they had lost the first. The two men met for dinner at Finley's apartment; among his other skills, he is a good cook.

Finley said, "I'll take over the campaign organization, but you have to agree to take over the OLO."

Contemplating the Office of the Leader of the Opposition, Brodie chuckled grimly. "The OLO's a fucking disaster."

Finley said, "Well, the party was a disaster when you took it over too."

Brodie: "This is a bigger mess than that one was."

Finley, mournful: "Well, yeah. But we both have another year to do our jobs at this point." They figured the public-relations drubbing they had suffered over the failed confidence motion had put Martin into the free and clear, at least until the spring of 2006.

Brodie pondered the chore ahead. They'd come this far; what the heck. "If you're willing to take over the campaign organization, then I will take over the OLO." Finley accepted. It was a kind of pact. Neither would leave the other in the lurch. One last chance to knock this misbegotten party into shape before showtime.

Finley, Brodie, and Tom Flanagan met with Harper and told him the OLO had to be cleaned out. Finley would take over as campaign manager from Flanagan, who would return for an election but not in a key structural role. Brodie would run the leader's office. Phil Murphy was dismissed. Dozens of Conservative staffers were fired. "That produced all sorts of terrible headlines about chaos," one Harper associate recalls. "It wasn't chaos, it was the beginning of order." The shakeup also made possible the arrival of the last major player on the Harper team: Patrick Muttart.

Muttart had worked at Navigator, a Toronto public-relations firm run by Jaime Watt, the dapper Conservative image-maker behind Mike Harris's 1995 and 1999 Ontario election victories. Muttart had nothing resembling his boss's public profile. Even today he can walk through a crowded

Parliament Hill restaurant without most of the reporters in the room noticing him.

"He's a bit of a nerd," one Conservative staffer says. "He has no hobbies. Politics is his hobby. He likes to study winning election campaigns. Especially in the English-speaking countries."

Muttart assumed responsibility for strategic planning, the election-readiness component of Harper's office, with about half the staff. (The rest worked on issues management, the day-to-day slog of Question Period preparation, legislative debates, and parliamentary committees.) In a way his job was to think like Harper and Boessenkool – concocting a blend of strategy and policy – but to put a sharper and more flamboyant point on it all.

How does a conservative party win an election? Muttart identified four campaigns over the past half-century where conservative parties, once viewed as the tool of fat cats to line their pockets, had moved aggressively to capture the middle class and, through it, power. Richard Nixon's 1968 election was the first. Margaret Thatcher's 1979 landslide in Britain was next. Then there was the 1994 breakthrough of Newt Gingrich and the Republicans, who broke the Democrat stranglehold on the U.S. Congress with a ten-point plan called the Contract With America. When it came to Gingrich, Muttart was particularly interested in the idea of concocting a digestible list of projects with which the new team would be associated. *What do you stand for? I'll tell you what I stand for*, bang bang bang bang. It all seemed crisp and professional and, as a bonus, a handy shield against being defined by one's opponents.

Muttart's last election precedent was the one least known to Canadian voters and, perhaps, most useful as a model for the

Conservatives: the 1996 victory of Australia's conservative-leaning coalition under John Howard, over Paul Keating's Labour Party.

At times Canada and Australia can seem like funhouse-mirror images of each other. They are huge former British colonies with federal constitutions, small populations, a steady influx of immigrants, and troubled aboriginal populations. Muttart would have found a lot of relevant lessons while studying the 1996 Australian election. A decade ago, Australia had a strong economy led by a former finance minister, Keating, who had knocked off his predecessor in an internal party feud. His opponent, Howard, was seen as a right-wing mediocrity who presided over an opposition crippled by a decade of disarray and policy vacuum. Howard's pollsters found that when you scratched the surface of prosperous Australia, you found a middle class that was sullenly convinced it was paying for the perks of the rich and the benefits of the down-and-out.

Howard prepared for the campaign by throwing off lots of right-wing ballast. He had once favoured greater use of private medicine, but he transformed himself into a champion of state medicare. How did he explain the flip-flop? "I changed my mind." During the campaign, he pitched his message straight at middle-class voters whose obligations seemed forever just a little bigger than their wallets. He revealed his platform, not all at once but one plank a day, for the duration of the campaign.

When it was over, Howard had won a resounding, durable victory. Like Nixon, Thatcher, and Gingrich in three very different races before him, Howard owed his victory to a big shift of working-class and middle-class voters. And, Muttart noticed, in all four of the cases he studied, Roman Catholic voters had migrated from the liberal parties that had become their home toward conservative parties that had formerly struggled to appeal to anyone except Protestants.

In collaboration with Dimitri Pantazopoulos and Perry Miele, Muttart started working on the sophisticated polling analysis that would allow the Conservatives to identify voter groups that might prove to be within their grasp, and the advertising strategy that could help reach them. Details of how they did that lie ahead. But first, a bit of a caveat.

When I wrote about Muttart for the first time in *Maclean's*, shortly after the 2006 election, one or two Liberals from the Martin camp grumbled that I had made the young Tory strategist look like a genius for doing what any modern, professional campaign team does: use market research and comparative politics to identify and attract classes of voters whose support for other parties isn't absolutely nailed down. To my surprise, Tories who have worked closely with Muttart agreed. There was, indeed, nothing tremendously novel or insightful in the contribution Muttart made to Harper's team. The only difference was that nobody had ever made such a contribution before.

"There's nothing profound about what [Muttart] did," says one Harper advisor. "What's profound is that he did it, and that we executed it. The fact of the matter is, the Alliance – and Harper said this, from the first day he ran for his first leadership – he wanted to professionalize the party. And that was why we brought Patrick on. We never had anyone in Harper's inner circle who understood political advertising the way Patrick does."

There was one last step for Harper to make before he tried once again to take this Liberal government down. He needed to practise campaigning. While Finley and Brodie reached into the OLO and started hauling parts out, Harper planned a coast-to-coast summer barbecue tour accompanied by his wife, Laureen Teskey. "He needed to do it because he needed to show the media that he was doing it," Norquay recalls. "Because the media was getting very, very close to writing him off."

It was a gruelling trip, or at least as gruelling as an endless succession of corn roasts can be. When she saw the schedule, Marjory LeBreton, the Conservative senator, shook her head. "Aren't you even going to take one weekend off?" she asked Harper.

"This is how I have to do it," Harper told her. "Laureen said to me, 'This is our last chance.'"

Harper's summer of glad-handing got him pilloried in the national press. *Hey, look, boring guy's out pretending to be fun.* But it is surprising how many Conservatives now say the tour filled in the last missing piece of the pre-election puzzle for him. A man who had always been awkward in crowds developed more confidence and poise in the only way that has ever worked: he threw himself into a lot of crowds.

⇧

Paul Martin's luck started running out for good when Gomery released the first volume of his report on November 1. Like Sheila Fraser's audit more than a year earlier, it said little that students of the sponsorship scandal didn't already know, but it said it portentously.

The judge found "a depressing tale of greed, venality and misconduct" and described "an elaborate kickback scheme" designed to benefit the Liberals' Quebec wing. Within days, Layton said he, too, could no longer prop up the Liberals in Parliament. With no other party on their side, the Liberals had no hope of surviving. The stage was finally set for a confidence showdown on November 24. Harper moved – seconded by Layton – "That this House has lost confidence in the government."

The lead story in that morning's *Globe and Mail* carried the headline "Liberals Plan Negative Campaign." The meat of the piece was a briefing that Charles Bird, the erstwhile 1990 leadership-campaign diarist – the one who had sworn the Chrétien hordes would "bleed" one day – and now a senior Liberal organizer for Ontario, had given his troops a few days earlier. Bird had said that the opposition parties, especially the Tories, would run a relentlessly negative campaign. As for the Liberals, "We will give as good as we get."

If Harper's speech on the non-confidence motion was any foretaste of the Conservative campaign line, the Tory attacks would be harsh indeed. Twice Harper told the Commons the Liberals had carried out their foul deeds "with the help of organized crime." He rattled off the same depressing list of Liberal misdeeds that had fuelled his Question Period attacks for more than a year.

"We have seen one minister of immigration have to resign over favouritism in giving out visas, while the next one billed taxpayers $118 for pizza, all defended by the prime minister," Harper said. "We have seen Art Eggleton, a man that Jean Chrétien fired from the cabinet for giving an untendered contract to a former girlfriend, get rewarded with a seat in the Senate."

On and on Harper went. He paused briefly to list Liberal failings on criminal justice, national unity, and budget-making. But there was no hint about what a Conservative government might do differently. For all the world it looked as though Harper planned to prosecute his way to victory.

And while all this was happening inside the Commons, something else was happening outside, across the nation.

It started raining money.

⇧

Newsrooms on Parliament Hill tend to be Spartan affairs. Reporters as a breed are not accomplished decorators. The typical Hill bureau comes decked out with only a few staple items: parliamentary phone directories, fax machines, piles of news releases, televisions eternally tuned to CBC Newsworld or CTV Newsnet – and, in every office, an ancient wall-mounted speaker.

The speakers bring reporters the texts of news releases read aloud by the staff of the Parliamentary Press Gallery, in the gallery's offices on the sixth floor of the National Press Building on Wellington Street. Every now and then, typically about three times an hour, the speakers crackle to life. "Your attention, please. We have three decisions from the CRTC . . ." or "Your attention, please. Just a reminder of the news conference by Jason Kenney . . ." Or whatever.

In the third week of November, the speakers started squawking more frequently. And on November 24, the day of Harper's speech on his confidence motion, the squawking became almost a running commentary as announcement followed announcement. Across Canada, Liberal ministers, ex-ministers, and wanna-be future ministers had fanned out to announce stunning amounts of new spending. On the first day of that week there had been eleven such announcements. Today there would be thirty.

Wayne Easter announced $483,900 for a theme park in Cavendish, Prince Edward Island. Robert Thibault announced

$2.6 million for a conference centre in Cornwallis, Nova Scotia. Then he delivered $201,500 for art gallery renovations in Yarmouth.

Aileen Carroll delivered $64 million for various international development-assistance projects. Belinda Stronach announced $1.1 million for police training. And $882,000 for "skills development in the international trade sector." And almost $8 million for "skills development in the technology and software sector." And $78,700 to integrate immigrants into the workforce.

For Stronach, it must have been a banner day: she had managed to spend more within a single twenty-four-hour period than she had on the night she had plied hundreds of Conservative convention delegates with blue martinis at the chic Hotel Godin in Montreal. And as a bonus, this time the money she was spraying around wasn't even her own. But given the scale of the money blizzard that was blowing, Stronach might as well have slept in. David Emerson announced $1.4 *billion* to prop up the nation's besieged forestry industry. Joe Volpe announced $700 million to modernize the immigration system. Scott Simms and Geoff Regan announced two different infrastructure deals, the first for $28 million in St. John's, the second for $37 million in Upper Tantallon, Nova Scotia.

Later, when the unprecedented blizzard of Liberal spending was over, the Canadian Taxpayers' Federation totted up the costs. In the first three weeks of November, the Martin government had announced $24.5 billion in new spending, about 15 per cent of total federal program spending for a year.

Ministers tried hard to put the best face on the feeding frenzy. "This didn't happen overnight," Stronach told reporters. David Emerson asked: "Are we trying to do what the public would like us to do? Yeah, that's what we're here for. And if people in an election say, 'We like what you're doing,' that's good."

Of all the ministers on the spending binge, perhaps only Reg Alcock came close to admitting what was up. "This is all within the fiscal plan of the government," Alcock told reporters. "But we are now moving harder and we are moving faster to get as many of the programs out the door. It was not planned this way. But we are not operating on our schedule."

"Cabinet was extraordinarily anxious to spit out the fruits of some of the labour that they had been undertaking for some time," Scott Reid recalls. And indeed: there was a visible pipeline stretching back from most of these announcements to earlier position papers, consultations, and so on. Little of this extraordinary orgy of spending was entirely improvised. "The second thing I should say is, there was about to be an election. And there was extraordinary pressure from cabinet and caucus to just jam stuff out the door." How much? One senior Martin staffer says some ministers simply profited from the chaos to announce new spending on their own, without even bothering to wait for clearance from the PMO. (Reid says he doesn't recall any such incidents.)

How can you spend multiples of billions of dollars without the principals being able to piece together, afterward, how it happened? One Liberal campaign official offers a partial response. "The structure and the process, and the way of operating, didn't even allow the person who was, on paper, the top dog to stop stuff from happening. I think that's another function of this group of people over the longer term. Whether it's Tim Murphy in the Prime Minister's Office, ostensibly running it, or David [Herle] on the political side as somebody running it – it's like they were running it, but they weren't. Things just *happened*, day to day. It's true. I know this to be true in my bones."

When the clock finally ran out on the Martin government, on November 28, it could hardly have been more anticlimactic. Members spent half an hour filing in for the confidence vote. For a long time they flooded the normally empty centre aisle, chatting, shaking hands, and gossiping across party lines. Jacques Saada, the Liberal minister for la Francophonie, spotted Don Boudria and hugged him hard. Boudria had been Chrétien's house leader, relegated to the backbenches by Martin. He was retiring. This would be his last night in the House of Commons. It would be Saada's last night too, although he did not know it yet. There were weeks of frustration still ahead before the Bloc would take him out in his Brossard–La Prairie riding south of Montreal.

In the Senate gallery, looking down across the House onto the Liberal benches, Senator Jim Munson watched the bustle below. Munson was a long-time CTV reporter who had become Jean Chrétien's communications director in 2002, and had been appointed to the Senate as one of Chrétien's last official acts. He shouted across open space to his former colleagues, packed three-deep in the press gallery: "Start the wave! Start the wave! Come on!" Munson tossed his arms skyward in an attempt to get the old football cheer going. He found no takers.

As the members stood to vote, those who would not run again received raucous applause from their colleagues. Conservatives Darrel Stinson and Dave Chatters, both fighting cancer, first and loudest of all. Then Ed Broadbent from the NDP, Claudette Bradshaw and Marlene Catterall from the Liberals.

When it was over, Peter Milliken, the Speaker, read the results: Yeas 171, Nays 133. The first Martin government was dead.

There's some old video footage of Joe Clark's government falling to a confidence vote in 1979. It ends with MPs and observers throwing a shower of loose-leaf and shredded paper into the air, celebrating the giddy uncertainty of an election many hadn't expected. Now a half-dozen Liberal MPs tried to recreate the moment, tossing skyward some sheets of paper they had taken pains to pre-shred. The effort seemed more pathetic than festive. There wasn't enough paper. There wasn't enough surprise. You can't recreate past glories. The chamber emptied within minutes.

8

MORE DON CHERRY THAN ARMANI

⇧

November 29, 2005, dawned in Ottawa the way November days usually do in the capital: grey, gloomy, not too cold but hardly promising. In the semi-circular driveway at 24 Sussex Drive, a familiar line of dark sedans formed the traditional prime ministerial motorcade: RCMP in front and rear, a couple of cars for staffers, and one for the prime minister. Sheila Martin sat by her husband's side in the back seat.

They weren't going far. Rideau Hall is only about a five-minute walk up Sussex Drive from the prime minister's residence. In fact, the last time Martin had gone to Rideau Hall to ask its occupant to dissolve Parliament, he had done it on foot. Like so much else, the 2004 stroll to Rideau Hall hadn't quite gone according to plan.

Martin had strolled up Sussex Drive, Sheila at his side, aides and bodyguards around them, with the usual clot of network camera crews just ahead, walking backward to capture the moment live for a waiting nation. The little gaggle promptly barrelled straight into a knot of tourists who'd hurried to the Governor General's house to watch Canadian history in action. PM, factotums, gendarmes, cameramen, and tourists made the most ungainly procession imaginable. Martin slowed to a snail's pace to ensure nobody got trampled.

The slow march opened up perilous empty moments of airtime, which the TV anchors filled by guessing about the True Meaning of It All. He's taking his time, Lloyd Robertson said on CTV. He mustn't have a care in the world. He's taking his time, Bernard Dérôme said on Radio-Canada. He must be terrified.

So much for that. This time, Martin's tidy little motorcade closed the distance between his front door and Michaëlle Jean's in three minutes. The newly appointed viceroy consulted in private with her prime minister for a little less than a half hour. Then Martin emerged back into the dingy morning to meet the waiting reporters.

In a brief prepared statement and his answers to questions from reporters, Martin sketched the themes of the campaign as he saw them: regret that it even had to happen; pride in a strong economy; and a clear warning that the best way to screw it all up was to vote for the parties that had recklessly forced this election in the first place. It was a profoundly stay-the-course message.

"A minority Parliament means the opposition can force an election whenever it chooses," Martin told the cameras, scowling faintly. "In this case, I believe ambition has overwhelmed common sense." He listed two bounties of good government that his scheming opponents had kept from Canadians' grasp by defeating the Liberals: "establishing benchmarks to reduce wait times in health care" and "making sure Canadians receive the full benefits of the tax cuts announced by the finance minister."

With that, the Liberal leader put an end to the morning's only remaining suspense by naming the date of the vote. "A general election, one forced over the holidays by the three opposition parties, will be held on Monday, January 23."

Eight weeks. It would be the longest election campaign since Brian Mulroney won in the landslide of 1984. Since then, to reflect the tempo of a nation made smaller by television and communications satellites, a new minimum length for campaigns had been set at five weeks. Every subsequent prime minister had stuck to that minimum. Until this one.

At the Conservative Party campaign headquarters on Albert Street, Ken Boessenkool put aside one set of briefing binders and planning books and opened a second. In 2004, Boessenkool hadn't had time to finish more than half the scripting for a campaign. Now he and Mark Cameron and their staff had done the entire campaign twice: once for a five-week campaign ending in the first week of January, the other for a full eight weeks. "If it's five weeks, we have a busy schedule," one Conservative said the night before Martin's trip to Rideau Hall. "If it's eight weeks, we have . . . less. Money is the limiting factor."

What was holding the Conservatives back wasn't how much money they had. It was how much they were allowed to spend. One of Jean Chrétien's last acts as prime minister had been to severely restrict corporate and union donations to political parties. The limits cramped the style of the Liberal Party, which was used to depending on a fairly small number of well-heeled donors. The Conservatives, on the other hand, were heirs to the Reform Party's extraordinary success at getting smaller donations from a much larger base of donors.

"We have *so much* money," a Harper aide would admit at the end of the campaign's first week, shaking his head in amazement. "We have shitloads of money. Way more than we can spend in a campaign. In a way we wouldn't have minded Martin's preferred schedule, which was to go in February, because we could have run this huge pre-writ campaign" – a blitz of television, radio, and newspaper ads, and direct mail, all of it unregulated by Elections Canada spending limits because it pre-dated the dropping of the writ.

Then why pull the plug before February? "Because you have to strike while the iron is hot. We're happy to do that. But now we're capped at $18.3 million for the whole eight-week period. We don't get any more money just because it's a longer campaign. So we have to be careful how we spend it."

The prime minister took five questions before leaving Rideau Hall to begin the long campaign. The first was from Peter Chura of Toronto's Citytv. "Prime Minister, many are predicting a negative campaign," he said. "Will your party use negative campaign ads?"

"I'm going to very much campaign on our record and where we want to take the country," Martin replied gamely. "And I believe in the country so much. And I am so optimistic about where we're going and what kind of a nation we can build. And I'm going to be talking about that record. I'm going to be talking about our promise and how we can achieve it."

So nothing but bright sunshiny days. Right?

"And of course in the course of that campaign I am going to be pointing out the differences between Stephen Harper and myself, the differences between the other leaders and myself," Martin continued. "And I will be pointing out where our values are, where their values differ. I'll be pointing out our record and the kinds of things that we support. Fundamentally,

I believe in this country and I'm going to be talking about the kind of nation that we can build."

The reporters at Rideau Hall chuckled – mostly to themselves, this time. Not out loud as they had when Martin had announced that Belinda Stronach's vote wasn't what he liked about her. "Pointing out where our values differ?" Translation: *You bet your life I'm going to use negative ads.*

"Our thesis was that the campaign was going to be broken into two pieces – before Christmas and after Christmas," Scott Reid told me much later, after the election. "Before Christmas we were going to have three objectives. One was to sink the record." Note that this doesn't mean the Liberals wanted to bury their record without a trace, but to embed it in the public consciousness. The Martin camp had little faith in their ability to actually win many yards with an engaging tale about how the Liberals had pulled the economy back from the precipice in 1995, polished it up all nice and shiny, and turned it into the envy of the world. But they figured if Martin kept hammering away at the theme for a while, they might get some of it to sink in.

"In a campaign this long, we're going to try to be osmotic. And maybe we'll lose a day or two, but hopefully we'll gain something. And maybe after a few days, people will say, 'These guys are being *dogged* about it. It may not be getting reported every minute, but they're not letting the slipper out of their clenched teeth, and they're *on* about the economy.' So that was objective number one. Own the economy, own health care and benchmarks, own child care.

"Secondly, we wanted to put a couple of new policy commitments in the window. At least a couple, before Christmas, that sank the record – allowed the record to be reportable – and created important differentiation with the Conservatives.

"Our third objective was to hold our own in the debates and to try to win them if we could. But the debates were more about Quebec. Both sets of debates" – French and English, before and after Christmas – "were about Quebec. You didn't want to lose, but where you wanted to create presence for yourself was Quebec."

That was the strategy for the first part, before Christmas. "And in the New Year? Our fundamental objective for the New Year was – having sunk the record and tried to establish differentiation – we would then try to talk about the future. And/or, respond to the circumstances we were looking at." The Liberals were well aware that by January, the campaign might have changed in ways they couldn't predict. So they built a lot of room for shimmy and improvisation into their game plan. But the basic plan was not just a hope, but a strategy to pick up seats.

This is not an easy business, talking about your plan for winning after you've run the plan and lost. Reid paused, considered how to sum it all up. "What we wanted to do – in our heart of hearts, but we dared not speak it out loud, for fear of jinxing ourselves – what we wanted to do was sink our objectives; win the debates; start to pick up some mojo in Quebec; and then *bring it on* in the second half of the campaign, as you neared voting day, with new, specific policy offerings that would generate news, drive the agenda, and cause people to say, 'Hey man, I can see how that extends out of what these guys are about, and I'm for it.'"

Campaign organizers almost never wait for the writ drop before they begin to deploy their campaign plan. For Martin, so much depended on gains in Quebec that he kicked the Quebec strategy into gear five days before the November 28 confidence vote. The venue was a meeting of the Montreal

wing of the Laurier Club, the national network of big-dollar
Liberal donors.

A few hundred Liberal swells milled around a ballroom at
the old Windsor Station on Peel Street in the early evening,
waiting for Martin to arrive. Even in a Liberal room in the
anglophone-dominated west end of Montreal, the dominant
language in the crowd was French. Very few of these people
were *brebis égarés* – the lost sheep of Canadian federalism who
had flirted with separatism and whom Jean Lapierre was supposed to both symbolize and attract, back when the goal of
Martin's Quebec game was to look right past solid Liberal
seats, taking them for granted, and grow into Bloc strong-
holds. No, these people were old school. They had been federalist in 1990 and 1992 and 1996, when believing in Canada
wasn't trendy, when Jean Lapierre was sitting next to Lucien
Bouchard in the Commons or working talk radio up the street
from Windsor Station, at CKAC.

These people belonged to a tiny and heroic demographic:
indefatigably federalist francophone Quebeckers. They and
people like them had saved the country twice, in 1980 and
1995, but they had spent the last two years wondering whether
the Liberal Party still wanted anything more from them than
their annual cheques. Tonight Paul Martin's mission was to
call them home.

Francis Fox was the prime minister's warm-up act. The
former Trudeau-era cabinet minister had come back to politics
for six months as Martin's principal secretary, then retired to a
seat in the Senate, part of the same crop of appointees as
Dennis Dawson. Fox was here to symbolize continuity and to
remind the Laurier Club members that they did too. He con-
gratulated the crowd for "participating in this great democratic work, the Liberal Party of Canada."

"We've seen majority governments and minority govern-ments," Fox said, "and I have to tell you, we prefer majority governments. What we need is stable government. We can't have elections every six months."

Fox wound up his pitch with a long introduction for Martin. "The only one who can stand up to the greats of this world – and I don't have to tell you who they are – is Paul Martin," Fox said. A dig at George W. Bush, and another measure of how far the Liberal leader and the nation had come. In 2003, Martin had grown thickets of committees and drafted armies of advisors to fix relations with Bush's Washington. Now the American president was a goblin who came out at night to keep scared Quebec Liberals in line.

Martin arrived, to hearty applause. Like the crowd, his speech was old school. Mock the opposition. Sing the praises of Canada. Remind federalists that, once again, they were all that stood between the separatists and victory.

In 1999, the night before Stéphane Dion tabled the Clarity Law in Parliament, Paul Martin had sworn a blue streak at the young staffer who'd been sent to brief him on the anti-separatist bill's contents. Now Martin was Clarity's defender. "The time has come for Gilles Duceppe to say publicly whether he puts himself above the law and the Supreme Court of Canada!"

Then Martin rehearsed the pre-Christmas campaign play-book by making a game attempt to "sink" the Liberal fiscal record: Healthy public finances, debt repayment, job growth. "These are the successes of a Liberal government. These are the successes of a country that works. And it's from this that the Bloc wants to separate us."

The Bloc claims to defend Quebec, Martin said. "But against what? . . . The separation of Quebec is the rejection of Canada's assets. The separation of Quebec is the rejection of Canada and I tell you, Quebeckers will never reject Canada!"

This stuff wasn't rocket science. Pierre Trudeau and Jean Chrétien could have delivered this speech in their sleep. But Trudeau and Chrétien had always been able to count on federalist Quebeckers, and Martin had given up on trying to accomplish anything fancier. The game here was rough but reliable: divide Quebec into "us" against "them," and hope to collect all the votes from "us." The assumption – reasonable as Martin spoke, but soon to collapse – was that, as in every federal election since the founding of the Bloc Québécois in 1990, Quebec would be a two-party game.

⇧

Day One of the campaign of his life, and here comes Stephen Harper, barrelling toward glory as if shot from a cannon. Or, more accurately, not.

At his opening news conference, in the lobby of the House of Commons, the Conservative leader rang all the classic challenger bells: time for a change, an end to corruption, a brighter future. The reporters who would spend the first week travelling with him asked him a few questions. One was about same-sex marriage. Another, from a reporter who spoke at the same time, was about some less thorny topic. Harper took the easy question. Nobody would have been surprised if that was that, at least for the first day. But at the end of his remarks, Harper made a point of coming back to the same-sex question.

"We were committed at the time of the [party policy] convention and through the last debate to put a free vote to the next Parliament on this issue," he said. "If that motion is defeated, we won't proceed. If it is passed, we will proceed."

Across Canada, Conservative supporters watching on television must have felt a brief moment of panic. Was it happening again? Already? The campaign had barely begun and Harper seemed to be getting caught up in another controversy over divisive social issues. At the end of the week, a Liberal warroom insider would point to this moment and predict that antics like the same-sex marriage outburst would seal Harper's fate. "At the end of the day, people don't like him," the senior Liberal said. "You can shine him up but he's still the same."

Was Harper being clumsy or careless? Or had he made a point of picking at the scab of the same-sex debate on the first day of the campaign, when news organizations would have so much else to cover that his controversial statement would make relatively few headlines? The election campaign would be over before a few close Harper confidantes would acknowledge that yes, it was the latter. Harper had to deliver on a commitment to his party's social conservative wing. But he would rather not be talking about same-sex marriage at the end of the campaign, if he could avoid it. So he would take the hit early and give himself as much time as possible to recover.

The same instinct led to another first-day announcement designed to bury bad news quickly in hopes that good news would follow. Gurmant Grewal was a Conservative MP from British Columbia who had flirted briefly with crossing the floor to the Liberals, at precisely the time Belinda Stronach had made the perilous crossing. Grewal had taped his conversations with Ujjal Dosanjh, the Liberals' lead political minister for British Columbia, and with Tim Murphy, Martin's chief of staff. Then he had released the tapes. Well, part of them. Well, edited parts of parts of the tapes. What had looked like iron-clad revelations of Liberal skullduggery had turned into the tale of a Conservative MP who couldn't keep his own story straight.

As Grewal started releasing bits and pieces of his tape, some of them apparently doctored, formerly ecstatic Conservatives began to realize he might not be an entirely reliable witness, and that his revelations about the government might not be worth the headache. "The advice of Mike Storeshaw and Geoff Norquay, of the people around [Harper] with any sense, was to cut [Grewal] loose," one insider recalls. "And Stephen chose to defend him and hug him tighter."

The leader's suppression of dissent could be brutal. James Moore, the bright young Vancouver-area MP, publicly called the Conservatives' handling of the Grewal affair "Keystone Kops." Moore's reward for his candour was to be hauled into Harper's office, shouted at for letting the side down, and barred from speaking in Question Period for six weeks.

And yet as reporters were settling into the Harper campaign's media bus on the first day of the campaign, their BlackBerrys buzzed with a Conservative news release. It was the text of a letter from Grewal to Harper. "It has come to my attention that our political opponents intend to use certain unresolved issues to attack not only me, but yourself and our party during the national campaign," Grewal's letter said.

"While I would not hesitate to fight these issues personally, it would be unfair to have the battle of a single MP become a focal point of the election." So he wouldn't be a candidate in this election.

In two different ways, this is Harper at work. First, the errant MP or candidate who realizes the error of his ways and writes a public mea culpa. As a rule, when this happens, if you look closely you can see Ian Brodie's hand sticking out of the repentant MP's back. People who seek public approval for a living do not, as a rule, like to back down. The quick, abject, flawlessly timed apology is not a common spectacle in electoral politics. But it would become a staple among Conservatives who made life difficult for Stephen Harper. The pattern would prove to be characteristic: trouble-trouble-trouble-bad-headline-Oh-my-*goodness*-I-realize-the-error-of-my-ways-bye-bye-now.

Second, the willingness to buy trouble early, on Harper's own terms, rather than stall and have trouble later anyway. This is the disciplined application of a principle everyone acknowledges: you can't run fast enough to stay away from bad days. And yet just about everyone tries. Harper is able to make a decision, in the face of that almost overwhelming flight instinct, to stand and take his beating. It does not guarantee a better outcome than running would have. But sometimes it can tilt the odds a bit. This time it worked: Gurmant Grewal's withdrawal received almost no coverage. Harper's stand on same-sex marriage received a lot more. But this way, at least, there would be time to move on.

There were so many sideshows on Harper's first day that an observer could have been forgiven for missing the main event: a campaign pitch that was different from the endless prosecutorial harangues many Liberals were expecting. "Now, this election will not only be about Gomery," he said at a rally in west-end Ottawa. "Judge Gomery looked at the past. We are looking toward the future now."

Well, maybe not quite. The next morning in Quebec City, Harper stood in front of eight candidates and announced the first new plank of a Conservative platform. A new "office of the director of public prosecutions." A full-time prosecutor to decide whether and how to proceed with federal prosecutions. Why? To "decide on prosecutions arising from the sponsorship scandal."

Right away, Harper ran into problems. First, he couldn't name any of the candidates standing behind him – even though he had begun his campaign in Quebec City because he claimed the Conservatives had a shot at a breakthrough there. "My staff can get you that," Harper growled at reporters who asked the candidates' names. But his staff couldn't, not until the campaign stopped hours later in Halifax.

More trouble in Halifax. Harper's own deputy leader, Peter MacKay, cheerfully disagreed with Harper's claim that a federal prosecutor would prosecute sponsorship malfeasance. "There's no way," MacKay said. "This office wouldn't deal with Criminal Code offences." Whoops. Reporters traded knowing glances. There's nothing more fun to cover than a disaster.

And then, on the second full day of the campaign, Harper pulled out of his nosedive. He strolled into 2001 Audio Video in Mississauga, Ontario, where his staff had set up a fake cash register in the middle of a long, uncluttered section of the checkout counter. Harper picked up a "GST/TPS 5%" sign and slapped it onto the cash register, while news cameras captured the moment.

Harper hated photo opportunities. His staff had made him rehearse this one meticulously the night before, precisely because if he was not comfortable he would screw it up. They experimented with different sizes and shapes for the big sign. They experimented with adhesives: sticky tape? Velcro? Finally they found a combination Harper was willing to work with.

⇧

The policy had been a longer time coming. In September, Muttart and Brodie had sat down to read the platform they inherited from the departed Phil Murphy. Muttart was already convinced the platform was a shapeless disaster and would need to be almost completely replaced. But with what?

The spring platform had included a cut to personal income taxes – not particularly different, as it turned out, from the tax cuts Ralph Goodale would unveil in the Liberals' fall pre-electoral mini-budget. But it took pages to explain, and market research showed that nobody could understand what all these adjustments to rates and exemptions would mean to their own tax bills. After all the tax cuts announced with a flourish by Paul Martin, Ralph Klein, Mike Harris, and others, most people still felt their own taxes had gone up.

It was after Labour Day, three months after Harper had come within a single vote of bringing down the Martin government, that he started gearing up the platform process yet again. It began with a meeting with Muttart and Brodie. "All right," Harper said. "What's the centrepiece of the platform?"

Brodie said the centrepiece, such as it was, was a complex cut to personal income taxes. Muttart said there would be no way to make it saleable in a general election campaign. Brodie said that if Harper really wanted his best advice, it was to promise a cut to the Goods and Services Tax. Muttart smiled just a little. He said he'd independently reached the same conclusion.

Harper broke into a broader smile. He had already reached the same conclusion. "We can't talk about tax cuts except the GST cut," he said. "That will break through. That will be a piece that people will understand."

Brodie and Muttart weren't sure they'd found an ally or whether the leader was having them on. For economists, GST cuts are the ugly duckling of tax cuts because they encourage consumption, which was already going gangbusters in a booming Canadian economy, instead of saving. In his last days as Alberta treasurer, Stockwell Day had mused publicly about *increasing* sales taxes such as the GST and *eliminating* personal-income taxes. So even after they'd left the meeting, it took Muttart and Brodie weeks to decide that Harper's enthusiasm was genuine. Once they did, they briefly flirted with an even bigger GST cut, to 4 per cent. But each point they cut would cost billions, and they would not be able to promise anything else if they put all their bets on a GST cut. So 5 per cent it would be.

The GST announcement set the rhythm for most of the campaign. The next day in Winnipeg, Harper promised to implement the Kirby Senate report on health-care wait times, paying to fly patients to other jurisdictions if they couldn't get timely care at home. Finally, on Saturday in Burnaby, B.C., Harper promised tougher penalties for drug crimes.

In a truncated first week, the Conservative had made his way from Nova Scotia to British Columbia, releasing a policy plank a day and working far more diligently to define himself than to attack Paul Martin. The Liberal, meanwhile, had shuttled between Montreal and Toronto giving rousing speeches to campaign rallies and rebutting Harper's announcements one by one.

It was an oddly minimalist way to begin the campaign. Privately, Liberals admitted they were saving their ammunition for after Christmas. And many were surprised that Harper hadn't made the same decision.

Why hadn't he come out on ethics, corruption, and the Gomery report? "We fully expected to get absolutely hammered in the first couple of weeks," the Liberal war-room strategist said. "The Tories are saving the hard negatives for later in the campaign." Still, if all Harper was talking about was how he'd govern, the Liberals were relieved. "We're happier having the debate on policy than corruption."

For Martin, the first week ended with two moments that showed his greatest strength and his most enduring weakness. His greatest strength was his tremendously appealing personality. It had allowed him to recruit support from far outside the old Liberal family: Scott Brison and Belinda Stronach, both lured from the Conservatives; Ujjal Dosanjh from the NDP; even Bono, the crusading rock star who spoke at Martin's coronation as Liberal leader. On December 2, Martin visited a Canadian Auto Workers event in Toronto and basked in the lavish praise of the mighty union's president, Buzz Hargrove, who was supposed to be an NDP supporter. Hargrove hugged the prime minister, gave him a union jacket, and said the Liberals had delivered so much in seventeen months that they deserved a stronger majority this time. "I could listen to you all day," Martin said, beaming.

And maybe he should have. Because when he left the CAW event to speak to reporters, Martin stopped listening long enough to open his mouth, revealing one of his most intractable failings: a tin ear for Quebec politics. A reporter for *La Presse* asked whether the coming election would be an *élection référendaire* – literally, an election that would act as a referendum on Quebeckers' desire to stay in Canada or leave it. "I think it really is an *élection référendaire*," Martin said, "certainly according to the Boisclair–Duceppe duo." Gilles Duceppe and the young new Parti Québécois leader, André Boisclair, had recently been plotting federal-election strategy together. "There's now a pact between them," Martin said. "The first step is the election of January 23."

As was so often the case when Martin misstepped, it was easy enough to see what he was trying to do. Play up the separatist menace to galvanize the federalist base. Oldest trick in the book. But to announce that an election would carry the weight

of a referendum? It was an extraordinarily reckless position for
a Canadian prime minister to take, especially with the Bloc
hovering over 50 per cent in the polls. In the four decades since
the Parti Québécois had been founded, no sovereigntist party
had ever broken the psychological barrier of 50 per cent of the
popular vote. Now Martin was giving the Bloc a licence to
claim that if it did so, the prime minister himself had recognized the political impact of the outcome. And for Paul Martin,
it was only the beginning of his Quebec troubles.

⇧

The first Conservative television ads, when they came out,
were almost charming in their bargain-basement hokeyness.
Harper and a blandly pretty actress sat at a desk, pretending
to do an interview. She asked him a scripted question about
pensions or taxes or government ethics. He recited a scripted
answer. She invited him – well, actually, she barked a command
– to look at a video screen. Where a voter asked a second
scripted question. Harper recited a second scripted answer. It
all felt a bit like a training film shot at a Soviet tractor factory
in 1954.

The ads finished with a shot of a woman assembling the
message "Stand up for Canada" on a mobile roadside sign. A
passing car beeped its horn twice. Beep-beep.

Even Conservatives made no attempt to hide their embar-
rassment. "But one of the things I learned in politics along the
way was, effectiveness may not be in my eye as a beholder,"
Norquay said. "Example: there is an art to writing a fundraising
letter. Have you ever seen a fundraising letter from a political
party? It is the most hokey, stupid, hackneyed, badly written
piece of shit. And it raises millions and millions."

Perry Miele and the Tory admen, with substantial creative input from Patrick Muttart, were working on the same principle. In focus groups, the ads had been quite powerful in getting voters to retain the central messages. Even the little beep-beep was calculated: if you were making dinner with a TV on at the other side of the room, the car horn would make you look up, in time to see a Conservative logo.

"There's a school of thought that we're more Don Cherry than Giorgio Armani," Tim Powers said. Powers is a burly Newfoundlander who often speaks for the Conservatives on television panels. "And the ads reflect that. Look at the success Don Cherry has had with *Rock 'em Sock 'em Hockey*. A low-tech production, but a messenger with a product people wanted. And he's now in his sixth or seventh version of *Rock 'em Sock 'em Hockey*." Seventeenth, actually.

Once word filtered through their ranks that the ads were *supposed* to look cheap, the Conservatives developed a quirky sense of pride in them. But through a mix-up that has never been revealed until now, the ads nearly wound up destroying the Conservative campaign at the outset.

Campaign ads are sent to television stations as paid advertising, and also to news organizations in the hope that they'll do a story about the ads. A little earned media to go along with your paid media. On the night the first ads went out, Yaroslav Baran got a call at Conservative headquarters in Ottawa.

It was the Conservative ad people in Toronto. They'd sent out the wrong DVDs to news organizations. These discs didn't contain only the ads that had been approved for the first blitz, the hokey fake-interview Harper ads. These DVDs had *every Conservative ad* on them. Dozens of ads. Positive ads, attack ads, ads for contingencies that might never materialize. Mockups of ads the leader hadn't even seen. If they got out, the

Conservatives would have (a) sabotaged their own ad strategy for the rest of the campaign; (b) shown themselves to be plotting a negative campaign while Harper tried to recycle himself as Mr. Forward-looking Policy; (c) looked like idiots.

Baran started to sweat. How far had these tell-all DVDs travelled? Good news. The Conservatives had this much luck, at least: so far, the courier had delivered only one, to Sun Media.

Baran needed that DVD. What to do? Probably a heist was out of the question. Come clean? Baran called Lorrie Goldstein, the *Toronto Sun* columnist. His plan was to offer a major scoop down the road in return for a major favour tonight. But Goldstein wasn't picking up his phone. So Baran just called Sun Media's news desk.

"Let me guess," the person who picked up the phone said, "you're calling about the DVD." Yes indeed, Baran said, unsure how to handle what they'd say next.

"Yeah," said the person at Sun Media, "we don't know what the problem is, but we can't get it to play."

Saints be praised. "Well, that's why I'm calling," Baran said. "There seems to be a problem with it. We just want to assure you that there's a replacement on its way. All I ask is that you give the messenger the one you have, because we need to figure out what's wrong with it."

Oblivious, the Sun person agreed to the swap. The single DVD that would have revealed every Conservative secret was safely retrieved. And that's how Sun Media had, then lost, the scoop that could have derailed the Harper campaign from the outset.

9

"LIKEABILITY? JESUS CHRIST!"

⇧

After two weeks of campaigning, Harper's big strategic decision to talk about Conservative policy instead of Liberal corruption had the Liberals more surprised than worried. Policy-a-day "might work well in April but I think he's getting caught in the ho-ho-ho season," Roger Gallaway, the incumbent Liberal MP in Sarnia-Lambton, said. "It's just not penetrating."

That's most Liberals. Some actually were worried. "The fact that people are starting to debate the issues and not Stephen Harper is not good for us," a war-room insider said. But Martin had always planned to put some policy of his own in the window before Christmas. Now the time had come to do that.

In New Brunswick, the Liberal leader said his party would double the length of its five-year child-care program. In Montreal, he spoke to the global conference on climate change, where his environment minister, Stéphane Dion, was acting as chairman with considerable aplomb and a diplomatic grace that few Canadians would have expected from Jean Chrétien's pugnacious national-unity cop. In Toronto, Martin announced a "Canada handgun ban" while David Miller, the city's mayor, stood beside him.

But there was an air of virtual reality to Martin's announcements. In Montreal, he gave a blandly hortatory speech to the climate-change meeting, whose goal was to begin designing a sequel to the Kyoto accord on greenhouse gas emissions. He saved his punch for his opening statement at the news conference that followed. "To the reticent nations, including the United States, I'd say this: there is such a thing as a global conscience, and now is the time to listen to it."

It was a striking choice of words. A "conscience" is normally understood as a sense of one's own responsibilities. But Canada, which had signed and ratified Kyoto, had increased its greenhouse gas emissions by 24 per cent since 1990. The United States, which never ratified Kyoto, had increased its emissions by only 13 per cent. If the United States had been as profligate over the same period as Canada, it would have spat an extra 662 million tonnes of carbon products into the air in 2005. That's more than Britain's total emissions in 2003. The gap between Martin's remarks and the truth is as big as *Britain*. Usually when a politician utters a whopper, you can't actually give the whopper a name. But you can name this one. You can call it *Britain*. Say hello to *Britain*, the whopper.

In New Brunswick, Martin announced extra daycare spending. Again there was something odd about it: The money Martin was announcing today wouldn't begin to flow until 2009 – almost certainly after the term of the government

Canadians were about to elect. As a rule, historically, political parties prefer to concentrate on their plans for the coming mandate, not the one after. "Our announcement was that we were going to make this a permanent program," Scott Reid explained later, after the election. "It [was] now a permanent social program that [was] here to stay. And no, it wasn't a tweaky little policy thing, it was a symbolic thing."

As for Martin's handgun ban, for a "new" and "total" ban it was both familiar and porous. Most handguns had been banned from the possession of most Canadians, except collectors and handgun owners, for decades. Even under the new regime Martin was proposing, individual provinces would be able to opt out of the ban. And this is the funny thing about a country: if you can get handguns into any part of it, you'll have no trouble transporting them to every corner of the land. But it was clear that the Liberals hoped that merely talking about gun control would goad a few backward Tories into making intemperate remarks that could be turned against the whole party.

Harper's campaign team knew this, and had prepared for just such a moment. The Conservative war room had a separate telephone number for "candidate support." Nearly a dozen campaign staffers were assigned to candidate support from early in the morning to late at night. All candidates had standing orders to call the hotline when any news outlet requested an interview about anything. A pre-interview conference call would ensue, with the candidate being coached long-distance by campaign staffers on policy and media relations. These sessions could last a half hour.

When news of Martin's handgun "ban" leaked, the same process worked in reverse. Joan Bryden, a reporter at The Canadian Press, caught wind of the next day's announcement.

When Bryden's quickly written story moved on the CP wire, reporters on the Martin campaign tour started assailing Scott Reid with questions. Rather than let the story dribble out like this, Reid decided to leak it more broadly, to major newspapers and broadcast networks, to broaden the playing field.

So the news was out almost twelve hours before Martin's announcement. As details started to appear in evening news-cast and wire-service stories, the Tory war room telephoned candidates across the country, urging them to stand down and make no public comment until Harper had had a chance to set the tone himself the next morning. Meanwhile, the war-room researchers worked overnight, gleaning details of Martin's impending announcement from the news accounts, and lining up arguments against it.

In the end, Martin's gun announcement produced more criticism of the Liberals for opportunism and sloppy policy design than coverage – pro or con – of the Conservative response. "That was a very telling moment in the campaign," a Conservative war-room insider said later, "because the Liberals thought this would be their first nuke. Just chuck this grenade into our camp and watch us scurry in all directions. And we didn't fall for it.

"Furthermore, we proved to ourselves and to the outside world that we have discipline. And in the end, our response was reasoned and reasonable. So that was a very important day, maybe more so internally than externally."

This was all going pretty well for the Conservatives. "The first two weeks," Jason Kenney said, "we're watching the news at night saying, 'What is this? We won this day free and clear. What do the other guys have up their sleeve? Tomorrow must be a big day for them.'" And it never was. "We got the message out. And they didn't. Day after day."

Which is what made the first big gaffe of the campaign so destabilizing when it arrived. Especially because the gaffe came from two Liberals.

⇧

Scott Reid is famous for his short temper, but he didn't blow up on *CBC News: Sunday* on December 11. He just let his mouth get ahead of his brain.

The topic was the fascinating difference between Martin's child-care plan and Harper's. Martin would send transfers to the provinces in return for high-quality, state-operated daycare centres for the children of a fraction of the child-rearing population. Harper's would abandon such grand schemes and simply send each parent twelve hundred dollars a year for each child under the age of six. Martin's plan emphasized formal structures for working parents. Harper's emphasized choice: parents could stay home with their children, send them to daycare (and foot most of the bill), have Aunt May babysit part-time, or any other arrangement.

It was a classic clash of values and priorities. Each party found the other's scheme appalling. Scott Reid simply found an unusually picturesque way to say so. "Working families need care," he said on the CBC. "They need care that is regulated, safe and secure and that's what we're building here. Don't give people twenty-five dollars a week to blow on beer and popcorn. Give them child-care spaces that work."

Later Reid would say he realized immediately that the "beer and popcorn" phrasing was a huge mistake. Before the end of the day he would be apologizing profusely. So would Martin. Typically, the Martin campaign quickly settled on the adjective they would all use to describe Reid's sortie: "Dumb."

But John Duffy didn't get the memo in time. Less than two hours after the CBC panel aired, Duffy spoke for the Liberals on a panel on CTV's *Question Period*. Tim Powers asked whether Duffy agreed with Reid's beer-and-popcorn analogy. The very strong instinct, at such a moment, is to avoid letting light show between two members of a campaign team. So did Duffy agree with Reid? "Absolutely!," Duffy said. "There's nothing to stop people from spending it on beer or popcorn or a coat or a car or anything."

The assumption behind the Liberals' comments was that parents cannot be trusted to spend money in their children's interest. It was an explosive accusation. Among precisely the working-class and middle-class voters the Conservatives were targeting, it would sound like government-knows-best nanny-statism of the worst sort. The Liberals needed a distraction, fast.

And along came David Wilkins.

⇧

Wilkins is George W. Bush's second ambassador to Ottawa. In person, he is a Southern charmer, swapping political gossip with visitors and sending them on their way with a can of boiled peanuts, a South Carolina delicacy of dubious culinary value. But as Speaker of the South Carolina legislature, he delivered his state for Bush in the 2000 Republican primaries with a campaign of unparalleled nastiness against Bush's main opponent, Senator John McCain.

Wilkins had watched Paul Martin lecture the United States on greenhouse gas emissions. Wilkins knew that emissions from Canada have grown more rapidly than emissions from the United States. And he watched Martin return two days later, flying back to Montreal from Windsor, Ontario, in a

snowstorm, to share a stage at the Montreal climate conference with former president Bill Clinton. Wilkins didn't like
Bill Clinton. And he was not at all pleased that a sitting prime
minister seemed intent on campaigning against the administration he represented.

Martin's Montreal appearances were on Wednesday and
Friday, December 7 and 9. That weekend, Wilkins sat at home
alone in the U.S. Ambassador's sprawling Rockcliffe residence
and hand-wrote a twenty-minute speech. He delivered it on
Tuesday, December 13, to a lunchtime crowd at Ottawa's
Fairmont Château Laurier. His theme would have been familiar to Benjamin Franklin: don't tread on me.

"It may be smart election-year politics to thump your chest
and constantly criticize your friend and your number-one
trading partner," Wilkins said in his fabulously languorous
Southern drawl. "But it is a slippery slope, and all of us should
hope that it doesn't have a long-term impact on the relationship." There was more. "What if one of your best friends . . .
demanded respect but offered little in return?" he asked.
"Wouldn't that begin to sow the seeds of doubt in your mind
about the strength of that relationship?"

What happened over the next few days could only happen
in Canada. Liberal support, which had been sagging, took a
bounce. Martin, remember, had once campaigned for the
Liberal leadership on a promise of a "more sophisticated relationship" with the United States. Now he was disinclined to
spend more time on sophistication. He showed up at a B.C.
lumberyard, wearing a leather jacket and talking tough about
the Yankees. "I'm going to call them as I see them," he said,
jaw thrust out. "I am not going to be dictated to."

It was one of the campaign's most vertiginous, through-the-
looking-glass moments. Martin had tweaked the Americans

for their behaviour on greenhouse gases. Now here he was in a lumberyard. (Perhaps Martin's advance staff could find no smokestacks.) And Wilkins, who had asked only that the United States be left out of the campaign, was pilloried for sticking his nose into it. And far from pushing Martin around, teaching him a lesson, the ambassador had given the Liberals a tidy little boost.

Amid all this, a veteran U.S. official took a telephone call from me. Speaking on condition of anonymity, he said Wilkins cared very little about the effect his speech might have on the election's outcome – although he had taken pains to speak before Christmas, so any uproar might have time to die down. "He would not have thought of doing this after Christmas," the official said.

Wilkins's message was not aimed at the Liberal leader or at any other campaigner. It was aimed at the Canadian state. "We are not going to watch the U.S. get pummelled any more," the official said. "Whether or not there is a campaign on, we're not gonna take it." Wilkins hoped any controversy might die down by voting day. "But we're not going to not respond. This is not a field day at our expense."

⇧

Let's pause to consider how scary all of this was becoming for Jack Layton.

The NDP leader knew better than anyone how gravely his party was endangered by the clash of dinosaurs now underway. In 2004, the Martin Liberals, more or less out of desperation, improvised a strategy that involved playing up the scary Conservative rise in the polls. Martin poached terrified NDP supporters by telling them they had to "stop Harper" by abandoning their party to vote Liberal. It worked. New Democrats never forgot how they wound up losing a dozen seats by fewer than a thousand votes.

So Martin had learned what a great strategy it was to treat the NDP as a bag of spare Liberal votes he could dip into if the going got tough. So far things weren't that bad. But while the party-preference numbers in the polls weren't budging, Harper was starting to get strong reviews for his campaign. If he rose, he would become more of a threat to Martin than in 2004 – more familiar to voters, with a better-prepared and more unified party. This big, looming Harper threat would put a great big chunk of the voters Layton needed into play, tempted by the Liberals.

To which New Democrats could only respond: Uh-oh.

Brian Topp, a soft-spoken man with an unruly shock of curly black hair, is an executive at ACTRA, the film industry union. He was Roy Romanow's deputy chief of staff when Romanow was premier of Saskatchewan. He worked on Layton's first national election campaign in 2004. In 2006, he was back as the NDP's national campaign director. He embodies a characteristic New Democrats have to an extent no other national political party does: when there is a campaign anywhere in Canada, they drop everything to travel in large numbers from wherever they live to wherever the fight is. In the rabbit warrens of the NDP's Ottawa campaign headquarters, upstairs from a Shopper's Drug Mart on Laurier Street, you could find people who had worked with NDP premiers and party leaders in Ontario, Manitoba, Saskatchewan, and British Columbia. Many had no Ottawa experience apart from their periodic trips to the capital to fight for Jack Layton. Most came in 2004 for their first national campaign. They came back in the spring of 2005 and went right back home after the false-alarm confidence vote. They came back again in the fall.

The NDP, Topp said, went through its own post-mortem exercise after the 2004 election. Most of the changes they settled on weren't huge; the NDP had, after all, nearly doubled its share of the popular vote in 2004, even if that had translated into only six more MPs. Layton's campaigners decided that, next time, they would target more people and money at the regions where they had narrowly missed and fewer people and less money at areas where they had no chance. They would make sure the party's ads, tour operation, and platform were saying the same thing at the same time. And they decided Layton's 2004 platform, a numbingly long laundry list of promises, needed to be much tighter and more coherent.

But that was all secondary. "The first rule," Topp said, "was *Don't get clobbered.*"

Topp is a student of minority parliaments in which the NDP sits in opposition. They're nice, while they last. The NDP has disproportionate influence over what governments do, especially Liberal governments. But then things get dangerous quickly. "History teaches that the Liberals run on our record – on the things that we managed to get accomplished. And we get our heads handed to us by the electorate if we're not very careful," he said. Not since Tommy Douglas in 1968 – thirty-eight years ago – has the NDP won bigger at the federal level after a minority Liberal government than before it.

"So we decided not to fight a two-front war," Topp said. "We basically switch votes with the Liberals. So we were going to concentrate on the Liberals."

Harper had met Layton frequently, as he had met Duceppe, to plan opposition strategy in the minority Parliament. In his meetings with Layton, Harper urged the New Democrat to be far more aggressive in grabbing the political centre. The goal was to supplant the Liberals altogether. The model was Manitoba, or today's United Kingdom, where the social democrats and the conservatives had left no room for the centrist party to breathe. But in private, Harper despaired of Layton's ability to pull off anything that bold and ambitious. "You can't teach an elephant to dance," the Conservative leader sighed.

Even the far more modest attack on the Liberals that Layton and Topp were planning carried risks. If there's anything most NDP voters like less than a Liberal, it's a Conservative. By focusing his attacks on Martin, Layton was hoping to keep NDP supporters from seeing the Martin Liberals as an acceptable alternative. The danger was obvious: that Layton would face a backlash for concentrating his attack on the lesser of two evils. In a way, that backlash was already upon him. Its name was Buzz Hargrove.

The CAW leader gave Martin his union jacket in Toronto on the campaign's first Friday. Joe Fontana, the Liberal labour minister from London, Ontario, had spent months softening Hargrove up in preparation for just such a moment. The union boss is susceptible to flattery and Fontana made it his business to ensure that Hargrove stayed flattered.

After he finally put on the big show for Martin on that Friday in Toronto, Hargrove seemed surprised by the criticism he received from NDP supporters. He quickly wrote an op-ed piece for the *National Post* insisting that he wanted CAW members to vote NDP wherever the party's local candidate had a chance to win. The advice seemed simple enough: If you lived where the NDP was strong, you should still vote NDP. Buzz Hargrove's own advice.

But now here's Buzz Hargrove, once again at Martin's side, on the campaign's second Friday. In Windsor. A city with two

NDP MPs. Two NDP MPs who were running for re-election. Two NDP MPs who couldn't be stopped unless, say, a nationally famous union boss plopped his supremely self-satisfied butt down in their town and told anyone who would listen that they should vote for another party.

New Democrats simply tossed up their hands at the antics of a man who had been one of the party's most persistent internal sources of dissent, not all of it entirely coherent, for years. "His job between elections is to make the party as far to the left – and unelectable – as possible," said Topp. Hargrove supported Svend Robinson for the leadership in 1995 against Alexa McDonough. In 2003, when McDonough finally gave up the leadership, Hargrove supported Joe Comartin, the left-wing Windsor MP, to replace her. And now here was Buzz campaigning with Paul Martin in Comartin's hometown. Thanks a lot, Buzz.

But this was precisely the problem. *Of course* Hargrove was in Windsor. The only people who would listen to the advice of a Buzz Hargrove on anything were, disproportionately, people who lived in ridings where NDP candidates had a fighting chance. There weren't a lot of people in plummy Rosedale or Outremont taking their cues from a union boss. "His endorsement of the prime minister only hurts us where we can win," one New Democrat said.

⇧

The parties had barely budged in the polls when Martin, Harper, Layton, and Duceppe flew to Vancouver for the first round of televised debates on December 15 and 16. Nobody expected record-breaking audiences. It was the eve of the last full weekend before Christmas. The 2004 debates, with the same protagonists, had been run on minimal rules with an eye toward direct confrontation among leaders. Good idea when there are two candidates on the stage. Not so good when there are four. The debates had degenerated for minutes at a time into pointless, incomprehensible shouting matches. At least everyone involved, even the TV networks, had the grace to be embarrassed about it all. So this year's versions were more or less designed to be as soporific as possible. The leaders had been warned that their microphones would be cut off if they tried to interrupt one another. Nothing would get in the way of earnest policy discussion. Flee, audiences! Flee!

But while the debates would be hard to win, nobody wanted to be declared the loser. Ever since Brian Mulroney made himself unstoppable by rounding on John Turner over patronage in 1984 ("You had an option, sir"), surviving the debates has been among every leader's highest priorities. The Liberals' opening gambit was to try to knock Harper off balance. Their plan went into action on the eve of the opening French-language debate.

On political chat shows on CBC Newsworld and CTV Newsnet, Liberal spokesmen affected dismay at the news that a 1997 speech by Harper had surfaced. In the speech, Harper calls Canada "a northern European welfare state in the worst sense of the term." He urges his audience "not to feel particularly bad" for Canada's unemployed. "They don't feel bad about it themselves, as long as they're receiving generous social assistance and unemployment insurance."

Harper had delivered the speech in Montreal to a meeting of the Council for National Policy, a right-wing U.S. think-tank. It was tailored to their political frame of reference, and it was jokey in the manner of an after-dinner address. And of course the Liberals had leaked it. In Vancouver, it was Martin's

British Columbia campaign co-chairman, Mark Marissen, who delivered a copy to the CBC. In Ottawa, the Liberals had Alex Munter, a former city councillor and an advocate for same-sex marriage, send a copy to The Canadian Press. Munter had watched from the NDP opposition lobby, behind the curtains, on the night the same-sex marriage legislation had passed its final vote in the House. New Democrats thought he was with them. But now he was working with the Liberals, even playing Layton in the mock debates Martin used to rehearse for the real thing.

The Conservatives had been waiting for the Liberals to start digging up the leader's past statements. Harper's campaign staff, divided between the Vancouver debate venue and the Ottawa party headquarters, had a quick conference call. Marjory LeBreton, the long-time Tory senator and Brian Mulroney confidante, was travelling with Harper and on the call.

To say the least, LeBreton had taken a long time to warm to Harper. When the Progressive Conservatives and Canadian Alliance were separate and at each other's throat, she had been one of the PCs' most effective weapons. When Harper became Alliance leader, reporters started receiving long emails from LeBreton detailing her point-by-point disagreements with Harper on questions of public finance or foreign policy. But to her amazement, Harper had come to rely on her, and then even to invite her to join his touring campaign staff. She offered two assets Harper's Calgary friends didn't bring to the table: institutional memory and a willingness to charm reporters.

But the asset she brought to the table on this particular day was a disinclination to give in to easy panic. "What are we talking about here?" she asked as the other Conservatives discussed Harper's 1997 speech. "Look. This speech has been around for a long time. Belinda Stronach tried to shop it around when she ran against Stephen for the Conservative leadership. The only way this is going to be a story is if we allow it to become a story."

Harper agreed. In the end, the speech would turn into a two-day wonder. Ignoring it reinforced a novel pattern that was starting to characterize this election. Harper, the challenger with no experience at a federal cabinet table, was spending most of his time talking about how he would govern. Martin, the veteran of a decade of Liberal control of government, was spending most of his time talking about Harper. That's a *brutal* dynamic if you're on the wrong side of it. Harper was already the topic of conversation. The Liberals would need luck and skill to change that. Luck, at least, would not be with them.

⇧

The debates themselves offered few surprises. Each man gave a good account of himself, with perhaps only Gilles Duceppe showing unaccustomed sluggishness in the English debate. Not that he had many English votes to lose. Layton, who had been forced by the wide-open 2004 debate rules to transform himself into a yappy little terrier, nipping at the others' heels until Martin, at least, clearly wanted to swat him, was far more poised now that nobody was allowed to interrupt anyone. Many commentators called him the winner.

But it was Martin who produced the most memorable clip. Rounding on Duceppe in the English debate, he berated the Bloc leader on the secession question. "This is my country and my children were born and raised in Quebec, and you're not going to go to them and say that you're going to find some backdoor way of taking my country or dividing Quebec family against Quebec family," Martin said, while Duceppe squirmed. "You're not going to win, Mr. Duceppe. Let me tell you that."

Great stuff. Better still, it fitted the strategic goal of the debates, which was to position Martin as a credible leader of Quebec's patient federalist base. Martin pursued the theme in the scrum room after the debate, where reporters were waiting to quiz the leaders on their performance. Did he want to have another go at Duceppe? You bet. Martin said he would meet the Bloquiste "on every street corner, in every city and in every town and village in Quebec."

It was a classic Martin answer in at least three ways. First, it agreed with the premise of the question. Would he (fill in blank)? Why, by God, you bet he'd (fill in blank)! Second, it included a supplementary dose of enthusiasm. Debate Duceppe? On every corner! In every city! And town! And village!

Third, Martin's answer promptly got him into trouble. Two days later in Montreal, Duceppe said he considered Martin's boast a formal offer. And he was going to take him up on it.

Breaking into English, the language in which Martin had issued his challenge, Duceppe shouted hoarsely: "If you're ready to meet me everywhere in Quebec, Mr. Martin, be my guest. I'm in Montreal today. I'm waiting for you! Come on the North Shore to talk about softwood lumber, Paul Martin. I'm there Tuesday! I will be waiting! Come on!"

Martin, of course, demurred. When he said he would meet Duceppe on every street corner in every village, he didn't mean he would actually meet Duceppe on any street corner or in any particular village.

And then something happened that, today, figures in nobody's five-minute history of the 2006 election. An event no strategist, Liberal or Conservative, spontaneously mentions now. But I persist in believing it was an important symbolic moment.

Harper offered to debate Duceppe, on television, in French. "If Paul Martin refuses to stand up for Canada, Stephen Harper will," a nameless Conservative strategist told The Canadian Press.

The moment was over almost before it began. Harper had shown no particular strength in Quebec polls. Duceppe dismissed Harper out of hand; he wanted to debate a prime minister, not some guy from Calgary. But even if Harper's offer didn't move polls, it illustrated something. The first job of a prime minister, going all the way back to John A. Macdonald, is to defend national unity. Harper had not yet proved he could do it. Still hasn't today. But this showed that he was at least willing to try.

On that inconclusive note, the first period of the campaign drew to a close. The Liberal and Bloc campaigns shut down almost completely for Christmas. Layton went to the Northwest Territories, a long trip worth making because the NDP had hopes of picking off the Liberal incumbent there. Only Harper kept his campaign running, almost uninterrupted, through the Christmas break.

"Stephen's credibility numbers started to go up," one senior Conservative says. "Our ownership of the tax-cut issue changed overnight. 'Which party is best positioned to cut your taxes?' After the GST thing it was no contest – and the Liberals had been ahead of us before the campaign. Those trend lines just crossed, and if you were interested in taxes, you were voting Conservative. That's retaking traditional conservative ground, but Martin had made huge inroads into that population.

"The child-care thing. Two parents with kids: 'Which party is the best party for your financial situation?' They (the Liberals) tanked. We went through the roof among that group of people on that particular score.

"And then after the first English-language leadership debate. 'Which leader do you think would be the best leader for Canada?' or whatever. Stephen's leader numbers had always lagged the party numbers, ever since he was elected leader – particularly after the 2004 campaign. Not by much, but by a few points. That flipped. The party numbers remained constant – but his popularity numbers went up. And that was the beginning of a constant, monotonic increase in his personal popularity, credibility, leadership numbers. Before the Christmas break, we were even pulling even with Martin on likeability. Likeability? Pulling even on *likeability*? Jesus Christ!

"So all of these numbers below the top line were starting to change before the leaders' debates, and then after the first English-language leaders' debate, there was a firm trend that had emerged."

A senior Liberal recalls sensing the same trends, not as strongly, from their side of the fight: "On the daily calls, David Herle did a summary of where we were and the imperatives going forward. I know that he, in particular, was very anxious – and this was probably code for a deeper anxiety, in retrospect – but he was very concerned that that first week back (after Christmas) be credible on policy and on substance. And there was an implicit recognition that Harper had connected with average middle-class families with his set of initiatives and that there had to be some ground regained there . . . I think he was feeling very anxious about how Harper had occupied that ground."

And then Harper kept on occupying the ground. The Conservative leader didn't want to go home to Calgary and stew over the holidays. He hadn't spent much time in Vancouver and up the west coast. Brodie wasn't sure there was room in the budget for Christmas campaigning, but Finley cut it as close as he could to make it work. They gave up the Air Canada plane and got a much smaller Canada Regional Jet. Reporters travelling with Harper were told there was no room and they'd have to catch up on their own if they wanted. (This gave the Parliamentary Press Gallery bigfeet a welcome break from Harper's campaign. And it ensured that most of the coverage would come from regional reporters, a state of affairs Harper had always preferred.)

Finley was convinced of something Brodie didn't buy: that people would be talking about politics over their Christmas turkey. Harper's lead had collapsed in 2004 for a lot of reasons, but one was that it was built on air. There was no strong sense of identification with Conservative policy or with Harper as a guy you could learn to like having around. So their numbers fell almost as quickly as they had shot up. Finley thought that if the fundamentals were strong going into Christmas, and Harper kept popping up on TV screens, folks who were already sick of talking about the bundt cake would mention that this guy Harper might not be so bad – and hear some agreement around the living room. "If we did get to that point," one Conservative said, "we could come back in January and hit it home."

The Liberals were betting it pretty much the other way around. Turn it on after the New Year. Take the top of the news right when people were starting to pay serious attention. To work, it required that the last week of 2005 be calm. Martin couldn't come out of the gate playing defence. Events refused to co-operate.

⇧

On Friday, December 23, the *Toronto Star* ran a little item noting that Mike Klander, a senior Ontario Liberal organizer and a key member of Martin's 2003 leadership team, had amused himself with an Internet weblog on which he compared Olivia Chow, the Chinese-Canadian NDP candidate for Toronto's Trinity-Spadina riding, to a chow-chow dog. NDP supporters, apparently forgetting that the Martinites expected them to ignore politics over Christmas, chewed on the news all weekend on various NDP-affiliated blogs. A few posted comments asking whether more prominent bloggers were aware of the story – "has anyone told Warren Kinsella, Paul Wells, Andrew Coyne?" On Christmas Day, Klander's dubious witticisms – he had also called Chow's husband, Jack Layton, "an asshole" – were chronicled on the *Maclean's* Inkless Wells blog. Klander resigned from his party functions a day later. For Martin the trouble was only beginning.

On December 26, thousands of shoppers were chasing Boxing Day bargains on Yonge Street, in the heart of downtown Toronto, when dozens of gunshots rang out. A half-dozen shoppers were wounded. Jane Creba, a bright and popular high school student, was killed. The death shocked a city where crime had been falling but deadly gun crime spiking. It's not as though the Liberals or anyone else had ignored gun crime. Martin had announced his tenuous handgun ban in Toronto precisely because of such concerns. But after the shootout, police seized one reportedly illegal gun. Suddenly gun bans seemed even less pertinent. By the end of the week, according to senior Conservative John Reynolds, internal Conservative polling showed crime as a top-five voter concern, for the first time.

Bonehead bloggers and tragic crime are, sadly, the way of the modern world. Neither incident would have rattled Martin profoundly. Only the income-trust affair could do that. On December 28, it blew wide open.

The affair had been a long time brewing. In the wake of the dot-com crash, investors looking for reliable investments flocked to income trusts, which pay most of their cash flow directly to investors in monthly cash distributions. The market value of trusts surged. Hundreds of companies rushed to restructure themselves as trusts to reduce their tax burden and appeal to ready capital. But the Finance Department in Ottawa was highly unamused by the loss of hundreds of millions of dollars in tax revenue.

In his first budget in 2004, Finance Minister Ralph Goodale announced limits on the amount of money Canadian pension funds could invest in trusts. The idea was to limit market demand, but the plan immediately backfired. Large, powerful funds like the Ontario Teachers' Pension Plan screamed in protest, saying the government had compromised their ability to provide benefits to retirees.

Goodale backed down, but Finance remained concerned about tax revenues lost to trusts. On September 19, 2005, Goodale dropped another bombshell. His department would no longer provide advance tax rulings for companies considering converting into income trusts. This was a signal that the Martin government was considering fundamental changes to the way public companies, including trusts, were taxed. The announcement had the same effect as putting up a stop sign in the middle of a four-lane highway without any notice. Brakes squealed. Trust prices plummeted. An arcane accounting matter had become a political crisis.

On November 23, five days before the confidence vote that brought the Martin government down, several of Canada's biggest income trusts suddenly jumped in value. After markets closed that day, Ralph Goodale announced a cut to dividend taxes. But he added that Ottawa would not impose any new taxes or restrictions on trusts. It was precisely the decision investors were hoping for.

Or was it the decision some had been told to expect? The NDP had its war room up and rehearsing, upstairs from the Ottawa drugstore, when Goodale made his announcement. Party staffers noticed the spike in trading. "We saw right away that this looked like a classic example of market interference," Topp said. The RCMP has a special unit that investigates this sort of business. "We felt there was enough evidence that they would bite on it."

Judy Wasylycia-Leis, the tiny, chipper Winnipeg MP who served as her party's finance critic, wrote a letter of complaint to the RCMP. The NDP was used to getting a flat No when they asked the RCMP to investigate the government, and in any case they were used to waiting a month for an answer. This time, truth be told, they kind of liked that delay. While they waited, they took care not to call for Goodale's resignation. They wanted to be able to kick the drama up a notch if they got lucky. They did get lucky. And they almost missed it.

On December 23, the RCMP faxed a letter to Wasylycia-Leis's Parliament Hill office, telling her that they had launched a criminal investigation based on her request. Problem: the office was closed for the duration of the campaign. Apparently the police were surprised not to get a response to such momentous correspondence, because on December 27 they telephoned Wasylycia-Leis's Winnipeg constituency office. A quick call to Ottawa and a staffer was sent to fetch the fateful fax. On December 28, Wasylycia-Leis, who was spending her Christmas vacation near Toronto, hurried to the Ontario capital. She scrummed outside the provincial legislature, in the rain, without pausing beforehand for a drink of water. Her throat dried up so badly she couldn't talk. A reporter discreetly passed her a mint so she could finish the announcement.

The news of a police investigation presented Martin with an unwinnable dilemma. He could fire Goodale and make big news bigger. Or he could protect him and make Goodale's woes his own. He stood by his friend. "I have the honour of knowing Ralph Goodale," he said, by way of explanation.

History has a shorthand for complex events, and history will record that the income-trust investigation put paid to Martin's re-election chances. That explanation pays too little attention to the way Martin's underlying poll numbers had deteriorated before word of the police investigation got out. And it understates the problems that would follow. But shorthand is like that.

On December 30, the Conservative national campaign co-chairmen, John Reynolds and Michael Fortier, sent a letter to every candidate and campaign manager in the party. "The final three weeks of this campaign are going to be, to quote Thomas Hobbes, 'nasty, brutish and short,'" Fortier and Reynolds wrote. "Paul Martin began this negative campaign by accusing Stephen Harper of being unfit for public life. His supporters have followed suit by attacking Conservative candidates in personal and unacceptable ways. And there will be more. In the last election, they got away with such unsubstantiated attacks. But it will not happen again. This time we will vigorously defend ourselves."

The letter promptly leaked, and accounts of it appeared in newspapers across the country on the last day of the year. Which was the point. The Conservatives had learned early that if they sent something to every one of their riding organizations, it would leak. They didn't know where, but they didn't much care. The Reynolds and Fortier letter was designed to be read by ordinary voters, not by its nominal insider audience. Putting it out this way was just cheaper than buying ads. In a successful campaign, paid media and earned media are supposed to work together. For the Conservatives, they had become indistinguishable.

10

WE DID NOT MAKE THIS UP

⇧

H appy New Year! Welcome to 2006! New hope, new phase of the campaign, new momentum. Or so the Liberals wanted to believe. Probably it was not a good sign when their airplane broke down.

When Campaign '06 began – with several Conservative campaign staffers wearing blue ski jackets with "Campaign '05" written on them, because somebody had paid for campaign jackets earlier in the year and by God, the Tories were not going to waste that money – one of the worries was that Canadians couldn't survive a winter campaign. Martin even tried to blame the winter campaign on the opposition parties, as any of the other leaders would have done in his place. But as it turned out, this was a mild winter. In Ottawa, there were very few really cold days. January 2 was one of them, a bright, clear, miserable, unsentimental icepack of a day.

Stephen Harper was in the capital to list the Conservatives' top five governing priorities. The Five Priorities idea had appeared, in embryonic form, in one of Patrick Muttart's first memos to Harper after the 2004 campaign. Newt Gingrich's Contract With America was an obvious model, a list of ten campaign pledges Republican candidates had signed on the steps of the Capitol building in 1994. The idea was to nail the whole party's colours to a mast in the simplest, boldest fashion possible. Then the other side couldn't make up wild stories about what you'd do. You'd *said* what you would do – said it and repeated it ad nauseam.

For the Harper Conservatives, the Five Priorities also offered a handy contrast with the drift that had accompanied Martin's arrival at 24 Sussex Drive and which the Liberals couldn't seem to end. Of course, Martin had talked a good game when he arrived. "It is not difficult to keep multiple balls in the air. Nor to make rapid-fire decisions," he said in a *Maclean's* interview in December of 2003, five days after he was sworn in. "I'm surrounded by very good people. That's the first thing. The second thing is, you come into this with very strong convictions and a context: this is how I see the world, this is how I see the country, this is how I see the priorities, and this is what I want to do, short, medium, and long term. The decisions flow almost automatically."

Yeah, not so much. Very little had flowed automatically while Martin was prime minister, and now Harper was going to turn that to his advantage. "If you don't have a clear idea of what you want to accomplish, you probably won't get much done," the Conservative leader said at his morning campaign event. "You need to know what you believe in, what you want to do, and have a plan to do it."

With that, Harper listed his priorities. A federal accountability act for a post-Gomery Ottawa. The two-point cut to the
GST, from 7 per cent to 5 per cent. Tougher penalties for crime.
The "choice in child care" scheme to replace the Liberal
system of government-run daycares with twelve-hundred-
dollar cheques for parents of small children. And a reduction
in health-care wait times.

The Conservative war room, not an organization prone to
cracking wise – humour being a difficult variable to control –
celebrated Harper's announcement by permitting itself a
moment of fun. The Tories sent out a news release bearing a
quotation from Martin. "If you have 40 priorities, you don't
have any." The line topped a list of fifty-six subjects Martin
had identified, at one time or another, as his priorities.

Meanwhile, Martin was buying bagels. This actually made
some sense. It was the day after New Year's and none of the
campaigns had a supercharged schedule. The Liberal leader
met reporters and camera crews at Kettleman's, an Ottawa
shop that produces a credible facsimile of the classic Montreal
bagel. Martin pretended to make bagels for the cameras for a
couple of minutes. Then he stood outside to take reporters'
questions. The real business was to begin that night, with a
flight to Winnipeg for a big Tuesday-morning breakfast
speech. But then the plane broke down. The symbolism of the
situation was probably less than ideal.

The flight was rescheduled to 5 a.m. the next day, always a
crowd-pleaser with the scribes. But the Martin camp wangled
a substitute plane, one usually booked by football teams and
rock stars. Its distinguishing feature was a large bar in the
middle of the passenger cabin. Flight attendants served coffee
and snacks from the bar to milling journalists and campaign

staffers. There was a vaguely festive atmosphere, despite the early hour.

Tim Murphy sketched the strategy for the campaign's back half. "I really do think there's a difference between our vision of government's role and Harper's," Murphy said. "And we're going to embrace that." It wasn't the most surprising strategy in the world. Murphy didn't have a problem with that. "It's like the old joke says: deep down, it's shallow."

Francis Fox was milling around the coffee bar too, schmoozing with the francophone reporters. He could hardly wait for the PM's Canadian Club speech in Winnipeg. "*Un maudit bon discours*," Fox said. Then, more wistfully: "But you people don't really cover speeches any more, do you . . ."

It all depends on the speech. This one really was a heck of a good speech, to paraphrase Senator Fox, as elegant in its prose style as any Martin had delivered. He methodically set out the differences between Harper and himself. "Mr. Harper and I differ on child care and gun crimes, we differ on medicare, on tax cuts and foreign affairs. We differ on issues right across the full spectrum of policy," he said. The biggest difference? Child care. Part of the charm of the cheques-versus-daycares debate was that each leader genuinely believed the other's plan was proof of his unfitness for high office. Martin could barely believe that Harper wanted to do away with his national network of daycares. "He would renege . . . he would terminate . . . he would deny . . . he would rip up," Martin said. "If you want a fundamental difference, this is it."

Any national campaign is a mix of appeals to target audiences – geographic, demographic, attitudinal. As Martin spoke in Winnipeg, his regional minister, Reg Alcock, was preparing to release a Manitoba-specific Liberal platform. Liberals in British Columbia would have a platform of their own, too.

Every national party had, and most have always had, a parallel organization for Quebec.

The parties' appeals are not tailored only along provincial borderlines. Layton's leadership of the NDP, in its entirety, can be seen as an audacious and hardly risk-free attempt to shift the party's appeal from its roots in agrarian populism and the shop floor, to a large new clientele that would be much harder to inspire and reliably hold: the urban bohemian creative class of Vancouver, Toronto, and a few other centres. So let Paul Martin squire Buzz Hargrove around southern Ontario. Layton would share stages with Steven Page, from the Barenaked Ladies.

In a sense you could say the Conservatives were making a regional play, too, although the map they stuck their flag pins into was a map of income brackets and lifestyle choices, not provinces and cities. Every party has a list of ridings it can hold, ridings it can hope to steal from rivals, and ridings that are beyond hope. Similarly, Patrick Muttart had done extensive polling to determine who voted Conservative, who might be persuaded to, and who would not be worth the wasted breath. Again, it's possible to overstate the novelty that Muttart's work represented. The Conservatives did not have a monopoly on this sort of sophisticated market research. It's closer to the truth, in fact, to say that for the first time since the late 1980s they were no longer letting the Liberals have the monopoly by default.

Muttart discovered that a couple with one or two children probably voted Liberal, but that a couple with three children was 50 per cent likelier to vote Conservative, and that the odds increased with every child after three.

He turned data like these into archetypes, imaginary people who would be either open or immune to Harper's appeals.

Everyone in the Conservative war room knew "Zoë," the name Muttart gave to a hypothetical single woman in her late twenties who lives in a condo in downtown Toronto and eats most of her meals in bistros on College Street. Zoë's voting allegiance, Muttart said, could not possibly be more utterly out of the Conservatives' grasp.

"And the funny thing is," Jason Kenney said, "our war room is awash in Zoës."

"Dougie," on the other hand, was the Conservatives' fondest hope. Dougie was Muttart's hypothetical tradesman, perhaps a construction worker, who was in his early thirties and lived in Yarmouth, Nova Scotia. Dougie didn't usually vote. But promise him a tax credit on the tools he needs to do his hypothetical job and his ears might prick up.

Muttart had several cases like Dougie and Zoë. "Mike and Theresa" had moved out of Toronto to suburban Oakville because they hated the bustle of downtown. They had a mortgage and two kids. Mike was a salesman and had to travel a lot. Only one of the two had a college degree. The Conservative policy book contained all kinds of appeals to Mike and Theresa.

But that other couple? The two-income, upper-crust downtown couple that didn't give much to charities and didn't volunteer? Forget them. They were Liberals. Always would be. Indeed, nobody in the Conservative war room could even remember the names Muttart had given them.

The Liberals were making many of the same demographic analyses that Muttart was busy making for the Conservatives. But mostly they were convinced of their mastery at playing the big, traditional regional play. Jean Chrétien had dominated Ontario, taken a larger chunk of Quebec at every election, and been competitive enough in Atlantic Canada to compensate for his weakness west of Ontario. The Martin 2006 strategy was an update of Chrétien's regional play.

Two months before the 2006 campaign started, John Duffy wrote a long piece for the *National Post* in which he explained that "Canadian politics are regional and Conservatives do the losing." Could that change? Duffy didn't offer much hope. His side was "weaker only in Calgary and the eastern half of Montreal." The biggest challenge facing the Conservatives, Duffy concluded, was that "today's Republican-derived conservatism is a tough sell in a country where 23 per cent of the population lives in Quebec."

This wouldn't be so bad, Duffy wrote, if only the Conservatives could learn to put up with life in the real world of hard knocks. "Like a bad golfer who curses the game for being too hard, Conservatives are prone in down times to grouse. They have a host of excuses for serial losing . . . 'We're just too principled for this place. If only Quebec weren't so . . . Quebeckish. If only Ontarians didn't keep an eye on Quebec's comfort level. If only we just gave all the money to the provinces and let them do what they want. If only the setup were different. If only the hole in the middle of the green were big enough for me to sink the ball there.'"

While Duffy was busy analyzing the Conservatives' lousy regional game, Harper had set about working on his shot-making. Even the Conservatives closest to Harper were surprised when it started to work.

⇧

On December 19, Harper gave a major speech to the Quebec City Chamber of Commerce. Very little of what he said would have surprised a campaign organizer from a half-century earlier, or a century. He began by flattering chambers of commerce in general, before moving on to flatter Quebec City as a region ("several reasons justify a generous federal contribution to Quebec City's 400th birthday"); the French language in general ("Quebec is the heart of Canada, and the French language an undeniable part of the identity of all Canadians"); and, with a detailed elaboration of his platform, every francophone Dougie, Mike and Theresa within the sound of his voice. Within days, Quebec pundits were referring to "*le discours de Québec*" as the sign that Harper had treated Quebec with a seriousness that would not go unrewarded.

"One of the things that's vital, that's been overlooked, is that Harper never gave up on Quebec," Geoff Norquay said. "Remember those angry letters he wrote to the *National Post* about a year ago, on a bunch of issues? That was really about Quebec. The *National Post* – a national newspaper! – had written that the leader of the Official Opposition was wasting his time trying to appeal to Quebec. It drove him crazy! 'Wasting my time? How can they say that?' He was angry. And he let it show."

More than that. Harper had been thinking hard about Quebec for as long as he had been in politics. Unlike Martin and, for that matter, Brian Mulroney, his study of Quebec politics had not always led him to flatter its assorted conventional wisdoms. He had been one of the first, as a rookie Reform MP, to insist that Quebec secession could only take place within the legal framework of the Canadian Constitution and that the Constitution must not be modified to recognize Quebec's distinct society. For most of the 1990s, when Reform was radioactive in Quebec, Harper was an enthusiastic advocate of the policies that made it so.

So when Paul Martin argued in the House of Commons that Harper represented a danger to Canada, because he would have to build a cabinet without serious Quebec representation, Harper scoffed, but he listened. When Belinda Stronach left the party, declaring Harper a threat to national unity, she could not have known how seriously he took that argument. That wasn't how *he* felt about the place Quebec would have in his thinking and his government. But he couldn't be sure. So, sources say, Harper organized a series of meetings, soon after he became leader of the united Conservative Party, with prominent francophone Quebeckers, including Paul Tellier, a former Mulroney chief of staff, and put the question to them: *what if a guy like me, an Albertan without Quebec roots or any serious Quebec caucus, became prime minister? Would that put an unacceptable strain on national unity?*

It was such an extraordinary display of humility that of course it stayed secret. Harper couldn't have let anyone see that he, himself, needed reassuring about his fitness for the top job. But now, as the campaign headed toward the home stretch, the very premise of the Harper-as-national-unity-threat argument – the belief that he would get nowhere in Quebec – was starting to erode.

⇧

From Winnipeg, the New and (Hopefully) Improved Paul Martin Campaign took its borrowed rock-star airplane west to Vancouver. The goal of the week was to draw fundamental differences between Harper and himself. In the event, it didn't go very well.

As Martin began to roll out the policy announcements that were to be the pillar of this crucial moment, it became clear

that most reporters weren't interested in anything except the
RCMP income-trust investigation. And the few who paid attention to Martin's announcements wanted to know why they
were so much like Harper's. Martin had a new wait-times
guarantee? Well, so did Harper, and he'd announced his first.
Martin would eliminate the landing fee for immigrants?
Harper would cut it nearly to zero – and it was odd that Martin
had rushed his own announcement, as though he was making
it simply because he'd caught wind of Harper's in advance.
"Embracing" different visions, to borrow Tim Murphy's phrase,
was turning out to be harder than it looked.

The lack of discipline of the Martin campaign's own message
machine was an even bigger problem. Reporters received the
full details of Martin's health-care announcement from the
Canadian Press news desk in Ottawa, via BlackBerry emails, as
they were being driven to Victoria from the airport. Somebody had leaked it. But Martin's campaign entourage reacted
calmly, leading most reporters to assume, wrongly, that it was
a planned leak.

The next leak was very different. The borrowed rock-star
plane was flying back east, from Vancouver to Ontario, for an
announcement the next morning in Waterloo. The Boeing 737
charter – one of the worst gas-guzzlers in the entire commercial air industry, as Tory and NDP war rooms had been eager to
point out – couldn't make it that far without refuelling. The
plane landed in Calgary to fuel up. And all hell broke loose.

While the plane was still rolling to the refuelling station,
Scott Reid came back from the closed-up section at the front
of the plane, obviously furious. He whispered urgently to
Véronique de Passillé, another Martin helper. Then every
reporter's BlackBerry started buzzing with new emails. The
next day's announcement in Waterloo, on post-secondary

education, had been leaked. And news had arrived that while in Vancouver Martin had given an interview to a Chinese-language radio station apologizing for the racist head tax Chinese immigrants once paid. And there was a third story. Martin's health-care announcement in Victoria had been boycotted by one of his own MPs, the floor-crossing ex-Conservative Keith Martin, who dissented from Liberal opposition to private health care.

Suddenly it seemed that the only place in Canada where you could be perfectly insulated from news about Paul Martin was Paul Martin's campaign plane. Bob Fife, CTV's Ottawa bureau chief, shouted forward to Scott Reid: why should news organizations bother paying to travel with the prime minister when the news was everywhere but here? "I sense your frustration," Reid said tightly. "And I share it."

"I gotta get on the air," Fife said. He telephoned CTV from his seat. The plane was already taxiing back into takeoff position. Fife recited a brief improvised commentary about the pandemonium on the Martin plane. "You start to feel like an Irish poet in a dark bar on this plane," he said to Newsnet viewers from coast to coast. Other reporters – some angry, some, if you must know, a bit giddy at the chaos of it all – pestered any Liberal they could find with questions, complaints, reproaches.

Back home in Ottawa, Ken Polk, a veteran of the Chrétien PMO who had been brought in to run the Martin campaign's media operation, was just getting home from another long day at the war room. "I made a practice of never watching the news, because I figured I'd watch it the next day. And besides, it was never very good for us, so why bother," Polk recalls. Suddenly the BlackBerry beside Polk's bed started buzzing. The emails were coming from Steve MacKinnon, from Scott

Reid, from Martin's press secretary, Melanie Gruer – from just about every Liberal on the plane.

"Have you ever seen *Platoon*?" Polk says, referring to Oliver Stone's Vietnam War epic. "There's a part in *Platoon*, near the end, where they're trying to get communication with a group of soldiers at a certain distance. And it's clear by the communication that they're in the middle of a firefight. And the last thing you hear is actually someone speaking Vietnamese into the microphone. So it's clear that it wasn't a very good ending."

That's what the avalanche of email from the Martin plane that night was like. "It was like little bits of communication from a firefight. It was like, 'They're coming at me! They're coming at me again!' and all I could think of was, 'There's really nothing I can do for you at this point.'" So Polk went back to sleep. Another rough day at the office.

Every single Martin announcement, for the rest of the week, was leaked in advance. Without fail, the Canadian Press office in Ottawa broke every story the night before Martin's announcement. Later, Liberals would speculate that CP had obtained an early draft of the party's platform and rolled it out in pieces, one step ahead of the Liberals. The Liberals could get no traction for their actual announcements; what fascinated reporters was the fact of the leaks. The first week of 2006 was a dead loss for the struggling Martinites. Time to reach into the tall hat and poke around for another rabbit.

⇧

The next week would kick off with the second round of debates. For years, Scott Reid had had a theory: why not use the debates – when the entire nation, or as much of it as could be made to care about federal politics, was watching – to launch a new idea for government? There wouldn't be time to lay on a lot of detail, of course. But one attention-grabbing idea might change the momentum of the campaign.

Since before the start of the campaign, Martin's advisors had had their idea. Martin would propose a constitutional amendment to ban the federal use of the Constitution's "notwithstanding" clause to override Charter rights. At lower levels in the Liberal campaign office, staff heard vaguely about the notwithstanding-clause amendment, without it ever being clear when it would be rolled out. The idea didn't go into the platform, which was finally being printed: the Martin campaign was too leaky and his staff figured the value of secrecy was too high to let it leak out of his inner circle.

Privately, those who did hear about the notwithstanding-clause amendment were entirely unimpressed. "Once you introduce constitutional scholars into a political debate, the energy pretty much leaves the room," one Liberal recalls. "It's not, 'Oh, yeah, let's march!' It's, 'Hmm, what an intelligent thought.'"

But the Martin campaign was nothing if not spirited in its use of gimmicks. On January 9, at the second-round English-language debate in Montreal, Martin ignored the first question put to him and announced that his "first act" as prime minister would be this constitutional amendment he had never before discussed with the Canadian people. In the days afterward, it would become clear that such a unilateral federal amendment might not even be feasible, because the provinces might need to give their consent too; that the proposal failed completely in underscoring real differences between Martin and Harper; and that it excited almost no Canadian.

Things were getting dire. Harper's appeal to the Dougies and Mikes and Theresas of the nation, with their workaday concerns, was working. In response Martin had reached out to an incredibly narrow target demographic. Call Martin's target voter "Dexter." Dexter's defining characteristic is that he flunked constitutional law.

⇧

Back the Liberal hand goes into the tall hat. Where's that damned bunny? On January 10, the day of the Montreal French-language debate, restless Internet browsers discovered something new on the Liberal website: a series of new Liberal ads. Eight different spots at first, then twelve. Each showed a fuzzy photo of Stephen Harper resolving slowly into focus while a woman's voice read, aloud, a message that rolled across the screen in stark typeface. Depending on the ad, the messages revealed the Conservative leader's ties to extreme U.S. right-wing groups; to the former Ontario premier Mike Harris; to Quebec separatists; and to assorted other horsemen of the apocalypse.

"People usually don't like negative ads. And they're usually bored by ads, period," one Liberal says. "But people became more energized, watching these ads. They were like, 'Show me the next one.' They were fascinated by it."

But then, several hours after the ads went up, one came right back down. The link vanished from the Liberal website. A few bloggers noticed. But if the Liberals were hoping nobody would see what they'd posted, they were too late. CTV News had archived all the ads on its own website – including the one that had vanished almost as fast as it had appeared.

"Stephen Harper actually announced he wants to increase military presence in our cities," the woman's voice says, while the photo comes into focus over a soundtrack of military parade drums.

"Canadian cities. Soldiers with guns. In our cities."

Just in case someone had missed the point, the voice added: "In Canada." Then: "We did not make this up." Drum roll, bass-drum crash, tubular bells like on the soundtrack of *Rocky*. And the tagline: "Choose your Canada."

If the ad referred to any fact or object in the real and comprehensible world, it was the Conservatives' plan to keep a standing military presence in or near the largest Canadian cities, in case natural disaster struck an urban centre. It was one of Harper's least persuasive policy ideas. The little garrisons would be underemployed for months or years on end. Then when a real emergency hit, they would in all likelihood be overwhelmed beyond their capacity to respond. But that wasn't what this ad was about. This ad wasn't meant to spark a debate about the proper deployment of scarce military assets. Its plain goal was to make Canadians afraid of their own armed forces.

The Liberals are actually pretty convincing when they swear that the ad wasn't supposed to get out. And that, until the moment it *did* get out, nothing had gone wrong. The Liberals, like the Conservatives, gave the creative guys in their ad consortium a very broad set of ad-campaign objectives and then let them squirt their creative juices all over the place. Some of the results were gripping. Some were just bad. "You basically give a brief to your agencies, and they go out and they create all kinds of stuff," Reid says. "And sometimes they have weird insensitivities to the politics of things because that's not what they *do* for a living. And then you go, 'No, no, can't do that.'"

So *making* a terrifying ad designed to turn Canadians against the men and women who risk their lives to protect us – well, that was just a bug in the system. *Letting it out* was the mistake. But as the Conservatives had learned in the campaign's first week, not entirely an incomprehensible one.

After the last debate, Martin had to put up with questions about the ad instead of questions about his performance. (Twenty-four hours after he had proposed a radical amendment to the heart of Canada's Constitution, nobody was bothering to ask about that.) When John Duffy tried to guide a CTV pundit panel back to the substance of the debate, the show's host, the considerably larger and unrelated Mike Duffy, descended on him, berating him and accusing him of trying to intimidate his host out of discussing the pulled ad minutes earlier, during an off-camera commercial break. Within an hour, journalists were emailing transcripts of the Duffy–Duffy cage match all over Ottawa.

Mike Duffy's harangue was part of a general collapse of mutual goodwill between the Martin claque and the Press Gallery. For more than a decade, some reporters had pulled their punches when they wrote about Martin, in the expectation that he would be prime minister any day now, and they would want to be in his good books. When Martin became prime minister in 2003, the Martinites had enjoyed a reputation as media-relations pros. Now they couldn't catch a break.

It showed on camera. Reporters and non-combatants couldn't stop talking about how heated, tense, urgent, and humourless the designated Liberal spokespeople were. The only reliable exception was Mike Eizenga, the party president, a Protestant clergyman from London, Ontario, who used his rare appearances as a chance to display a chipper, aw-shucks demeanour. As for his colleagues, not so much. Scott Reid's beer-and-popcorn line had got him pulled from the airwaves for the rest of the campaign. John Duffy, a formidable rhetorician, kept trying to win every TV debate in a slam-dunk. The result was more heat than Marshall McLuhan's cool medium could take.

In the Tory war room, meanwhile, a sign hung in plain sight of all the staffers who had to deal with reporters on the telephone. It reminded them of their obligation to proper phone etiquette. The four questions they should never stop asking themselves were:

1) What are we accomplishing with this? (That is, were they accomplishing political goals when they said something, or simply making themselves feel better?)
2) Are we debating on our ground or theirs? (Were they talking about what *they* wanted to talk about, or what *Liberals* wanted to talk about?)
3) Are we taking their bait? (The second rule restated, for emphasis.)
4) Is our tone neutral?

The point of the fourth question was that angry people don't win debates. The thought did not seem to have occurred to Martin's spinners. A striking example was Susan Murray, a long-time CBC reporter who left broadcasting after the 2004 election to become communications director for Scott Brison, the Minister of Public Works. In her broadcasting days, Murray had been genial. Now, as a combatant on CBC Newsworld's *Politics* with Don Newman, she teetered constantly at the brink of outrage.

The Tories spotted this early and decided to egg Murray on. Sandra Buckler, an Ottawa lobbyist with little previous media exposure, was Harper's representative on the same panel. Nobody played even-tempered better, and she soon settled on a neat trick. Murray would lean forward and try to catch Buckler's eye. But Buckler simply refused to look the other woman's way. For the duration of the campaign she never looked

Murray in the eye while the two of them were on camera. It made Murray angrier and angrier. She would lean forward, staring past the amused NDP spokesman, Brad Lavigne, sometimes waving her hand to catch Buckler's attention. Buckler kept talking, tone neutral, taking nobody's bait.

⇧

Anyone wondering how the screw-up over the parade-drum ad was possible would not have to wait long for another screw-up to worry about. The parade-drum ads, and attendant confusion, came on a Tuesday. The next morning, a Liberal campaign staffer showed up early to work, as usual. (Liberals worked the traditional absurd hours common to campaigns everywhere, dawn to midnight, day after day plus weekends. Conservatives worked shifts and were encouraged to leave work behind them and sleep soundly when they went home.) Outside the Liberal headquarters on Metcalfe Street was a row of newspaper boxes: *Globe, Citizen, National Post, Dose.*

On this Wednesday morning, there were no copies of *Dose.* Instead, there was a neatly stacked pile of mimeographed and paper-clipped copies of the Liberal platform.

The Liberal platform was not supposed to be released until six hours later.

Across Ottawa, political reporters staggering downstairs to collect the morning paper found their own hand-delivered photocopies of the platform waiting at their front doorstep. Emails were bouncing around the Internet announcing that the *Western Standard*, a political magazine published by the young Conservative gadfly Ezra Levant, had received a leaked copy of the platform the night before. "My first thought when I got the document was, 'Who else has it, too?'" Levant said.

So he posted the file on the magazine's blog and sent word to the thirty-three thousand addresses on his email list.

To this day, rival campaigns insist they had nothing to do with the platform's distribution all over Ottawa. The denials seem implausible: whoever hand-delivered copies to reporters had to know where they lived. Some of the recipients have unlisted phone numbers. But we give the party offices our home addresses when we travel with the leaders' tours. Whoever the culprit, the prank profoundly destabilized the Liberal campaign. "Absolute and utter shock," one war-room insider said.

What was slightly less surprising was how little news was in the platform. It was a repackaging of Ralph Goodale's November mini-budget, along with a repackaging of the glut of announcements made in the week before the confidence vote.

The platform was the brainchild of Peter Nicholson, the business executive who had signed on as a senior policy advisor in Martin's PMO. Nicholson was the guy Martin turned to for the thirty-thousand-foot chats the Liberal leader loved to have about the long-term trends in public policy. When you heard Martin talking about the competitive challenge from China and India, or the demographic challenge from an aging population with low birth rates, that was the sound of Nicholson's influence. When you noticed how rarely Martin talked about China, India, or demographics in any sustained way, that was the sound of Nicholson's lack of influence. The lack of influence was, as a rule, louder. It was Nicholson's lot in life to re-enact, endlessly, the 2002 meeting when Elly Alboim had schooled a roomful of Order of Canada recipients on the distinction between what mattered and what a government should talk about. In the end, the Liberals had let him write the platform, with input from John Duffy and a few others. What they weren't going to do was run on that platform.

"You come into this with very strong convictions and a context," Paul Martin had told *Maclean's*, only twenty-five months earlier. And now, the Liberal campaign to make that principled, ordered case for Paul Martin, *to the extent it had ever existed*, had collapsed in a heap. It was all so sudden. The parade-drum ad had leaked on January 10. Four days later, a few Liberal war-room staffers convened at Hy's on Queen Street for beer and cheese toast. They wore the vaguely haunted gaze of the suddenly, unexpectedly powerless. The only question was how bad the thrashing would be.

"Our offensive in January was utterly smashed," John Duffy recalls. "It was like something in *A Bridge Too Far* where you've got this huge tank army, and there are a bunch of tanks at the front of the narrow roadway through Holland that are all shot to pieces. And the entire army is sitting there, behind these burning tanks, going, 'Can't we go in and fight?'

"The burning tanks were the RCMP investigation, the leaks, bad vibes on the airplane, one damned thing – beer and popcorn, right? – I mean, just the number of shot-up tanks. Some of them our fault. Some of them happened to us externally. And we just couldn't get our offensive going. It just sat there and revved and never made it.

"It was the saddest thing I ever saw."

But then something beyond the control of the Liberals happened. And this time, unlike so many forces beyond Paul Martin's control, this one actually *improved* Liberal fortunes.

Stephen Harper ran out of scripting again.

⇧

The 2004 campaign had been only half over before Harper ran out of prepared messages. This time he did so much better. But at some point he had to finish announcing the platform. The thing wasn't endless, after all. But by timing the pacing of announcements, the Conservatives did have some control over when they'd finally run out of news. Harper had always wanted to wait until after the second set of debates. Others wanted to get the platform out to local candidates earlier, in the first week of January. As it turned out, that choice would have left the Conservatives competing for headline and broadcast space with the collapse of the Liberal campaign, a violation of the cardinal rule that in politics, you never want to interrupt an opponent when he's busy beating up on himself.

In the third week of December, Muttart and Brodie sat down with Finley and Ray Novak, Harper's poker-faced young executive assistant, to try to figure out how to stretch the platform until after the second debates. It was hard. Everyone was tired. The middle of a campaign is a lousy time to start rethinking big parts of your strategy. The best they could come up with was to re-announce the GST cut. Harper didn't like that idea one bit. "I want to be making fucking news until the platform comes out. Every goddamn day, you've got to have something there."

They made it all the way to the campaign's second-last Friday, ten days before the election. "Keep in mind that the platform was designed for a thirty-seven-day writ period," one insider recalls. "Five weeks. Instead we're up against eight weeks. We were really squeezing the tea towel, by the end, to make news." So what if the big announcement on tax treatment of tradeable securities donated to charities didn't exactly rocket across the headlines? It protected Harper from improvisation for one more day. Which was the point.

When he finally ran out of scripting, Harper lasted fine. For about a day. The Conservative leader kicked off the last week of the campaign just across the border from Ottawa in a Knights of Columbus hall in Buckingham, Quebec, talking up the virtues of his new Quebec lieutenant, a former junior provincial minister named Lawrence Cannon. Harper was buoyant. Cannon and as many as three other Quebec Conservatives might actually win their ridings, if you could believe the polls. Maybe even more. The Tories had sent the networks an ad mocking the Liberal martial-law ad. Footage of Liberal MP Keith Martin complaining that "some idiot" had approved the ad. Footage of Paul Martin telling a CBC town hall that "I approved the ads, there's no question."

The Liberals were furious, certain that the ad must violate the CBC's copyright over the Martin interview footage. No problem: the Tories hadn't actually bought airtime to run the ads anywhere. Giving it to the networks was enough. It played on the news. Earned media and paid media, indistinguishable once again.

Harper's home-stretch strategy was to close the deal with the reluctant object of his most ardent affections, the francophone Quebec voter. "Quebec's place isn't in the bleachers," he said. "Quebec's place is on the ice!" And, "We don't want to spend our time asking questions to others. We want to give answers!"

Two days later, *La Presse* endorsed Harper in a long editorial signed by the Montreal daily's chief editorialist, André Pratte. It was almost unheard of for even a federalist newspaper like *La Presse* to endorse a party led by a non-Quebecker. At a rally in Lévis, across the St. Lawrence River from Quebec City, Harper was introduced by a gangly candidate named Steven Blaney, who announced to the crowd in rapturous tones: *"Avez-vous vu le ciel? Le ciel est bleu!"*

Have you seen the sky, or perhaps, the heavens? The heavens are blue. It was the war cry of Quebec's traditional conservative *bleus*, going back a century and more. The priests used to finish by reminding their congregations that *l'enfer est rouge*, that hell was painted Liberal red. Blaney left that part unstated. Then Harper gave a lovely speech, everyone applauded, and he went downstairs to blow a news conference completely

It's possible to see what he was *trying* to say. Success was catching up to him. On his campaign plane the night before, the campaign press had organized their election pool. Most of the scribes had bet on a Tory majority. Harper couldn't put off the question of a majority Conservative government any longer. Fear of Tories could no longer save the Liberals from defeat, but if Canadians did not feel comfortable with a Tory majority they were never going to give him one.

So Harper set out to calm the waters. What he meant to say was that even a majority would not mean that the hordes would be unleashed to pillage and burn. Canada would remain a complex polity, with formidable institutional momentum and dispersed political legitimacy. NDP and Liberal premiers would have to agree with Harper's intergovernmental projects. The laws of men and nature could not be repealed at his whim. The skies, however blue they might be, would not fall.

It came out badly.

"I'm not sure there is such a thing as a true Conservative majority in the sense of a Liberal majority," Harper told reporters. "The reality is that we will have, for some time to come, a Liberal Senate, a Liberal civil service and courts that have been appointed by the Liberals. So these are obviously checks on the power of a Conservative government."

It was supposed to sound soothing. To many ears it sounded petulant. Or worse.

To Martin's ears it sounded like a lifeline. The PM's entire campaign had depended on voters' fears of a hidden Conservative agenda. Here at last was evidence. Or close enough. "The question is, if he raised it, it's because he's worried the courts are going to stop him doing something," Martin said in Saskatchewan, where he was campaigning to save his embattled minister, Ralph Goodale. "I don't know what that is, but it's up to him to let us know."

The Harper campaign wasted two days before they understood the impact of the boss's gaffe. It was a rare case where they couldn't hear what Harper had said through the ears of ordinary Canadians – or, crucially, of the slightly left-of-Conservative Canadians who would need to vote Conservative if Harper was to hold his potential majority. Liberal civil servants and courts? Ian Brodie's *doctoral thesis* was about entrenched Liberal bias in the Charter arguments that make it to the Supreme Court. Brodie was pretty much the wrong guy to see red flags when Harper started talking about Liberal judges.

Meanwhile the Liberals, after being cowed briefly into silence by the mistaken release of the armies-in-the-streets ad, had bought major TV time to air eight stop-Harper ads from the same series. Conservatives and Liberals now agree the Liberal ads stopped Harper's momentum cold. Meanwhile Martin tossed out his platform, for the second election in a row, to transform his home-stretch campaign into a defence of a woman's right to choose an abortion. If it ever does happen that a new Conservative government bans abortion; stacks the Supreme Court to make the ban stick; and survives mass defections from its pro-choice MPs – in plain defiance of its platform commitment not to initiate any such action – Martin's last days on the hustings will seem heroic indeed. If not, not.

What's clear is that Harper hurt himself with his comments. Greg Lyle of Innovative Research Group conducted the Canada 20/20 election panel online survey for *Maclean's*. He measured the emerging Harper constituency in the campaign's last week.

"First, the Conservatives secured this victory through a campaign focused on a targeted group of voters," Lyle says. "They did not try and be everything to everyone. Instead, they attempted to maximize their vote within a Conservative universe."

This reflects the influence of Tom Flanagan and Patrick Muttart on Harper's thinking. Flanagan, the game theorist, wrote that larger-than-necessary coalitions are ungainly, although even Flanagan must have hoped for a larger Tory caucus than the one Harper would end up with. Muttart's willingness to zone in on winnable voters – the Dougies, Mikes and Theresas, to the exclusion of the Zoës – was efficient, but it put a low ceiling on the Conservatives' growth potential.

"One immediate and striking observation is that the Conservative universe" – the total number of voters who would even consider voting Conservative – "is small, less than half the electorate," Lyle says. Harper did expand his base so that it included more women and francophones at the end of the campaign. But he was still playing hard for half the pie, instead of playing clumsily for all of it.

But that other half of the pie remains. And it would prove to be a problem for Harper. Lyle found that 55 per cent of his online panelists "remain unimpressed with the incoming prime minister."

More than unimpressed. "Most of our panelists remain concerned that Stephen Harper and the Conservatives are too extreme and scary," says Lyle. In the home stretch of the campaign, while a chunk of the electorate was still uncertain about how to vote, Harper had succeeded in reinforcing the fears of the very voters he needed to close the deal.

⇧

That was Harper's problem. Martin's was that he was fighting a two-front war. Not three: Martin had long since conceded the Quebec front, and Gilles Duceppe's final campaigning was designed to beat down the Tory vote. Outside a handful of ridings in Montreal and western Quebec, the Liberals were no longer a factor in Martin's adopted home province.

But Martin's last stand against Harper depended on his ability to suck NDP voters away from Layton. It had worked last time, and Liberals made no secret of saying they needed it to work this time. His big mistake was assuming that everyone else felt like joining him in replaying the 2004 campaign. "We decided to take the fight to them," Brian Topp of the NDP said. "So once the debates were over and we had our platform out, then basically our next throw was to say, 'The issue isn't, should New Democrats go to the Liberals. It's, shouldn't the Liberals come to the NDP?'"

The Liberal and NDP strategies to swipe each other's votes had this much in common: both depended on the probability of a Harper victory. Martin needed NDP voters to panic and flee to him. Layton needed Liberal voters to give up on Martin. "As soon as there was a pretty clear consensus in our universe that it was going to be a Conservative government," Topp said, "then we went to that message: don't waste your vote on the Liberals. They're going to be a smoking hulk."

Layton spent three straight days in British Columbia, the most competitive market in which his party had realistic hopes of making gains, to hammer his message home. "The Liberals are going to be too busy thinking about themselves for the next two years to think about you," Layton said mournfully. To Liberal voters he made a direct appeal. "Give us your vote, this time."

On the last Saturday of the campaign, several staffers from the NDP war room had a quietly celebratory dinner at Mamma Teresa's, an ancient and dependable Italian restaurant on Somerset Street in downtown Ottawa. The choice of venue was anything but accidental. Mamma Teresa's was the most notorious Liberal gathering spot in the capital. Its entry was lined with autographed photos of Jean Chrétien, Paul Martin, Brian Tobin, and several other prominent Grits. The New Democrats had made a point of gathering here to eat a Liberal dinner, in the hope that two days hence, they would eat the Liberals' lunch.

Martin found a new emotion colouring his desperation: indignation. Stealing other parties' votes was what *Liberals* were supposed to do. "For a leader who claims to value the environment, our social programs, our commitments to Aboriginals, Jack Layton has been making some very strange comments during this campaign," Martin said in Burnaby. "He's attacked Liberals, not Conservatives. In fact, he's all but ignored Stephen Harper."

Martin had to go to the well one more time. He needed a physical demonstration of New Democrat support bleeding to the Liberals, the way it was supposed to. The Liberal leader who had persuaded Scott Brison and Belinda Stronach and Ujjal Dosanjh to cross party lines and get under the big Liberal tent staged one more meeting with Buzz Hargrove. It went the way meetings with Buzz Hargrove often do.

In southern Ontario, Martin and Hargrove teamed up to lecture voters on the vital necessity of voting Liberal to stop

Harper. Then Hargrove scrummed with reporters, and made it clear that as far as he was concerned, people could vote for anyone they liked if it would stop Harper. Including, in Quebec, the Bloc Québécois. "Mr. Harper doesn't have a sense of Canada and its communities," Hargrove said. "His view is a separatist view." Should Quebeckers vote Bloc to stop him? "Anything to stop the Tories."

Martin had to send out a news release to correct Hargrove's comments. But the damage to the already rickety Liberal comeback was done. In the NDP war room, Brian Topp could only chuckle. "People in the New Democratic Party have been working with Mr. Hargrove a lot longer than the Liberals," he said. "And I have to say, respectfully, having watched what happened in this campaign, that nobody in the NDP was the least bit surprised about how that worked out."

Harper, meanwhile, had reverted to the form he had always shown – and would always show – when he ran out of scripting. He went into a shell. He had all but stopped speaking to reporters. The lockdown on candidates, already heavy-handed, became absurd as the Harper campaign worked over-time to make sure no candidate said anything controversial. Or for that matter, anything at all. Lina Dib, a scrappy reporter for Quebec's TVA television network, followed one candidate out of a Harper event, firing questions at him. A local campaign staffer put a hand on Dib's shoulder to dissuade her. Big mistake. The TV reporter rounded on the staffer: "Don't you *touch* me," she snarled. The staffer looked properly mortified. Too late. The incident was on camera.

The last week of the campaign had come down to one leader on the prowl for votes and three others in trouble and bailing water as fast as they could go. Layton's own ceiling was low, of course. But within that tidy universe he was pressing to consolidate gains. Martin had lost that luxury two weeks earlier. Now he was fighting, ungracefully but with all his strength, to save the Liberal Party. Duceppe toured ridings that should have been safe, to parry Conservative advances. And Harper was playing a sullen defensive game, terrified of another gaffe in the home stretch. But he was already too late. Hope for a majority was slipping away.

THREE SISTERS, NO WAITING

⇧

"**F**riends, I have never been so proud of our great country, and I am honoured and overwhelmed to be asked to lead it," Stephen Harper said at the Telus Convention Centre in Calgary on the night of January 23. "We will do all that we can. We will give it all we've got. From time to time, we will even make mistakes."

It was a superb little speech: plain-spoken, optimistic, gracious, devoid of oratorical affectation. "Our Canada is rooted in our shared history, and in the values which have and will endure," the country's next prime minister said. "Throughout this campaign, I have been inspired by the thousands of Canadians I met who embody those values.

"Individuals, families, workers, and business people trying to get ahead. Parents doing their best to teach their kids right from wrong. Immigrants discovering new opportunities in a new land. Seniors seeking security. The young promoting their ideals. East and West, English and French, city and country, men and women, new Canadians and old."

He was describing the sort of grand coalition Paul Martin had sought to call to the Liberal banner when Martin stood on a similar stage in Toronto in 2003. But never in his journey to his own triumphant night had Harper been permitted the luxury of self-deception. So Harper did not claim or kid himself that all of the nation's cliques, clubs, and tribes were on his side. He had come a long way. But if he had touched the brass ring, it was only with his fingertips. Much of the real work was still ahead.

It was as though somebody had put the word *eke* into the English dictionary in anticipation of this moment. If ever victory had been eked out, this was it. Harper's Conservatives had 124 ridings out of 308, 31 short of a majority. The Liberals had hung on to 103 seats. The gap between the two parties was 15 seats narrower than it had been, in the Liberals' favour, after 2005. The Conservatives had gained only a handful of seats in Atlantic Canada. They took 40 of Ontario's 106 ridings, but the Liberals managed to hold 54. And the Conservatives were shut out of Canada's three largest cities, Toronto, Montreal, and Vancouver.

The Liberals' strong finish owed a lot to the efficiency of their vote distribution rather than to genuine popular support. The Martin Liberals' share of the popular vote was 30.2 per cent, lower than the party had scored in any general election in Canadian history apart from the John Turner rout of 1984. In Quebec, the Liberals salvaged thirteen seats, three more than the Conservatives. But the Liberals won only 20.8 per cent of the Quebec vote, their lowest share since Confederation. In a late-breaking but gracious concession to the facts, Paul Martin told Liberals in his own Montreal riding he would not lead the party into a third election.

The election gods have a knack for subtle games. As Conservative strategists did the arithmetic, they found a House divided in tantalizing fashion. In most confidence votes in a minority Parliament the parties vote monolithically, sometimes with the government, sometimes against. Look at Martin's experience: Liberals plus New Democrats (plus a few independents and one party-hopping heiress) had survived a confidence vote. Then the NDP changed sides and a united opposition brought the Liberals down. So how would it play this time? In some ways the numbers weren't dire. Harper could hang on to power if either the Bloc (51 seats) or the Liberals (103) voted with his 124 Conservatives. It was only the NDP who wouldn't be much use to him. Jack Layton's game-closing assault on the Liberal vote had worked out nicely, growing the little NDP caucus by 10 seats to 29. But 124 plus 29 is only 153. If the Speaker, the Liberal Peter Milliken, kept that job, that would leave 307 MPs for most votes. And 153 votes would be one short of a majority. You might be able to get André Arthur, the jovial and mustachioed talk-radio host who was the new Parliament's sole independent, to vote with the government. But who wants to depend on an independent for survival?

Harper was only one MP short of a situation in which the support of any opposition party could ensure his survival. One lousy MP. Still, what could he do?

⇧

Beyond the mixed results in Parliament, the broader national landscape was also a mix of good news and bad. With Patrick

Muttart's strategic help, Harper had spent the campaign zeroing in on voters who might be willing to give the Conservatives a chance. And writing off everyone else. The result had matched the effort: while Harper was genuinely popular among a segment of the population, a narrow majority was unmoved. Or worse.

Pollster Greg Lyle spent the campaign running a large-sample Internet panel for *Maclean's*. They're the latest craze. You sign up several thousand people over the Net, control for any differences between their demographics and the broader population's, then ask the same group a consistent series of questions over the course of the campaign. It's like a focus group as big as the audience at a Nelly Furtado concert at CNE Stadium. Also the focus group lasts eight weeks. Whereas the Nelly Furtado concert only seems to.

Lyle tracked a 22 percentage-point swing in the difference between Paul Martin's favourables and Stephen Harper's favourables. But at no point in the campaign did more than 45 per cent of Lyle's "panellists" ever consider voting Conservative. Some were rock-ribbed Conservatives who never looked at another party. A few started Conservative before Harper managed to lose them. The rest were attracted to another party and Harper managed to woo them. Add all those cases up: 45 per cent.

In the 1995 campaign that got Mike Harris elected premier of Ontario, Lyle says, Harris's campaign team worked hard on what they called the HOAG variable, for Hell of a Guy. They needed voters to warm to Harris, so they set about portraying him as the kind of fellow anyone would enjoy spending time with. Of course many Ontarians never believed Harris was a HOAG. But enough did.

"The federal Tories delivered HOAG big time in this campaign," Lyle says. If you look only at respondents to Lyle's Internet panel who were willing to consider the Conservatives – the so-called Tory universe, about 45 per cent of the total – most of that subgroup became much more impressed with Harper over the course of the campaign. That's true even for respondents who didn't vote Conservative in the end, but who had the Tories as their second choice. "Second-choice Conservatives are twice as likely to like Harper as to say he would be the best PM," Lyle said, "which sets the stage for growth if he convinces those voters of his competence in the job."

As for consistent Conservative voters, well, by the end of the campaign they were in love. The proportion of Tory voters with a *strongly* favourable view of Harper grew from 34 per cent to 64 per cent.

Jaime Watt of the Toronto consulting firm Navigator – Patrick Muttart's old stomping grounds – found something similar when he conducted focus groups in cities across Canada two days after the election. Nowhere was the strength of the Harper bond stronger than where voters had come to their Conservative allegiance latest: in Quebec City. "To our surprise and that of our Quebec partners, Léger Marketing, for some voters Stephen Harper has moved beyond the 'my kind of non-politician' status he has in English Canada," Watt wrote. "To some in our groups he has become an object of deep affection. . . . It does seem to represent the beginning of an affair between some deeply disenchanted Quebec voters and the new Prime Minister."

Likeability? Jesus Christ. But silver linings often come in clouds. "More than half the public – 55 per cent – is not in the Conservative universe," Lyle said. "Those voters remain

strikingly unconvinced that Harper is a Hell of a Guy."
Panellists who had never considered voting for Harper were 86
per cent likely to agree that "the Conservative Party is too
extreme for me," and 83 per cent likely to agree that "Harper
scares me."

Now, the majority of confident leaders actually like knowing
who doesn't like them. Jean Chrétien took great pleasure in
hearing he had upset somebody who was never going to vote
for him anyway. But Chrétien won majorities. If Harper was to
have any hope of a majority, he needed to grow his voter coalition. Given the skepticism about him in the land, at times it
would feel like chipping away at a rock face.

⇧

The Harper team wasted no time. Six days after the election I
was buying breakfast at an Ottawa café when the guy in front
of me at the cash-register line turned to introduce himself. It
was Patrick Muttart. I'd heard about him, written about him,
never met him. He doesn't talk to reporters. So, I said, making
small talk, ready for some downtime after the election? Nope.
Muttart was already at work on a Campaign '06 post-mortem.
What went right, what went wrong, and where in the rock face
of public opinion could Harper plant the pitons for his climb
to a majority?

But while the strategists worked on strategy, a new government had to govern. Ian Brodie had waited until six days
before the election before telephoning Alex Himelfarb, the
Clerk of the Privy Council, to start talking about the transition
to a Conservative government. The Harper campaign, determined to avoid leaks (except the intentional kind), had been
reluctant to reach out to the bureaucracy too soon because

they didn't want to read stories about Harper turning arrogant and presumptuous.

Harper's chief of staff had never met the country's ranking civil servant. "I'm Ian Brodie and I'm the chief of staff and I'm on the transition team," he said gamely into the telephone. "And there's a possibility that we could win this thing."

Himelfarb laughed. "There's a *possibility* you could win this thing?"

Brodie: "Yeah, it looks like there's a possibility we're going to win this thing."

Himelfarb: "Yeah, I think you've got a pretty good possibility of winning this thing. How are you feeling?"

Brodie: "Nervous. If we make it to Thursday without fucking up, I'll believe we might win this." Himelfarb laughed again. Brodie gave him the name of the contact person for the Harper transit team, should one be necessary: Derek Burney.

In a sense, the transition had already begun. The bureaucracy is a cumbersome machine, but it is more genuinely nonpartisan than some people believe, and it likes to do forward planning when its political masters are otherwise occupied. At every election, the platform of the main opposition party is dissected by armies of functionaries who put together plans for implementing the main planks. *Here's how much your proposal might cost. Here's how it fits or conflicts with what's been done on this file up to now. Here are potential obstacles.* Already the Conservatives were more popular with the civil service than they might have suspected, for the simple reason that their platform was so easy to turn into stacks of briefing books. The Tory campaign document was little more than a point-form list of specific plans on specific files. There was none of the highflown "vision" rhetoric that had taken up increasing amounts of space in Liberal platforms. You could love or hate this platform, but loving it or hating it was not a civil servant's job. Implementing it might be. And as platforms go, this one would be a cinch to implement.

Harper's campaign plane flew from Calgary back to Uplands Air Base, the Government of Canada airbase just down the road from Ottawa airport, on January 24. There was a motorcade waiting for the prime minister–designate outside Hangar 11. This would take some getting used to. A minivan took Laureen and the kids home. Harper was whisked to Parliament Hill with his executive assistant, Ray Novak; Bruce Carson, a veteran Tory who'd been a policy advisor for the Harper campaign; and Ian Brodie. On the Hill, they met the head of Harper's transition team, Derek Burney.

Burney had been Brian Mulroney's chief of staff in 1986, helping to rescue the still-inexperienced young prime minister from organizational chaos that had endangered his government. Burney would lead a small transition team including Ray Speaker, who had served with Harper in the Reform caucus from 1993 to 1997 and who had helped negotiate the Tory-Alliance merger on Harper's behalf.

The general organizing rule for the transition was that whatever Martin had done, Harper would do the opposite. Harper wanted only one direct subordinate, so Brodie would be chief of staff. There would be no principal secretary. Harper and Burney designed their cabinet structure to make and implement decisions swiftly. The outline would have been familiar to Brian Mulroney, but Harper's cabinet would have far fewer members. There would be two main cabinet committees. Priorities and Planning would be the guardian of Harper's five canonical campaign priorities and of other long-term projects that drew, more or less directly, from the platform. Operations was at least equally important but it was

dedicated to putting out fires, handling surprises, and inte-
grating short-horizon events into the government's work.
Brodie, meanwhile, set up a streamlined PMO in which – in
stark contrast to Martin's reign – almost everyone would have
specific files and would be expected to attend to them.

The first big meeting of the transition took place on
Wednesday, January 25, at 9 a.m. Alex Himelfarb had come to
visit Harper, Burney, and Brodie. Harper's people had reason
to be suspicious of Himelfarb: close to Chrétien, a key fixer
on some of Martin's most politically delicate files. Himelfarb
had already met Harper privately and told him he'd be leaving
the job. But the details of such an important departure, and
the identity of Himelfarb's replacement, would take weeks to
work out. Meanwhile they were stuck with him. How would
they get along?

"Mr. Harper, congratulations on your victory," the Clerk
said. "Can you tell me how long a transition you have
planned?"

"Two weeks," Harper said. This was roughly what everyone
had expected. There would be a new cabinet on February 6.
Himelfarb took note of the date. He paused.

Then he said the most extraordinary thing. "Can I say that
the civil service is not only prepared to help you with the transition – we *welcome* the transition of government."

It was not, the Harper team decided, an expression of party
preference, but of two other feelings: faith in the democratic
alternation of power from Liberals to – well, after thirteen
years, to anyone, frankly. And relief that two years of confusion, panic, improvisation, and scattershot administration
were coming to a close. "Every single official we saw around
the town in the first four weeks would start by saying, 'First of
all, let me tell you on behalf of everyone we work with, how

thrilled we are to have just five priorities to work with,'" one senior Conservative said.

A deputy minister summed up the same feeling, a few months into the new government, when I asked him what the biggest change from the Martin years was. The mandarin thought for a minute, then replied with real feeling. With this new crew, he said, "the agenda is actually a description of how the meeting is going to go."

Which is not to say the transition went perfectly. Whatever Burney and Speaker's virtues, neither the old Mulroney Tory nor the Reform pioneer had been in electoral politics for a decade. Neither was involved with the party on a day-to-day basis. Those characteristics had helped Harper in his paramount goal of keeping the transition team's existence secret. But they didn't help in what probably *should* have been his paramount goal, which was to have the smoothest transition to a government and one that most effectively deployed the party's human resources. Senior Conservatives now say one or two sitting members of caucus would have come in handy, and that a few members of the campaign team should have moved straight into the PMO to keep some continuity from the campaign. But the campaign team was exhausted. Which means that staffing for the new government – hundreds of hires across dozens of departments – didn't go smoothly. And Harper's biggest staffing decision, the composition of his cabinet, became his first headache, and one of the most enduring.

⇧

January 28 was a Saturday. Conservative MPs, veterans and rookies alike, flew to Ottawa from across the country for a succession of very brief meetings at a downtown hotel. Nobody knew why they were coming to town. Everyone was told to keep it quiet. Jim Prentice stifled the urge to talk by spending as much time as possible on ski hills. Then he boarded the flight from Calgary and found that just about everyone on the plane was somebody he knew. Cue four hours of awkward small talk.

In the hotel meetings, a surprising – and surprised – number of Harper stalwarts were told they wouldn't be in his cabinet. As they wandered around Parliament Hill in the random Brownian motion of the dejected, several of them – Rahim Jaffer, James Rajotte, James Moore, Jason Kenney – bumped into each other and shared their amazement at being kept out. Later they would get word that Monte Solberg had been let down hard too. Every prime minister has a tough time saying no to supporters and admirers. Paul Martin kept a fantastically large cabinet, partly to avoid letting anyone down. It turned out Stephen Harper wouldn't have that problem.

His home province was the biggest headache. "Look, this is a critical cabinet-making decision you have to make. How many members are you going to have from Alberta?" one Harper advisor says. "And Stephen had said, many, many, many times over the course of the preceding year – to Alberta caucus members collectively and individually – that cabinet wasn't going to be a meritocracy. Numbers being what they were, we couldn't have twenty-six cabinet members from Alberta."

In the end he had three, plus himself. Prentice's uncomfortable flight from Calgary wasn't a false alarm: he was in. Rona Ambrose, the personable young Edmontonian, would be the environment minister, a job she knew very close to nothing about. And, in the inevitable rejigging as rough drafts became a final list, the rejected Monte Solberg was asked back, to become minister of citizenship and immigration. Solberg and his colleagues could only speculate about the reasons. One theory was that there was a limit to how poorly rural Alberta could be represented at the big table before rural Albertans started to reject this government from the outset. Flanagan and Harper had written about conservatism's three sisters. At some point Harper had to stop tossing bouquets at the Red Tory sister and her intoxicating, hard-to-get sibling, *la bleue québécoise*. The prairie reform sister was the one what brung Harper, and in the end he had to dance with her too. Even if she did look like Monte.

But of course nobody thought twice about the presence of Solberg or the absence of Jaffer when the scribes and the newly minted ministers convened at Rideau Hall on the chilly morning of February 6, because what the hell was David Emerson doing here?

Of course you know what Emerson was doing there. But it sure took us a good chunk of the morning to figure it out, and then to wrap our heads around it. Paul Martin's star recruit to the Liberal cabinet of 2004 was Stephen Harper's star recruit to the Conservative cabinet of 2006. Oh, and Michael Fortier, the stubble-chinned Montreal lawyer who had served as Harper's national campaign co-chair and hadn't run as a candidate anywhere for any party? He was the new public works minister. He would serve from the Senate, as a Harper appointee. That would be the same Senate whose members Harper wanted to see elected.

Both appointments were breathtaking acts of *realpolitik*. Harper had done poorly in the three big cities? He now had ministers from two of them. He was one lousy MP short of a stable minority in which even the NDP could prop him up? Well, now he had that extra MP. But the appointments weren't only about strengthening Harper. They were about hobbling his opponents. British Columbia was the only region of the country where the Liberals had gained seats on both the 2004 and 2006 elections, the only part of the country where Martin's bigger-tent vision had paid modest dividends. The symbols of that bigger Liberal Party were Ujjal Dosanjh, a former NDP premier, and Emerson, a banker from the province's conservative business elite. By poaching Emerson, Harper could clip one wing of that, uh, big tent. Okay, so it doesn't work as metaphor, but it looked like it would work as strategy.

The Conservatives were helped by the fact that David Emerson is one of the most beatifically gormless amateurs ever to stumble into electoral politics without pausing to consider how it works. His excuse for switching parties wasn't political conviction but its perfect absence. He had run as a Liberal, he told pie-eyed reporters, only because a Liberal was offering cabinet seats. Now that Liberal, Paul Martin, had quit as Liberal leader, so David Emerson was a free agent again.

"You're saying that if Mr. Martin had become prime minister you would have stayed with him and become a minister in his cabinet?" one reporter asked.

"Yes, absolutely," Emerson replied cheerfully.

Oddly this sort of answer didn't impress many voters in Emerson's Vancouver-Kingsway riding. Hundreds of them launched a protest that would last for months and decorate many of the riding's lawns with DE-ELECT EMERSON signs. To one newspaper interviewer, Harper would admit that he had expected "some superficial criticism." Privately, Conservatives admitted that they thought Fortier's appointment to the Senate would be more controversial, and that at any rate they never expected the firestorm they had to withstand after the Emerson appointment. In the campaign Harper had shown a preference for controversy early rather than later, by stating his gay-marriage policy on the first day. The Emerson and Fortier appointments showed more of the same instinct. But the controversy Harper got was more than he had bargained for.

While they watched the Emerson firestorm, the other new ministers settled into their jobs as best they could. Harper had told Prentice that in addition to serving as Indian Affairs minister, he would also chair the Operations committee of cabinet. "I didn't really understand what it was. I just said, 'if that's what you'd like me to do, I'd be happy to help out. We'll talk about it when I get to Ottawa,' says Prentice."

At the reception after the swearing-in ceremony, Alex Himelfarb buttonholed Prentice and said, "You're the chairman of the Operations committee. Do you know what that means?"

"And I said, 'Well, I think I do.' And he said, 'Well, I just talked to your wife, and I don't think you do. Come over here.' So he took me over to the side." And then the Clerk informed the new minister that the only people who'd ever chaired the Operations committee before had been deputy prime ministers. Harper wasn't naming anyone with that title. But in terms of structural responsibility, Prentice was it.

One moment at the swearing-in ceremony, ignored by everyone else, struck me with particular clarity. Peter MacKay took his oath as Foreign Affairs minister and returned to the rows of seats where his colleagues sat. The last leader of the Progressive Conservative Party reached out one of his boat-sized hands and wrapped it around the hand of Monte Solberg, Day One Reformer, Preston Manning loyalist. They smiled the slightly abashed, now-we're-in-for-it smiles that all new ministers seem to get with their titles. And my memory flashed back to a night at Darcy McGee's, the Irish pub on Sparks Street that serves as a redoubt for all manner of Hill denizens.

This would have been a Wednesday night in 1999 or 2000, and Peter and Monte had picked this night to try and talk through the gulf of philosophy and recrimination that separated their parties. They stood at the end of the bar, near the servers' station. Each man had his tie loosened and his sleeves rolled up. Each held a pint of Keith's India Pale Ale in one hand and used the other to point accusingly into the other guy's chest as they hectored and remonstrated and blamed, teetering all the while at the very outer edge of civility. I am sure that the argument lasted at least two hours. There were hundreds like it between Tories and Reformers over more than a decade, the protagonists varying, the positions never budging. And now here they were, running the country.

It cannot be a coincidence that Conservatives discovered the knack of getting along just as Liberals were losing it. Solberg and MacKay can't have changed their minds about who was right or wrong ten years ago, but they finally grew tired of using that resentment as a basis for organizing their political lives. Eventually they had lost so many times, they decided to act as winners act. The Liberals, meanwhile, made the opposite exchange. A large number of the people around Paul Martin had gathered in Calgary on the *first anniversary* of Martin's 1990 leadership defeat for something they called "Bitterness Weekend '91." Eventually the bitter crowd won power, and they did their best, but many of the people who watched them govern were amazed to see that getting what they had wanted for so long did not make them substantially less bitter.

Several hours after the Harper government was sworn in, parties sprang up all over Ottawa as rookie ministers celebrated the arrival of new Tory times. The Empire Grill, a fancy steak joint in the Byward Market, became the headquarters for

transplanted ministers from Mike Harris's old Ontario government, for John Baird and Jim Flaherty and Tony Clement,
all now pillars of the Harper government, along with assorted
Toronto lobbyists and business types. But a few blocks away at
Métropolitain, an ersatz Parisian bistro, a quieter, less festive
crowd gathered. The ones who hadn't made it. James Rajotte,
James Moore, Jason Kenney, and Rahim Jaffer shared dinner
and contemplated the news of the day, which they had learned
from TV like everyone else. Bitter? No, bittersweet. These
young men had been out of power for as long as they had been
in politics. Now the boss had left them just outside the inner
circle. It wasn't perfect. But given where they'd been until now,
they'd take it.

12

LIBERALISM: YOU BREAK IT, YOU OWN IT

⇧

If the history of an organization as complex as the Liberal
Party of Canada in the last third of the twentieth century
can be boiled down to a contest between the Trudeau and
Chrétien camps on one hand, and the Turner and Martin
camps on the other, then this is where it ends: in a bit of a rout,
actually. Six majority governments for the Trudeau–Chrétien
team. Zero for the Turner–Martin team. That's gotta hurt.

On February 2, 2006, reporters packed the National Press
Theatre on Wellington Street to watch Paul Martin give his
last news conference as Prime Minister of Canada. He had
held the job for a little less than twenty-six months. "The fact
is that – does anyone leave office with a feeling that there is
unfinished business?" he asked, not very clearly. "Very clearly.
But I feel very proud of what we have accomplished."

He mentioned the strength of the economy, whose broad
direction had been set before he moved against Jean Chrétien.

Or, if you prefer, before Chrétien moved against him. Liberals were now free to debate that question in perfect leisure while somebody else governed the country. "We have also, I believe, a strong list of accomplishments – accomplishments which in fact we thought we would do over a much longer mandate but, in fact, [were done] in about eighteen months," he said. This seemed to be a new interpretation of events: the decade of history-making achievement Martin had promised at the Air Canada Centre *had happened*, but it had been compressed into less than one-fifth of the time originally planned, like coal into a public-policy diamond.

What feats were woven into the diamond's crystal structure? Child care, first. "When you think of an agreement with all of the provinces, or the vast majority of the provinces, on an issue such as child care – something that I wish we had been able to do ten years ago; we didn't have the resources – I think that we're going to find that that child-care agreement is going to happen. And that it's going to have a significant effect on the success of our nation." As Martin spoke, today was Thursday. On Monday, Stephen Harper would leave his first cabinet meeting to announce a date for the cancellation of the Martin child-care agreements with the provinces.

But it wasn't only Harper, the Conservative, who was rendering the Liberals' accomplishments in child care so ephemeral. Even now, in his last days as a political leader, Martin the Liberal preferred to stick with a delusional agent-of-change narrative instead of acknowledging that Liberal virtue had existed before December 12, 2003. Martin wished he could have done child care ten years earlier. A less short-sighted man would have pointed out that child care was something Liberals had been doing for pretty close to ten years. The National Child Benefit, a system of payments to low-income parents, had existed since 1998. The 1999 throne speech contained a commitment to "increase resources and further strengthen supports for early childhood development," through agreement with the provinces, by December 2000.

And the government of Canada came through. Under the 2000 federal-provincial health accord, Ottawa paid $500 million a year to support everything from healthy pregnancy to early childhood care. When little of that money actually wound up getting spent on producing child-care spaces, the government set aside a further $900 million over five years specifically to improve access to early learning and child-care programs (and a further $320 million over five years for similar programs for aboriginal children). To be fair, that money was set aside in a budget delivered by John Manley, not Paul Martin. Maybe Martin didn't notice.

But at least one of his briefers had urged Martin to bring up that Liberal record during the 2006 campaign, when the difference in child-care philosophies became the central policy debate in the fight of Martin's life. If you put the Martin-era daycare agreements in the context of nearly a decade's work on support for kids, they start to look like the culmination of a pretty good story. You see a government that began by concentrating on the poorest families. It ramped up support for them as money became available. It extended its efforts into early childhood care for all sorts of families, drawing steadily on lessons learned as it moved toward greater levels of ambition. At many points in the narrative, choice in the *manner* of child care, which Harper would turn into a Conservative trademark, had been built into Liberal policy. Surely, Martin's briefer argued, this was a better story than a massive, statist, untested daycare behemoth pulled out of your ass in the last days before an election?

"The answer," Martin's briefer recalls, "was to sort of shut off at that point. The discussion went back to just the stuff we were going to announce the next day."

Back to the career-ending news conference. "There's no doubt in my mind," Martin continued, "that the cities and communities agreement is going to change very much for the better the way in which Canada is governed, the way in which it addresses its problems. That was a major breakthrough. The Health Care Accord, I think, is going to lead inevitably to a strengthened health-care system. We're already beginning to see that – the dramatic reduction in wait times and the fact that the provinces have come together in a measurable basis."

Once again, if Martin's voice was muffled, it's because he was speaking from inside his change narrative. Before Martin and the provinces had ever signed their health-care accord, the provinces had twice reported on comparable health indicators, under the terms of the 2000 and 2003 federal-provincial health agreements. New organizations to measure and coordinate the country's health-care systems – the Canada Health Council and the Canadian Institute for Health Information – had been set up under the 2000 and 2003 agreements. Some of the best research into wait-time reduction strategies had been funded by the Canadian Institutes for Health Research, now nearly a decade old. Which may help explain why wait times had already begun to shorten before Martin signed a deal promising to shorten them.

"And I've got to say that the Kelowna agreement, in which Canada is finally in a measurable way addressing what is one of its most shameful legacies, I think is something of which all Canadians can be very proud." Not a dime of money had yet flowed under the Kelowna accord. Jim Prentice would soon announce that the Conservatives' broad model for relations with First Nations on reserves would be the First Nations Governance Initiative, which a Liberal Indian Affairs minister, Bob Nault, had introduced in 2002, before Martin's government withdrew it.

"So the answer to your question is I think that we accomplished a great deal," Martin said.

Well then, why'd he lose? Paul Hunter from the CBC phrased the question in the most congenial way imaginable. Martin had explained the rationale for calling the Gomery inquiry a thousand times, Hunter said, and yet accountability had become a key campaign issue. "So is it fair to say that the hard lesson there is that in politics, doing the so-called right thing comes with a price? And that you paid it?"

Had he paid the price for doing the right thing? Gee, what was he going to say – no? "In the long run of history I don't think doing the right thing is ever the wrong thing to do," Martin declared, tautologically enough.

"Look, there's no doubt that political analysts are going to debate both sides of that issue. The strategy, was it the right thing to do politically, was it the wrong thing to do politically and how should you have handled it differently? And I suppose there'll be as many opinions on that as there are people. But I can tell you one thing on which there should be no dissent. And that is . . . from a moral-imperative point of view it was the right thing to do. And I don't think that there is another alternative morally."

This would depend on your definition of morality. There's a line of thought among engineers and architects that *efficiency* is a moral imperative, too. That you really don't have the right to kick up an almighty storm of crap if it adds nothing measurable to the sum of human good.

⇧

What was Judge Gomery's mandate? To follow the money. To find the bad guys. To fix the system so the sponsorship program could never be repeated. And how'd that go?

Well, when it came to following the money, Gomery could not have face-planted more spectacularly. For months Gomery's spokesman, François Perreault, had made a great show of confiding to selected reporters that the forensic audit Gomery had commissioned from the accounting firm Kroll Lindqvist Avey would be the inquiry's main event. Reporters dutifully wrote dozens of articles promising the Kroll audit would dramatically reveal the money trail. There were a lot fewer articles afterward, admitting that the Kroll audit was one of the most spectacular wet firecrackers in the history of book-keeping. (Perreault also found no room for this wee detail in his "tell-all" book, *Inside Gomery*.)

Why the dud? To a great extent it's not Kroll's fault, nor even Gomery's. Inquiry lawyers told Kroll's accountants to stay out of the way of the police, who had also taken a considerable interest in sponsorship malfeasance. So the Kroll auditors were forbidden to look at transactions that were the subject of criminal charges or police investigations.

Criminal charges? Police investigations? Funny you should mention them. This gets to Gomery's find-the-bad-guys mandate. To be sure, it was a loose mandate. In return for enjoying sometimes comically lackadaisical rules of evidence, Gomery had no authority to assert criminal wrongdoing. But he was at liberty to "name and blame," an authority he exercised with relish.

But the heavyweight namers and blamers in our society are police and the law courts. The sponsorship abuses led to three convictions: Jean Brault, Paul Coffin, Chuck Guité. The RCMP investigations that led to those convictions, and in two cases the charges themselves, predated Paul Martin's arrival at 24 Sussex. Nothing Martin or Gomery did affected the course of those court cases.

Fixing the system so the sponsorship scandal could never be repeated? Gomery released two reports, one on what went wrong and one on how to fix it. In the *first*, he wrote: "It is reasonable to assume that if the guidelines and procedures introduced in 2001 by Communication Canada to manage the Sponsorship Program had been in place from its inception, the mismanagement and abuses that occurred from 1996 to 2000 would not have been possible." If those words in the first report have any meaning, it's not entirely clear why Gomery bothered to write the second. But he's a trouper, so he did his best.

And his best was dismissed as unconvincing by more than sixty of the country's foremost authorities on public administration. In a letter to Stephen Harper a month after Martin's last news conference, the signatories – including John Manley, Bob Rae, Barbara McDougall, Hugh Segal, Paul Tellier, Tom d'Aquino, a half-dozen college and university presidents, and dozens of others – said Gomery's recommendations would corrode the essential working relationship between politicians and senior officials. "The core problem of the [second] report is that he was working with a subject that I don't think he really understood," Arthur Kroeger, the highly experienced former deputy minister who, coincidentally, had worked on Martin's transition team, told reporters.

Martin, of course, had campaigned on a promise to implement every Gomery recommendation, in advance, sight unseen. Don't ever let anyone tell you Paul Martin wasn't bold: he had hitched his wagon to a revolution in public administration *with no idea what that revolution would look like*. At his last news conference he was sticking to that promise. "I think that in Mr. Justice Gomery's second report, as indeed with his first, that he has fully justified the expectations that were placed upon him," Martin said. "And I fully support his conclusions."

So Paul Martin was ending his term as Liberal leader more or less as he had begun it: in a fog of obfuscation and denial. But he did touch obliquely, just once, on a central truth of his party's predicament. It happened while he was standing up for the Board.

Hélène Buzzetti from *Le Devoir* pointed out that Martin had spoken, yet again, of his pride in his advisors. "Yet when we speak to many important organizers on the ground, many who, incidentally, did not participate in the last campaign, they say that a pre-condition of their return to the Liberal Party is the assurance that your entourage will fold its tents. That they won't be around any more. So how much responsibility do you think you take for the divisions that reign in your party? How responsible do you think you are, because of the way you acceded to the leadership?"

Of course Martin didn't like the question. "Look, in every party are there people who like each other and people who don't?" Those divisions, in his party, were "minimal," he said. "And I can tell you that the people around me have been members of the Liberal Party for a very long time. They know a lot of people and I've never heard anyone impose that condition."

And the hell of it is that here, at least, Martin was right. His advisors – all the Scotts, Terries, Davids, Tims, Johns, and Karls – might have their quirks and flaws, but they were not some alien body that had grafted itself onto the Liberal Party of Canada. They *were* the Liberal Party of Canada, as much as anyone else. They had grown up in it, contributed to its victories, and mastered its rules better than their opponents had.

And when they made their move against a three-majority leader, almost everyone in the party had thrown on a coat, grabbed a torch or a pitchfork, and joined the mob.

So it was a bit rich for Liberals to start blaming the clique around Martin now, in 2006. It was a bit easy to imagine the party's ills could be made to disappear simply by de-commissioning Scott Reid's BlackBerry. The party had bought Paul Martin's leadership. It would have to own his failure.

⇧

Denial is a hard habit to break. For years before Harper's victory, Liberals had been convinced he could never be prime minister. After January 23, Liberals were less comforted by cozy certainties. Some thought the Conservatives were, as likely as not, settling in for several years of power. Others were sure Harper had profited from two freak accidents, the sponsorship scandal and the income-trust investigation. Surely his victory was a fluke and his comeuppance would not wait.

The numbers do not comfort that hypothesis. Ever since the Kim Campbell wipeout of 1993, parties to the right of the Liberals have been rather steadily climbing: from 54 seats (if you add Reform/Alliance and Progressive Conservative totals) in 1993, to 80 in 1997, dipping slightly to 78 in 2000, then back up to 99 in 2004 and 124 in 2006.

If you look at popular vote, the story is a little more muddled: Harper's new Conservative Party won a sharply lower share of the popular vote in 2004, at 29.6 per cent, than the Alliance and Progressive Conservative parties had scored in 2000, at a combined 37.68 per cent. But that only demonstrates that uniting the parties was good strategy: despite the eight-point drop in popular vote, the merged party won 21 more seats in 2004. And because it stayed merged, it translated a five-point increase in popular vote into 25 more seats in 2006.

The Liberals? After Chrétien's 1993 breakthrough the Liberals managed to gain seats in only one subsequent election, in 2000. They lost seats in 1997, 2004, and 2006. They lost their share of the popular vote in those three elections too.

Harper's victory wasn't a fluke. It accelerated a decade-long trend by which conservative parties slowly displaced the Liberals as the party of the average working Canadian. Just as Jean Chrétien and Preston Manning had displaced the Progressive Conservatives after Brian Mulroney let that party vanish into the swamps of Meech and Charlottetown. Which is why Jason Kenney so quickly warmed to his task when I asked him to analyze the current health of the Liberals. True, Kenney is the Conservative MP for Calgary Southeast, where Liberals were hardly thick on the ground at the best of times. But he's also a canny political observer. And the Liberals have had mixed success lately from listening to their own instincts. Maybe they should pay some attention to their opponents' diagnoses.

"The Liberal Party, characteristic of most parties in power after a long time, became a bodiless head," Kenney said. "It's a leadership without grassroots." This was illustrated in particularly lurid fashion by Elections Canada figures for political donations for the first quarter of 2006. Six times as many Canadians donated to the Conservatives as to the Liberals in that period. *Twice* as many Canadians donated to the NDP as to the Liberals. True, a lot of the money that would ordinarily go to Liberals had begun to go to individual leadership candidates instead. But there's a serious, serious problem there.

"There are, I would estimate, no more than ten thousand real, honest-to-goodness Liberal activists in the country," Kenney said. "Outside of Toronto and some little regional pockets, it's not really a national party with any kind of grass-roots base. So they can end up with a brilliant, bilingual, articulate leader, but rebuilding has to be more than a slogan for them.

"And of course, having lost completely their traditional chunk of support in francophone Quebec, the math is impossible for them to form a government. They have to regain that. I think that becomes more and more unlikely by the day.

"And finally, if you look at the brilliant slate of decent people running for the leadership, we'd love to run against pretty much any of them. I can't see Gerard Kennedy or Michael Ignatieff or Bob Rae or Stéphane Dion – all smart, decent people – selling with a forty-year-old plumber in Peterborough who makes forty grand. The spectrum of first-tier leadership candidates there reads like the perfect list of attendees at a cocktail party in the Annex or Cabbagetown. It's not Main Street. It's not the kind of slate that can connect with a broad middle-class constituency.

"We were joking this morning. What's Ignatieff's wife's name again?" I couldn't recall, but I remembered her name sounds vaguely Central European. (I checked later. It's Zsuzsanna.) "Exactly. So in the next election it's Steve and Laureen vs. Count Michael and What's-Her-Name. It's almost a dream for us."

⇧

Which may help explain why, when I met with Ignatieff a few days later, he was workin' so hard at soundin' like ordinary folk. I haven't heard anyone drop so many g's from the ends of his participles since *Hee Haw* went off the air.

"Yeah, people have got questions about – bein' out of the country," Ignatieff said. Here, "bein' out of the country" is a genteel euphemism for the fact that until he moved to Toronto to run for Parliament in 2005, the rookie MP for Etobicoke-Lakeshore had not resided in Canada since 1969. He spent some of that time teachin' at Harvard. "I genuinely get a lot of people sayin', 'It's great. It's great. Good for you.' Behind the you've-been-out-of-the-country question, it's not really – I think Canadians rather like the fact that somebody's been out and has *done* stuff and has come back. What they want to be assured is that the guy knows the *country*, right? He's not some kind of *Martian*."

Oh, surely that's a bit harsh. Where would any Canadian get the idea that Michael Ignatieff is a Martian? I mean, where besides the preface to his book *The Rights Revolution*, published in 2000? In that preface, Ignatieff admits he is writing about the Canadian conception of rights and that it "may read oddly" to an audience of actual Canadians. "To them, this book may seem like a report by a visitor from a distant planet," Ignatieff writes. "I want to alert readers that I am a Martian outsider."

On a campaign poster, that phrase would at least have the virtue of novelty. But at the end of his preface, Ignatieff hurries to reassure Canadians: writing *The Rights Revolution* "has deepened my attachment to the place on earth that, if I needed one, I would call home." These Liberals, they are masters of patriotism. O Canada! My home, if I needed one, and native land!

But if Michael Ignatieff could be boiled down to an exotic c.v. and a fairly transparent just-folks act, he would be easy to dismiss. His opponents have learned he is more tenacious than he appears. The first to learn was Stephen Harper, who visited the good professor's riding just after the New Year in hopes of stealing it from under Ignatieff's loafer-clad feet. No dice. "I'm a very combative person," Ignatieff says. "I've been workin' hard since I was a teenager."

Under David Smith, the ageless Grit strategist appointed to the Senate by Chrétien, and Ian Davey, an architect of John Manley's resoundingly unconvincing leadership campaign in 2002, Ignatieff has been workin' hard at wooing Liberals. Many have been wooed, despite early skepticism. (I don't know how many. I'm in the exquisitely delicate position of writing, in July, about a leadership race that will reach its climax some weeks after this book hits the shelves. What follows may read oddly. I want to alert readers that I am an outsider from the distant past.)

"What you hear in the small rooms of the leadership contest – and sometimes they're very small, like a hotel room where you're sittin' on the bed and there's a riding association, it's like ten people, and sometimes it's a hundred people; it's a small-room process – what you hear is: 'We have suffered from our divisions,'" Ignatieff says.

"'We have suffered from the tribal war of the chieftains. We must be united. We must be credible outside of metropolitan, downtown Vancouver, Winnipeg, Toronto, Montreal, Halifax. We have a big credibility problem in developing a policy that says to rural Canada, "You're not left behind. We're not ignoring you. We care. You matter to us."' I've been tryin' to say that this party is not just an election machine, it's a national institution."

Ignatieff isn't shy about acknowledging that in that particular mission, the Conservatives are ahead. Have been ahead for some time. "We've got to become a mass-based party, we've got to become a $50, $75, $100 party in financial terms. We're possibly ten years behind the Conservatives in our vision of ourselves as a workin' man's and woman's party who, you know, because they care about public issues, they sign a cheque. We've gone to the forty-fourth floor for our money for too long and it had a bad effect on us. We gotta be gettin' our money from the kind of dinner I was at in PEI on Friday night. We give you a little lobster and a glass of wine, you pay your money and three hundred people come out. It's kind of great. It's kind of – *popular*. That's the kind of party we've got to become again."

But a party will never hear from ordinary Canadians unless it learns, or relearns, how to speak to them. That means relevant policy, communicated clearly. Once again, Ignatieff refreshes because he sees a lot worth emulating in his opponent. "This is where Harper, I think, has taught us a significant political lesson. I'm supposed to be this, you know, public-policy wonk. But what I have seen from him is he has a very considerable capacity to produce very clear promises, and very clear messages that resonate with Canadians. In our best hours as Canadians we have been able to do that too. We just need to remember: that's how the game of Canadian politics is played. And that that's the way it should be played. I salute Harper for the clarity of his five priorities. I just don't happen to agree with them."

Very good. So what would down-to-earth Ignatieff policies look like? Here, it must be said, there's work to be done. On crime: "I'm not soft on crime at all. I wanna put people in the slammer with the best of them." Oh dear. "But I spent my graduate-school years going to a medium-security prison on Tuesday nights. And one of the things I came away from that knowing is that prison makes almost everybody who goes in worse, not better." So a Prime Minister Ignatieff, one presumes, would work to contain his urge to put people in the slammer.

On taxation? "For God's sake, you know, just think of what we" – i.e., the government – "could have bought with that GST cut, instead of just more DVDs and TV sets. Now I understand, I understand, I understand the electoral appeal of this. I'm not an elitist. You know, I pay taxes like everyone else. But it goes down to a very deep vision of government."

This is a pattern that conversations with Ignatieff often take. He stands strongly on one side of an issue, while leaving open the possibility that he might stand strongly on the other. After the first debate among Liberal candidates in Winnipeg, I wrote on my blog about Ignatieff's suggestion that the party should consider a carbon tax. Now, there aren't three ways a carbon tax can work, there's one: it's designed to discourage people from burning hydrocarbons by making that activity more expensive. Hydrocarbons, in this country, dispropor-tionately come from Alberta. (That's why it was so funny when some observers applauded the Quebec government's "leader-ship" in introducing a carbon tax. Quebec has *waterfalls*. It was showing as much leadership by introducing a carbon tax as Manitoba would be if it introduced a mountain tax.) So anyway. I wrote on my blog that Ignatieff was courting con-troversy by flirting with a carbon tax. His staff responded by sending me the text of an Ignatieff speech on energy policy in which he didn't mention carbon taxes. Ah. So he's for carbon taxes unless you'd rather he weren't.

I asked Ignatieff who his political model is. Ignatieff named Franklin Roosevelt. "Why? For one sentence. 'We have nothing to fear but fear itself.' The great function of political leadership is to make people feel that great visceral feeling in your gut that we are a great people."

But maybe you don't like Roosevelt? No worry. "It's not so much particular leaders as political courage. You can forgive errors in judgment, but political courage is what draws people to leaders. Because people are willing to say, goddammit, this is where we are and we're going to go this way. So I admire political courage above all virtues."

But maybe you think courage can go too far? That's OK, so does he. "You know, there's a very, very fine line between courage and obstinacy, between courage and wrong-headedness. I'm praising a very subtle virtue that knows the difference between arrogance, obstinacy, blockheadedness and real courage."

Now, this is all great fun, but in a way Ignatieff is only showing the flexibility that is common to front-runners in political races. All things to all people? You say that like it's a bad thing. Still, it's in the context of Ignatieff's general reluctance to draw sharp edges on issues that his stance on Afghanistan starts to look like an asset. Here is his great big neon rebuttal waiting for anyone who says he won't stand firmly for something unpopular.

Afghanistan is an odd issue for the Liberals. Canadian soldiers are there because Jean Chrétien sent them. They are in Kandahar, some of the most dangerous territory in the world, because Paul Martin sent them. Bill Graham, the party's interim leader, voted with the Harper government to extend the mission. It's a pretty Liberal mission. Now, there's room for legitimate debate over whether the deployment should be extended past the beginning of 2007. Or about whether it was appropriate to make that decision almost a year early, as Stephen Harper made MPs do when he put the question to a vote in Parliament in the spring. But you get the impression that a lot of the sudden Liberal opposition to the Afghanistan mission doesn't come from procedural disagreements. You get the impression it comes from squeamishness and the usual Opposition obsession with tactics. Military deployment would have been a good point of principle to quit cabinet over, if Stéphane Dion, Joe Volpe, Ken Dryden, or Carolyn Bennett had felt like it.

Which is why it is so striking to see Ignatieff standing nearly

alone on Afghanistan (the only other candidate on his side is
Scott Brison). "I'm as tactical and strategic as the next guy,"
Ignatieff told me. "But my judgment tells me that a Liberal
Party that initiates that mission; warns the country in a responsible manner that there are costs to be paid; and then votes
against a resolution for the extension of the mission is contra-
dicting its own previous record. [It] sends a message to the
country that when the numbers go south and the casualties
rise, this party runs for cover."

On any other issue, this would be the point in the conversation where Ignatieff would begin to equivocate. And for a
moment, he seems true to pattern. "Now let me make it very
clear. Many members of the caucus are profound supporters of
the mission and just hated bein' jammed by Stephen Harper. I
have respect for those who voted the other side to mine. Please
put that on the record."

But then he gets back on message. "But I want us to be a
party that is committed to a strong, combat-capable military to
provide human security. I want us to be, beyond that, a serious
country – so that if you ask Canadians to do somethin' hard,
we do it. And we have the capability to do it. This serious-
country stuff is not idle talk to me. The part about my country
that worries me most is, we're big on the hot air and we don't
follow through. And Afghanistan is a test of how courageous
we are as a country."

Well. There's conviction, if Liberals want it. Not that the
only conviction is on Ignatieff's side of the Afghanistan debate.
That became pretty clear when I interviewed Bob Rae, in the
back of a campaign volunteer's car as we rode from a backyard
picnic to the Ottawa airport.

I had a pet theory. The basis of my pet theory was the fact
that Bob Rae and Michael Ignatieff used to be roommates

together at the University of Toronto, and the fact that most of the other Ottawa pundits had decided that Afghanistan would be the issue that divided the leadership candidates. That seemed too easy. So my theory was that Afghanistan wouldn't be determinative, and that when the Liberal leadership contest came down to the final moments, Rae might support Ignatieff, or Ignatieff, Rae.

That theory survived until I saw Rae's reaction when I mentioned Ignatieff's name. Rae winced noticeably and shook his head. "The party has some choices to make," he said with impressive finality. "I haven't agreed with a lot of what Michael has written about in the last few years. So there is going to be a debate about foreign policy and Canada's voice in the world."

What you hear most often about Bob Rae when Liberals discuss the leadership race is that they, personally, like him, but his catastrophic five years as Ontario premier in the early 1990s makes him a hard sell in the biggest province. Rae is unimpressed by the notion that he's radioactive in Ontario. "Quite the opposite, I think, actually. In 1995, I was still running ahead of Harris in terms of who'd be the best premier, right up to the last week. When I left Ontario politics, there were the warmest of editorials saying what a great contribution I'd made to public life. I went into my law practice, I was immediately asked to do all kinds of things that were positive and high profile. Never needed a bodyguard. Walked around, did things in all sorts of communities. At a personal level I've always felt a really warm connection with the people of the province."

So that's Ontario. What about Quebec? Rae's campaign manager – his formidably taciturn brother John Rae, the Power Corporation executive who ran Jean Chrétien's national campaigns – lives in Montreal. Bob Rae was premier through the Charlottetown accord mess. We were speaking on June 24,

Quebec's Fête Nationale. So I put it bluntly: Does Quebec constitute a nation?

"Yeah," he said. And here I thought I was asking a hard question. "Nation, people, distinct society – it's all the same. It just means that you recognize the distinctiveness of the collectivity called Quebec. And that's something that we should have done in 1987 at Meech, it's something we should have done in 1992 in Charlottetown, and it's something we should be doing."

As we spoke, Harper was in Quebec, dancing as fast as he could around the question Rae had answered so bluntly. Rae said: "Harper's problem is, he fought against Meech. And he fought viscerally against Charlottetown. I've always thought that the love affair between the people of Quebec and Stephen Harper made less sense than Britney Spears's first marriage. There's no durability. It isn't based on any long-term deep compatibility and affection. And I think that will become clear as time goes on. As someone who fought hard for Meech and Charlottetown, I can certainly tell you who the opponents were, what kind of arguments they were using. And their essential view of the notion of the French fact in Canada. It's not very generous."

With Rae, a discussion of national unity often seems to turn into a discussion of his low regard for the Harper Conservatives. "The two things that have always driven me politically have been the need to counter the arguments of separatism and the need to counter the arguments of the new right." In fact, Rae sees Harper as precisely the galvanizing antagonist the shaken and stumbling Liberals need.

Rae was talking, as all the candidates do, about the need to transform the Liberals from a party funded by fat cats into one that rallies the grassroots. Problem: Liberal grassroots don't rally easily. "Somebody said to me the other day, actually making a good point: when New Democrats and Tories raise money it's usually to fight something," Rae said. "They're angry at something. The Tories are always mad at something. They're mad at the gun registry, they're mad at this issue, they're mad at that." Liberals, on the other hand, "are very well-adjusted people. They're not that angry at anything, they're just *people*. So the question is, how do you create a popular base? I think Harper is the one guy who can actually mobilize Liberals. And I think that's what we're going to begin to see over the next while. It's really where we have to focus our time and attention."

It's odd that the only candidate with experience as a head of government would fall so naturally into a dynamic of opposition. My hunch is that it has something to do with Rae's NDP upbringing. He doesn't just have more experience in government than the rest of the leadership pack – he actually has more experience in opposition too. The weight of circumstance makes most New Democrats more comfortable levelling a critique than coming up with a plan. Rae was famously a little amazed to actually win power in 1990.

But maybe it's not just his upbringing that makes Rae so eager to take Harper on. Maybe it's the moment. The Liberal Party of 2006 can agree on very few things. By the end of the parliamentary session, Conservatives were whispering to each other that the Liberals had essentially ceased to function as a coherent parliamentary group. But Liberals can agree on this much, at least: they don't like the guy who ended their thirteen years in power.

At the leadership debates in Winnipeg and Moncton in the spring, any candidate was guaranteed a round of applause for calling Harper's five priorities trivial or simplistic. Ken

Dryden, the former hockey goalie and minister, seems to have captured many Liberals' affection by transforming himself into a kind of balladeer of Liberal self-regard. His speech has begun tumbling out in urgent haikus of wounded virtue, and the Liberal crowds I've seen proceed to eat it up. Here's an excerpt from an interview he gave a blogger named Arnone, whose Next Face is one of dozens of Liberal blogs that have sprung up since the leadership race began. Transcribing Dryden's comments as prose didn't seem to do them justice. Here's the way they seemed to want to order themselves.

Unhappy
a found poem by Ken Dryden

That is what is so disturbing about the Conservative government.
It is so small.
It is so pinched. It is so
ungenerous.

It is so unhappy.

It is a government that is so about now
and so about me.

And "now" and "me" are so important
but we want tomorrow to be part of it
and not just now.

And we want our neighbour to be part of it
and not just me.

And we feel better if both are a part of it
and I don't think that is what
the Conservatives offer.

So this is one of the surprises of the Liberal race: that its
only poet is a lumbering ex-jock whose neck barely fits his
dress shirts and whose sentences last longer than most
working Canadians' summer vacations. The other surprise is
Stéphane Dion.

⇧

Actually, I'm not surprised. A few of us toiling in the Quebec-
politics salt mines noticed Dion even before Jean Chrétien did,
when the owlish prof was publicly disagreeing with most of his
province's intellectual elite before the 1995 referendum. It
was Dion's unshakeable faith in Canadian federalism and his
skill in defending it that won him a phone call from Chrétien
after the vote. His open letters to assorted members of Lucien
Bouchard's government won Dion a reputation for clarity,
conviction, fearlessness, and a bottomless capacity for annoying his adversaries – and a good number of bystanders in the
bargain. But after he introduced the Clarity Act in 1999, Dion
disappeared from most Canadians' radar screens, even in
Ottawa. When Paul Martin punted him from cabinet in 2003,
nobody complained.

But every week at Liberal caucus meetings, backbench MPs
– Dion now among them – would line up to give their opinion
on the issues of the day. Senator Percy Downe, who hadn't
picked a leadership candidate when he told me this anecdote,
said the response each intervention received was a matter of
close attention. "The caucus members called it 'the claps,'"

Downe said. "They'd measure it. An applause meter, like you're at a karaoke bar. Dion would get the strongest claps after every intervention. And everybody sitting around would say, 'Well, why is that man not in the cabinet?'"

After the 2004 election he was. Martin made Dion his environment minister. But old habits die hard. When the tenth anniversary of the referendum approached in 2005, Paul Martin telephoned Dion and instructed him to write commemorative op-ed pieces for Quebec newspapers. A wag might note that Martin didn't bother to task his intergovernmental-affairs minister, Lucienne Robillard, or his Quebec lieutenant, Jean Lapierre, with that particular bit of outreach.

Still, there's a big difference between a minister whose competence makes him necessary despite a long catalogue of annoying traits, and a leader. At first, Dion's candidacy for the leadership seemed custom-designed to illustrate that difference. At his Montreal campaign launch, almost every staffer who had ever worked for him was on hand and on board, but almost no sitting MPs. His powers of attraction seemed to work only at extremely close quarters. Not good enough for a serious candidate.

The only way forward was for one of the great loners in Canadian politics to exercise his atrophied social muscles. Dion threw himself into the same small-room process as the other candidates, meeting individual Liberals in dozens of hotel cafés, backyards, and kitchens. The surprise was that he started to get some traction. His first coup was to land Mark Marissen, the British Columbia organizer who helped the Martin Liberals make their only regional gains in two elections. Left to his own devices, Dion might have run an intellectual's campaign of op-ed articles and university seminars. Marissen persuaded him to keep pressing the ground game instead.

As a minister, "you spend a lot of time reading briefing books and discussing with your officials," Dion said, "whereas you're always with Canadians in a leadership race. Canadians who are Liberal. You don't have to persuade them to be Liberal, you have to persuade them to come to you. It's much more personal. And because I've been there for ten years, there are a lot of ideas about me that are sometimes very flattering. But there are also myths I have to work on."

Which myths? "That I'm a cold person, or I have no charisma, or I don't know how to speak English. Or that I couldn't deliver in Quebec. Or that I couldn't deliver in the rest of the country. So I have to give people a chance to see me. And because expectations are sometimes very low, it gives good results." The only condition he imposes on his schedulers is that he needs downtime before he delivers a major speech – to write it. "I may have some political skills. But I don't have the skill that consists of being comfortable with texts written by others. I have to write for myself."

He remembers the first time he met Stephen Harper, on a TV current-affairs show's set during the Charlottetown referendum. Even then, the young Reform strategist, not even an MP, had an eye out for the reception he would get from Quebeckers. "I remember the first question he was asked," Dion recalls: "'*Quelle est la position du Reform Party?*' And he answered, in the French he had at the time, '*Je m'excuse mais nous avons un nom: c'est le Parti réformiste du Canada.*'"

I put to Dion the case that Conservatives so often put to me when Dion's name comes up: that Dion won the credit for a hard-line stance against Quebec separatism that Harper had pioneered in Parliament before Dion even went into politics. Dion smiled. "If that were our only disagreement, I'd be delighted. What's true is that before I arrived in politics, these ideas were circulating. A former clerk of the Privy Council, Gordon Robertson, had written a paper. Several academics had written on these issues. The Quebec Cree had a great big campaign about why they couldn't go along with a referendum victory in Quebec against their will. . . .

"The difference is that at that moment, Stephen was in politics and he could speak as a politician. He was in politics before me. So he spoke about it as a politician before I did, that's for sure. But Dion the political scientist was discussing these questions too."

What does he make of Harper? "At the moment when he had to look like an honest young man, whom people could imagine as their son-in-law, he had that. Very precise words. And concise. He worked on his image, improved his French. You can't underestimate him, absolutely not."

Okay, but that's Harper's style. What about the man himself? "He admires George Bush a bit the way I admired Jean Béliveau when I was five. It's nonsensical how completely he copies him in everything – in the style, in the speeches on Iraq, in the way he muzzles his ministers, in the way he manages the press like a president – he wants to *be* president."

What did Dion learn from his two political bosses, Chrétien and Martin? "It would be good to have a blend of the two, no?" He paused to consider. "The big difference, perhaps, is that one of them seemed to like it. Mr. Chrétien looked happy in politics. Sometimes he was in a murderous mood, but he gave the impression he was enjoying it. Mr. Martin was able to be relieved, but to be happy?"

⇧

This is what some of us learned a decade ago, and what most Liberals are only beginning to learn: that a conversation with Stéphane Dion almost inevitably goes in surprising directions. But don't take that as either endorsement or prediction. The Liberals have a deep field of candidates and a leadership-selection process that virtually guarantees surprises on the convention floor, in Montreal in December. Can a front-runner make it to the convention without making so many enemies that he loses any hope of growing after the first ballot? If the front-runner can't close the deal, does the convention turn to somebody blandly acceptable, so the winner is everyone's second choice? It's how Joe Clark won the Progressive Conservative leadership in 1976, and Abraham Lincoln became the Republicans' man in 1860.

Is the Liberals' next leader a Lincoln, a Joe Who, or something else? They will find out when the delegates get to Montreal. Not before. In 2002, Liberals believed they were trading a sure thing for a surer thing. They turned out to be wrong. On January 23, Canadian politics became a new world, a world whose contours cannot yet be mapped with any precision. Stephen Harper's opponents can do no better than to listen to their hearts and play their hunches.

13

PMSH

⇧

"**P**rime Minister Stephen Harper." The first time a reporter addressed him by that title in public – before he was sworn in, so before it was strictly accurate – he admitted he liked the way it felt to hear it.

One reason Prime Minister Stephen Harper found it relatively easy to do what he had said was that he had said what he would do. If you offer Canadians a twenty-first-century economy and a place of pride and influence in the world, it's kind of hard for them to tell when they've arrived. If you offer to cut the most annoying tax in Canada and send every parent a cheque, it's easier to tick off the little boxes.

Jean Chrétien had the same idea when he was elected in 1993. But his quick-delivery promises had more to do with halting the mad momentum of the Mulroney years (when on any given day you could find yourself asking, "The fate of the country depends on *what?*") than with getting much started.

Chrétien left his first cabinet meeting to announce that he had already delivered on two promises. The Canadian Forces wouldn't be buying new helicopters, shorthand for "no more extravagance." And the Pearson airport privatization was cancelled, shorthand for "no more cronyism." Both decisions caused no end of headaches down the line. But they may even have been worth the downstream hassle, because they created the immediate impression that finally, somebody was hitting the brakes.

Harper's Five Priorities (a good name for a band, actually) had the opposite objective. After the drift of Chrétien's government from 2000 to 2002, the civil war through 2003, and the swamp of the Martin years, Harper didn't need brakes. He needed to show that the old jalopy of state still had an engine in it. A sense of urgency informed both the choice of the priorities and the decisions about the government machinery that would deliver them.

On January 4, almost three weeks before the election, Harper sat for an interview in Toronto with journalists from several magazines published by Rogers. "The first four of the five things I've talked about are things that, quite frankly, we can do fairly quickly," he told the reporters. "And they will all have longer-term impacts. The country will be different because of them." Note that he said only four could be delivered quickly: the GST cut, the child-care cheques to parents, a package of tough-on-crime legislation, and the federal accountability act. The last promise, for a patient wait-times guarantee, was "more difficult," Harper allowed.

So four of the five priorities were designed to be quickly deliverable. The government was built to deliver quickly. "We made a decision early on – like very early on, before the election began – that in the event of victory we would not get involved in a complicated rejigging of the machinery of government," one senior Conservative said. "That was considered and rejected, basically for the reason that if you start to reorganize the machinery of government, kiss your productivity goodbye for the next two years as everyone figures out who reports to whom." Indeed, the only major machinery changes Harper made were to undo two of Martin's machinery changes. The botched division of the Department of Foreign Affairs and International Trade into two separate departments had soured almost the entire foreign-service apparatus against the Martin government. Harper cancelled it. He also reversed Martin's division of Human Resources Development into separate Social Development and Skills Development departments. Everything else he left much as he found it – with two key exceptions.

First, Harper installed new people. He would need a new Clerk of the Privy Council – even though he and the old Clerk had hit it off far better than either man had expected. In the weeks before his successor was named, Alex Himelfarb found himself going back to the prime minister's office at the end of most days for a second round of daily briefings, more or less just because both men liked the chats so much.

As a consumer of briefing books, the new prime minister seemed to combine the strengths of his two predecessors. Chrétien hated detail and would stare daggers into the heart of anyone who dared put a too-long memo under his nose. But he had an uncanny instinct for seizing the essence of a complex situation. Martin was an information bulimic, never happier than when he came up with a tough question to ask his officials about something on page 450 of a three-inch binder. But he seemed to view the act of ending a discussion with a decision as a sign of weakness. Harper combined Martin's appetite for drudgery with Chrétien's aptitude for synthesis. For a man with such a profound suspicion of government, he was a bureaucrat's dream. But he needed new bureaucrats. One day early in the transition, Martin telephoned Harper from overseas to remind him of a deal he had cooked with Himelfarb: upon Martin's departure, his Clerk was to become the new ambassador to Rome. Harper readily agreed. After considering several replacements he settled on a man who reflected the best administrative strengths of the Liberal government, before the wheels started to fall off.

⇧

Kevin Lynch had served as Deputy Minister to John Manley from 1995 to 2000, when the then-industry minister was wiring every school in Canada to the Internet and setting up the Canada Foundation for Innovation, the cornerstone of the Liberals' science and research strategy. Lynch had moved on to Finance for Paul Martin's last years in that portfolio. He was considered – with Eddie Goldenberg, Martin, Manley, Himelfarb, and Chrétien himself – one of the architects of the Chrétien government's unheralded strategy to transform Canada from a resource-based to a knowledge-based economy. George Russell, my old editor at *Time* magazine's Canadian edition, used to have a theory that Kevin Lynch secretly ran the government of Canada.

Now, after two years in Washington as Canada's representative at the International Monetary Fund, Lynch was ready to become Harper's senior bureaucratic lieutenant, the Clerk of the Privy Council. In announcing the appointment, Harper called Lynch "a highly focused professional," a description that said as much about the role Harper expected a Clerk to play as it did about Lynch's qualifications. "He understands our five-priority agenda and will greatly contribute to moving it forward."

But one of the things Lynch understood about the five priorities – a nuance that eluded many of Harper's critics – was that they didn't begin to encompass the scale of the change that was coming. Very rapidly, Lynch and Harper implemented a major facelift of the senior public service. The machinery didn't change, but there were plenty of new machinists. Deputy ministers are the top bureaucrats at each department, the leading figures in a permanent government that does not, automatically, change just because the party in power changes. But this new government made a point of changing deputies. By June there would be new deputy ministers at Finance, Industry, Human Resources, International Trade, Environment, Indian Affairs, Citizenship and Immigration, Natural Resources, Intergovernmental Affairs and Public Safety. Some of the moves were lateral, designed simply to give a senior mandarin a fresh set of problems to think about. Others were bolder. Richard Dicerni had left Ottawa for the Ontario public service in 1992, which meant he knew the Mike Harris Tory crowd who had now decamped, in large part, to Harper's cabinet. He would be the new deputy at Industry, a department that seemed to have lost its energy after Lynch had left it. And Samy Watson, the Environment deputy under the Liberals, was seen to be too closely wedded to the Liberals' Kyoto strategy on greenhouse gases. He was unceremoniously hoisted out of that spot into a bureaucratic limbo, awaiting a future assignment whose nature the Harper government did not bother to dangle hints about. The Conservatives still weren't entirely sure what they would be doing at Environment. But they knew they didn't want a holdover from the old regime to do it.

These changes, implemented in close consultation with Lynch, made an incalculable difference in cementing Harper's relationship with the senior public service. The Conservative leader's weird comments in the election campaign's final week about a "Liberal" bureaucracy had put official Ottawa on edge. But Harper's new Clerk was the man most civil servants would have picked, and his personnel decisions showed more concern for *orderly* change than anything his predecessor had managed. At every step along the way, Harper's office had announced these changes publicly. No news organization covered any of them. The silence only confirmed the prime minister's conviction that the Parliamentary Press Gallery wasn't interested in covering serious matters.

⇧

The other major organizational change of the Harper transition did get covered by Kathryn May, the *Ottawa Citizen's* redoubtable public-service reporter, but its significance sailed over the heads of most other journalists. Harper and Lynch began cleaning house in their own backyard, at the Privy Council Office, where the prime minister's own advisors work. While the Tories had been wandering through the wilderness, the PCO had developed a bad case of the bloat.

When Chrétien took over as prime minister in 1993 there were about 350 people in PCO. Despite the 1995 budget's program cuts and the subsequent years of relative restraint in spending growth, that number had roughly tripled to 1,100 by the time Harper was elected. Much of that extraordinary growth had happened during Martin's short term in office.

"Everything that Martin thought was a priority had to be at least co-managed out of the Privy Council Office," a senior

Conservative said. Aboriginal affairs, Canada–U.S. relations, regulatory reform, and several other projects had sprouted little secretariats at PCO – badly coordinated with, and sometimes antagonistic to, the more routine work at the line departments. So there were all these teams of crack bureaucrats sitting around waiting to provide expert, outside-the-box thinking whenever Martin wanted it. And doing considerable damage to the coherence of policy development and delivery the rest of the time.

Harper and Lynch decided to send them home. As a first phase, with more to come, Lynch sent 150 people from PCO back to their departments, principally Indian Affairs, Environment, and Industry. Here Harper's instincts ran precisely opposite Martin's. "If this prime minister thinks something is really important, he's going to trust it to a department and to ministers who can manage it on a day-to-day basis," the senior Conservative said. "Because otherwise you're not going to get anything done."

Note what happened here. Harper had developed, and in some ways had worked hard to earn, a reputation as a control freak. But there are different kinds of control freaks. Harper was at the centre of his government's policy direction and, especially, its communication philosophy. He would never be shy about stepping in to countermand a minister at a key moment. But he didn't kid himself that he could run thirty departments. He was determined that they would have the tools they needed to run themselves. "Of course we're conservatives," the senior Harper advisor said. "We're going to try to restore the best aspects of the way the system used to run."

"Governing requires a conservative temperament," Harper had told the Mortgage Loans Association of Alberta eight years earlier. "This temperament includes a respect for tradition, a penchant for incremental change, and a strong sense of honourable compromise." This was the temperament he had brought to his first big staffing and structural decisions.

As for the governing decisions, several of the big ones were already made. Priorities. Harper left the cabinet's first meeting to confirm that the first monthly cheques for one hundred dollars would go out to the parents of every Canadian child under six on July 1. John Baird, the young former Ontario cabinet minister, set to work with his department to write a Federal Accountability Act. It would be the first bill the new government would table, on April 11. Vic Toews, the former Manitoba justice minister, had the same job now in Ottawa and he set about drafting legislation imposing mandatory minimum sentences. Jim Flaherty, the former Ontario finance minister who looked uncannily like an Irish cop from central casting, started work on his first federal budget. Its centrepiece would be the first one-point GST cut. The fifth priority, the one Harper would allow to hang fire for a while, was health-care wait times. But here again he confided the job to a former provincial minister, Ontario's Tony Clement.

And if that were all Harper had done, this would be a short chapter. But the five priorities were only markers. Canada's new government had much more on the go than that, including two areas of eternal Canadian preoccupation: federalism and foreign affairs.

⇧

On February 15, Jean Charest flew to Ottawa for lunch with Harper at 24 Sussex Drive. Ottawa reporters caught wind of the meeting from their Quebec City colleagues, but attempts to confirm the news were stymied at every turn. When the meeting was over neither man met with Ottawa reporters. Charest scrummed with the National Assembly Press Gallery in Quebec. Why there and not in Ottawa? "Because I like you," Charest told his daily tormentors, smiling nervously. Subtext: somebody didn't like the Ottawa reporters as much. But the staging mattered less than the substance, which was that Harper quickly formed a partnership with the Quebec premier that was far closer than any since Lester Pearson's, forty years earlier, with Jean Lesage. Not that it was hard to improve relations. When Harper visited Charest in March in Quebec City, he set a modern-day precedent, because neither Chrétien nor Martin had ever gone to meet a Quebec premier in Quebec's capital city. It is impossible to tell you how many times Harper and Charest met face to face before summer: by the third or fourth meeting, both men's staffs simply stopped telling reporters when they were getting together.

Their most important file was the nebulous "fiscal imbalance," the belief that Ottawa had more money than it needed and the provinces, not enough. But before they crunched that one, they had an easy deliverable to put in the window first. In May, Harper travelled to the opulent Salon Rouge of the National Assembly, the site of Quebec public life's most important ceremonies, to announce that Quebec would have a special permanent post within Canada's delegation to UNESCO, the United Nations cultural organization.

It was a little short of what Harper had promised in the campaign. He had offered the province a chance to send its own delegation to UNESCO, but the organization's rules didn't allow that for sub-national entities like provinces. (Either the Conservatives hadn't bothered to check this point before the election, or they hadn't bothered to pass along the bad news to Quebec voters.) So Harper had offered as much as he could.

Charest's response was as important as the offer: previous Liberal premiers had, on occasion, made a show of disdaining the crumbs tossed their way from Ottawa, to shore up their nationalist street credibility. But now Harper and Charest were engaged in a conspiracy of interest. Harper didn't want to stop at ten Quebec seats. He had to demonstrate that his government would make an effort for a federalist Quebec government. Charest, battered in the polls almost since the day he had become premier, had to show Quebeckers he was good for something. He had to demonstrate that he could make progress for Quebec while a Péquiste premier wouldn't. So the two men pasted on smiles and did their modest announcement up big like Christmas.

All of which left Dalton McGuinty feeling a bit like the Maytag Repairman. For a decade Ontario had provided more than half of Chrétien's entire caucus. The premier of the largest province was used to pulling a lot of weight in Ottawa. Even when Mike Harris was premier and the Liberals found him far more annoying, from day to day, than Lucien Bouchard, they couldn't simply dismiss him. Now Harper was in charge. And while the Conservatives hoped to win more seats next time in Ontario, McGuinty's help was neither likely nor particularly useful in getting them. Which is why McGuinty's first meeting with Harper lasted twenty minutes and had to wait until the prime minister was coming to Toronto anyway – to speak at a fundraiser for McGuinty's rival, Ontario Conservative leader John Tory, whom Harper addressed before a cheering blue-chip crowd as "Ontario's next premier." This was a glimpse of the Stephen Harper whose strategic sense sometimes ran ahead of his manners, the guy who had written off Belinda Stronach when a little diplomacy might have kept her on board a bit longer. He knew he didn't need McGuinty. So he indulged the

urge to be a bit of an ass about it. It was not the new prime minister's best day, but neither was it out of character.

But all the meetings with assorted premiers were only
springtime preludes to the autumn's big task, which would be
finding a way to eliminate the "fiscal imbalance." Simply
admitting that there was such a thing as a fiscal imbalance had
been crucial to winning Harper acceptance among Quebec's
intelligentsia, who had always been amazed that the Liberals
refused to acknowledge the imbalance. Multi-billion-dollar
surpluses in Ottawa, deficits in the provinces – what more
proof did the Liberals need?

But if the truth be told, the Liberals weren't alone. This
would turn out to be part of Harper's problem. In 2005, the
Commons Finance committee struck a subcommittee to
examine the fiscal imbalance. And among the non-partisan
technical experts the subcommittee summoned, a majority
said either that Canada has no fiscal imbalance; or that ours is
smaller than in other federations and shrinking; or that if the
provinces need more revenue, they should just raise taxes
instead of asking for a handout from Ottawa. The provinces
have access to the same tax sources Ottawa does, the experts
said. Which meant Ottawa's spending habits weren't their
problem. "It may be useful for governments to blame others
for their ills," Richard Bird of the University of Toronto's
Rotman School of Management told the subcommittee. "But
generally you shouldn't believe them when they do so." As a
kind of bonus, there was a rock-solid consensus among
bureaucrats in the federal Finance department that the fiscal
imbalance was a province-built bogeyman designed to extort
money out of federal coffers.

Still, promising to attack the imbalance had a certain tactical allure. It made the Conservatives look open-minded

and generous, the Liberals pigheaded and stubborn. Which wouldn't make it any easier to fix the problem once elected, because simply *defining* it was such a challenge. Harper couldn't even sign onto the provincial consensus: there was none. When the premiers took receipt of an experts' report they'd commissioned on solutions to the perceived imbalance, Ontario's Dalton McGuinty stormed out of the meeting, furious that his taxpayers and Alberta's would be the only Canadians who didn't benefit from the experts' proposed adjustments to the federal equalization program.

So the imbalance was out there, somewhere, and Harper had promised to fix it. But its existence was disputed, and even the premiers who swore by an imbalance couldn't agree on a definition or a solution. Piece of cake. On May 2, with the tabling of the first Conservative budget, the Harper government began to hack its way through the jungle of the imbalance debate.

Finance Minister Jim Flaherty tabled both the budget and a separate discussion paper, "Restoring Fiscal Balance." That little booklet was aimed at framing the negotiations that would dominate the autumn's agenda. It marked the beginning of the Harper government's attempt to get back to reality after indulging in high-flown, province-friendly campaign rhetoric.

First, the definition. What was the fiscal imbalance? Well, it was complex. Ottawa had fallen into the habit of announcing surpluses far bigger than forecast; spending the windfalls in areas of provincial jurisdiction; refusing to make long-term spending plans, because all these surprise surpluses made planning difficult; and basically making a hash of consensual, rules-based fiscal federalism. Flaherty promised to address every component of this chain. He'd improve forecasting so billions of dollars didn't fall from the skies into Ottawa's coffers every spring. He'd take windfalls, when they happened, as his cue to cut taxes, pay down debt, or increase spending on clear federal matters like defence and public safety, rather than on provincial matters like health or education. And so on.

By this point, provincial officials must have been starting to scratch their heads. Where, in all of this, was Flaherty's promise to give billions of dollars to the provinces? Wasn't that what "fixing the fiscal imbalance" was supposed to mean?

By the eve of a June meeting with his provincial counterparts at Niagara-on-the-Lake, Flaherty was sounding positively mischievous. If the provinces wanted $10 billion to fix the perceived gap, they could keep waiting, he said. "They're unrealistic, pie-in-the-sky figures that do not reflect the budget realities of the various governments in Canada today," Flaherty said. Besides, if they really needed more money they could just raise provincial taxes, Harper's man said, sounding for all the world like the staunchest of Liberal hardliners on the fiscal-imbalance question.

And well he might. His "Fiscal Balance" discussion paper was the product of Conservative politics, but also of civil-service drafters in the Department of Finance. Its pedigree was clear. In 2002, Stéphane Dion had prepared a PowerPoint presentation proving, at least to his satisfaction, that there was no imbalance. Four of the charts from Dion's PowerPoint deck had found their way into Flaherty's plan to "fix" the imbalance.

The provinces were not pleased. "When Mr. Harper said, 'I'm going to fix the fiscal imbalance,' he never said, 'I'm going to fix it by asking the provinces to increase taxes,'" Charest said. Ah, but he hadn't *ruled it out* either, had he? Just as he hadn't ruled out giving British Columbia a strong voice at the cabinet table by poaching an addled Grit. Charest was learning what other Canadians were learning: that while Harper was a relatively straight arrow by the standards of recent prime ministers, it was never a bad idea to scrutinize the fine print.

By the end of Parliament's spring session, then, Harper had made several bold moves on federal-provincial relations without quite managing to suspend the immutable law that governs the field: the provinces always want more money than any sane prime minister can give them. Still, he had a shot at clarifying the rules of engagement. Martin had specialized in one-off deals with each province, a guaranteed recipe for bitterness and resentment because each province could persuade itself that the others' deals were sweeter. If he could lower expectations sufficiently by summer's end, Harper stood a good chance of restoring order and predictability to the way billions of dollars are distributed every year in the federation. A more prosaic goal than slaying some fiscal-imbalance jabberwock, but one still worth pursuing.

⇑

Perhaps the biggest opportunity for the Conservatives to establish a new brand identity, though, lay in foreign policy. It was not obvious terrain. Harper had travelled a few times to Europe but he was no globetrotter. Foreign diplomats around Ottawa were in a near-unanimous snit because, as Opposition leader, Harper had made almost no time to visit any of them. But within weeks after the election he started establishing a clearer, less hesitant tone for Canadian foreign policy.

Legislative elections in the Palestinian Authority had produced results that shocked Western observers when Hamas, the hardline anti-Israel party with links to terrorist organizations, won a strong majority. Like leaders around the world, Harper urged Hamas to renounce violence and recognize

Israel. That didn't happen. Who takes Canada's advice on anything? But then something novel did happen: Canada cut off aid to the Palestinian authority. Before any other government in the world had done so.

It was a little less bold than it appeared. Harper knew other governments would soon follow. "We had consulted with all our like-minded partners," a foreign-affairs official recalls. "We were all going to say the same thing. But the fact was, the EU had to have their EU meeting before they could announce what we had all agreed we were going to do. The Americans, for good reasons, didn't want to be off the mark right away." So Harper took the liberty of moving first instead of waiting. A sign of things to come.

In March, the people of Belarus voted in presidential elections. The incumbent, a scuttling little thug named Alexander Lukashenko, had prepared diligently – rounding up and arresting human-rights activists, arresting and beating opposition candidates and their staffs, sending commando squads to beat up reporters who tried to cover all of this. A squalid business. It was obvious as soon as the polls closed that Lukashenko's overwhelming re-election had been secured with the help of truncheons and jail cells.

All this would not only have been easy to ignore, there was virtually no downside to ignoring it. Belarus is a small country with a population barely larger than Ontario's. There is no large Belarusian community in Canada. But the promotion of multi-party democracy in Europe is a Canadian value. It is a value Canada shares with the U.S. State Department and the European Union, both of which had been monitoring Lukashenko's bully-boy tactics with mounting alarm.

The day after the Belarus election, Harper asked his senior staff for a statement about Belarus. One bubbled up from the

Foreign Affairs department in the ordinary fashion. "It said, you know, 'Canada notes with concern,' blah-blah-blah, or some crap like that," a Harper aide recalls. "It was a typical kind of Canadian, 'See here, don't go around killing your opponents any more.'" Harper took one look at the proposed release, swore, took out a pen and paper, and drafted his own version. "Just put it out. Don't even tell Foreign Affairs. They can read it later. Maybe learn something," he told his staff.

What they read was pretty blunt. The election "was not free or fair," began the communiqué, which went out in Harper's name. "I am shocked that a dictatorial and abusive regime such as this one can continue to exist in today's Europe."

But of course the most spectacular expression of Harper's new foreign-policy assertiveness was his secret flight to Afghanistan on the first weekend of March. Chrétien had travelled to Afghanistan too, at the end of 2001, but somehow this felt different. Kandahar, where Harper visited, was more dangerous territory than Kabul. Already soldiers had been killed and injured in their new role there. Harper was typically blunt when he told the Canadian troops on the ground that he would not let them down now. "We don't make a commitment and then run away at the first sign of trouble."

This new clarity in foreign policy didn't take long to get noticed in the foreign capital that stood at the centre of Harper's preoccupations: Washington. In April, Nicholas Burns, the U.S. Undersecretary of State, was in Ottawa for regular bilateral consultations. Now, Nick Burns is a pretty serious character. He is the ranking career diplomat at State, the Number Three figure on the State Department's organizational chart behind Condoleezza Rice and another Republican political appointee. The U.S. Embassy, in an unusually expansive mood, invited half a dozen Ottawa journalists to sit down with Burns during his visit. Through a comedy of errors too complex and trivial to chronicle here, I was the only reporter who showed up. And because I was on my way to a formal reception at Rideau Hall, I looked like a bit of a goof in my tuxedo and black tie. Which is neither here nor there, but it shows you that sometimes Ottawa can be a strange place.

Anyway. Burns made it clear that the State Department was tremendously excited to have an engaged, active new government to deal with. Harper's early move against Hamas, and Canada's designation of Sri Lanka's Tamil Tigers as a terrorist group, were "indications of a very self-confident foreign policy and of a government not afraid to make very tough decisions," Burns said.

"So we are very impressed. We are very impressed by the self-confidence and by the clarity of thinking in Canadian foreign policy."

I had to ask. "Does this clarity have the virtue of novelty in terms of Canadian foreign policy?"

Burns: "No, I didn't say that. I was just describing a state of affairs as they currently exist. No, I don't want to make comparisons. That's not fair." But. "But I will say, I think there's a real sense that there is a possibility for new beginnings."

⇧

By the time the Harper government's first one hundred days had passed in May – on May 2, if you counted from the January 23 election, or later if you started from the swearing-in of the Harper cabinet – the new prime minister had made progress on four of his five priorities; changed the face of the civil service in ways that did not turn the bureaucracy against him; made progress in reforming federalism; and brought a new assertiveness to Canadian foreign policy. Which is not the same as saying he had made a flawless start. In his handling of the Environment portfolio; of Canadian casualties in the Afghanistan conflict; of the Parliamentary Press Gallery; and of his own formidable temper, Harper showed weaknesses that might foreshadow his eventual undoing.

The environment was always going to be a bear for this government. Under Chrétien and then Martin, the relevant department had been turned into a full-time Kyoto think-tank, dedicated to coming up with schemes for meeting Canada's almost uniquely onerous greenhouse gas commitments under the global treaty.

From the beginning Canada's Kyoto targets had been set with almost whimsical disregard for what Canada might actually be able to accomplish. At a 1997 meeting in Regina, federal and provincial environment ministers agreed the Canadian delegation would go to the global conference at Kyoto with the goal of stabilizing emissions at 1990 levels by 2010. A daunting enough task, because by 1997 Canada's carbon emissions were well above 1990 levels. But Chrétien promptly abandoned the consensus he'd reached with the provinces, for one reason: because he had vowed that Canada would set a tougher target than Bill Clinton's U.S. government. So before even leaving for Kyoto, the Canadian delegation had a new target: 3 per cent below 1990 levels by 2010, with further reductions to come later.

But in deciding to outdo the Americans, Chrétien was chasing a moving target: Al Gore. The U.S. vice president was the head of his country's Kyoto delegation, and he never forgot that he would be a candidate for president in the 2000 election. He needed to nail down his credentials as a warrior against climate change, a subject that had preoccupied him a lot more before he entered the Clinton White House than since. So Gore set an extravagant goal: 5 per cent reduction below 1990 levels by 2010. Chrétien promptly set the Canadian reduction target at 6 per cent.

A commitment at a global talk-shop is meaningless unless a national government ratifies it. *Clinton never even bothered to send Gore's target to Congress for ratification.* He knew it didn't have a hope in greenhouse-gas-fuelled hell of passing. George W. Bush's formal repudiation of Kyoto makes him a handy villain for the environmental movement, but it did not change the fact that his Democrat predecessors had failed to ratify it – failed, that is, by not trying. Chrétien didn't send his own target to Parliament for ratification until the fall of 2002 – after Paul Martin had been bounced to the backbenches and Chrétien was on a quest to bolster his progressive legacy before riding off into the sunset.

So here's a plan that had zero provincial support (except in Quebec, which has waterfalls). A plan designed to outflank Canada's largest trading partner, which had already folded its tents. A plan that split the bureaucracy into warring camps: during Chrétien's last year in office, the Natural Resources department was a sieve of leaked reports arguing that Environment's Kyoto targets were impossible to meet. Stéphane Dion, Martin's own environment minister, has said that if the Liberals had won on January 23, he would have had to admit that Canada's targets couldn't be reached.

So spare a moment's sympathy for Rona Ambrose, one of Harper's youngest ministers, new on the file and handed a great big stink bomb. She didn't handle it well. Would you?

Part of Ambrose's problem is that her party is torn by interests that, on this file, sometimes complement each other and sometimes compete. First, Conservatives are ambivalent about the science. A lot of Conservatives, probably most of them, do believe the science behind global warming. But just about everybody in Canada who doesn't believe it votes Conservative. Second, the Conservatives have a value set that puts environmental virtue – even virtue honoured in the spectacular breach, like the Liberals' on greenhouse gas emissions – lower in the party's hierarchy of values than free markets and minimal regulation.

But the third interest is what makes things, well, interesting. It is strategic, and Stephen Harper is a strategist before he is anything else. The Conservatives know that every environmental advance they can post is a blow against Liberal claims of moral superiority at the next election. Ambrose, her department, and the Harper PMO were planning an ambitious set of environmental initiatives for the autumn of 2006 and beyond. It would target not only, or even primarily, greenhouse gases, but rather all the other toxins, junk, and effluvia that a less Kyoto-obsessed Environment department would consider the normal stuff of the portfolio. But in the meantime Ambrose was an unspectacular parliamentary performer, and the opposition was running her ragged.

But the environment remains an esoteric file for many Canadians, so Harper's Kyoto problems were peanuts compared to the issue that gave his rookie government its nastiest moments: the treatment of Canada's war dead.

⇧

There is no long-standing tradition of lowering flags to half-staff on government buildings when a dead soldier comes home. In fact, the country has gone back and forth on whether war remains should be brought home at all. The Commonwealth tradition after both world wars was to bury soldiers at Commonwealth gravesites near where they fell. The poppies grow in Flanders fields because nobody shipped Canadian soldiers home after they died in the trenches. More recently, partly because the logistics of repatriating war remains became less daunting, it became more common to bring Canada's fallen soldiers back to Canada.

But the death of a Canadian soldier did not cause the immediate lowering of government flags until Chrétien ordered it in 2002, when four Canadians were killed in Afghanistan by U.S. friendly fire. Under Paul Martin the practice became commonplace. Privately, senior Conservatives worried that the lowered flags and the endless live coverage of the returning caskets fed a maudlin and uniquely Canadian sentimentality about death.

Their argument – which few were willing to make, and none would make in public – was that soldiers are paid to do dangerous work. Some will die. But to romanticize their death is to cheapen their contribution in life – and the contribution of their comrades who managed to stay alive.

Look, I'll understand if you don't buy it. Especially because Harper never made the argument in public. At Conservative caucus meetings he would share with MPs and senators his concern that Canadians had lost the emotional toughness that came with dangerous military missions. But instead of making that case to the Canadian people, Harper simply ordered that flags stay up after combat deaths and that the return of soldiers' caskets to Canadian soil be off limits to reporters and cameras.

He then proceeded to make a hash of his explanation, claiming that soldiers' families had requested the changes when in fact the families were divided, and indeed many had argued forcefully against the new Harper rules. It was easy to conclude that Harper simply wanted to cover up the cost of his military adventures. He was vilified by opponents of military excursions. He'd have borne that burden cheerfully, because opponents of military excursions did not represent a growth market for Conservatives. But he also received countless complaints from Canadians who support the military and want it to handle tough jobs – but who failed to intuit Harper's belief that the moment of a soldier's death is not the right moment to pay attention to his work. Harper took his worst public-relations hit in precisely the field where he most wanted to inspire Canadian pride.

⇧

A much less serious obstacle to Harper's work was his continuing feud with the reporters who live in Ottawa and are paid to cover his work.

Harper had never had much regard for the Parliamentary Press Gallery, whom he considered lazy, incurious, sensation-obsessed, and biased in favour of big government. Conservatives, in turn, were obsessed with the number of reporters who fetched up in government jobs during the Liberal years. Susan Murray from the CBC wound up working for Scott Brison. Ian Jack and Al Toulin from the *Financial Post* worked for David Emerson (in his Liberal incarnation) and Tony Valeri. CTV's Jim Munson became Chrétien's communications director! He landed in the Senate! Vast left-wing conspiracy!

Never mind that reporters had found work with Tories when Tories were in power – Tim Ralfe, Luc Lavoie, Michel Gratton, Bill Fox, and many more. Never mind that as soon as the Conservatives got back in power, reporters disillusioned with the gallery grind started knocking on Conservative doors again. Dan Dugas from Broadcast News wound up in Peter MacKay's office, Robert Paterson from Global TV in Heritage minister Bev Oda's shop. A thoughtful observer might conclude that there is something about daily journalism that makes it profoundly unappetizing for serious professionals past the first flush of youth. But Harper was less inclined to discern workplace realities than a conspiracy.

He had also been badly knocked about by reporters during the last half of the 2004 campaign. I'll let a Harper aide tell the tale.

"Go back to the 2004 campaign – from which all of this comes, right? At the beginning of the campaign when things were relatively good for us and we had at least a certain amount of momentum on our side, he went out and famously did a press scrum in which the reporters ran out of questions," the Conservative says. "Unheard of. A forty-five-, fifty-five-minute scrum.

"And then comes a time where you want to have a ten-minute press scrum or a five-minute press scrum. For whatever reason. And you do the ten-minute press scrum and everyone says 'Oh, he's hiding.' Well, why? Because he used to do an hour? Ah. Right.

"So your toughest moment as a public communicator is the rule you want to set for whatever your relations are with the press. Because if you start to fuck around with the rules based on how tough the day's going to be, or how difficult your message is that day, that itself will become part of the story."

Harper's the guy who advertised his same-sex marriage policy and deep-sixed Gurmant Grewal on the first day of a national campaign. He's the guy who wheeled out freshman Tory David Emerson and Senator Michael Fortier on the first day of a new government. He's all about buying trouble early to minimize trouble later. He would do it again with his media management.

The Harper aide had one more part of the 2004 tale to tell. "Answering eight days in a row of lead questions about abortion is never going to happen again. Never. It is never going to happen again."

Sure, but how do you avoid that? Sometimes with perfectly benign methods. The first question on the wall of the Conservative campaign war room had been, "What are we accomplishing with this?", a reminder to speak only when the party's goals could be advanced. Harper would not step in front of a microphone unless he had something to announce. He couldn't demand that questions relate to his announcement, but in the normal order of things most would. You're going to cut the GST? But how? Why? When? None of those questions could be as hard as something random out of left field.

But Harper also wanted more control, and he wanted it early. So at his first news conference after the election, he walked to the foyer of the Commons and stood at a microphone in front of the green chamber's ornate wooden doors. And before he arrived, his press secretary, Dimitri Soudas, wandered among reporters collecting a list of those who wanted to ask questions. Then nobody's question would be acknowledged unless Soudas read his or her name first. Actually, just now, as I'm writing this, I recall that at that same, first post-election news conference, I shouted a question to Harper in the time-approved manner. Several of my colleagues whispered to me that there was a list, so keep it down, dork.

It took a while for reporters to decide they found Harper's method objectionable. Part of the objection was that the list was hardly the end of things. Reporters were banned from the third-floor hallway outside the cabinet meeting room, so we could not buttonhole ministers as they left. The PMO even stopped announcing cabinet meetings in advance, as well as meetings with premiers and even the visits of dignitaries such as Haiti's new president-elect, René Préval. Harper and his ministers shunned the National Press Theatre, purpose-built for news conferences and equipped with simultaneous French-English translation.

And on that April evening when Ian Brodie telephoned newsroom managers in Ottawa, Toronto, and Montreal to inform them of the secret Afghanistan mission, he told Rob Russo of the Canadian Press that the wire service could send any reporter it wanted – except Alexander Panetta.

Panetta is the same troublemaker who had written about Paul Martin rehearsing his acceptance speech in 2003. His instinct is to write about things when he learns them, which makes him a valuable journalist and a bane of politicians. He had caught wind of Harper's Afghanistan trip early, made inquiries, and been told by the PMO that if he wrote about it, he would be deemed a national security risk and barred from covering the trip. So he did sit on the story – until reporters on the ground in Kandahar saw members of Harper's advance team scouting the Canadian Forces base there. Now the story wasn't that Harper was going, but that he was coming. On such nuances are scoops built. Panetta wrote and delivered the story, which went to CP member papers across the country for publication.

Now, a dogged reporter is one thing, a security risk another. But there was no more room to doubt that Panetta was in bad odour for being the former, not the latter, when Russo told him to pack for the Afghanistan trip *because* Brodie had tried to bar him. The flight took off with Panetta. On the way back from Kandahar, he was even granted a brief interview with the prime minister. This is not how you treat a security threat. It's how you try to treat a reporter who resists being bullied.

Soon enough relations between Harper and Ottawa reporters collapsed into acrimony. William Stairs, Harper's campaign communications director, was replaced soon after the election with Sandra Buckler, the doggedly on-message spin doctor from the campaign war room. Buckler was the first communications director anyone could remember who simply wouldn't return most routine calls from reporters. After an acrimonious first meeting with the Press Gallery's elected executive, she stopped taking calls from Gallery executive members – even when the Gallery's new president, Yves Malo, was calling in his ordinary capacity as a reporter for Quebec's TVA network who was simply doing his job by asking about government business.

When Harper and John Baird were ready to release the Federal Accountability Act in the Commons foyer, the Gallery executive set up two microphones for reporters' questions. One for French, one for English. We would ask our questions in an orderly fashion, no shouting – but no PMO picking and choosing either. As soon as Harper's staff figured out the reporters' new gambit, the prime minister decided, on twenty minutes' notice, to move the announcement up the hall, to a room far too small to accommodate all the reporters. When the two microphones and the lines of unruly reporters moved too, Harper took two questions and then stomped out of the tiny, cramped chamber.

Finally in May, Harper wanted to announce development aid to Sudan's strife-torn Darfur region. Reporters showed up in the Commons foyer to ask questions. They lined up behind the two microphones. Soudas showed up to take our names in his list. No, he was told, there didn't need to be a list. We had microphones and lineups. We would be *so good*. Soudas scooted upstairs to Harper's office for a minute, then returned to say that the prime minister would make his announcement but field no questions from anyone. "That's it," Yves Malo said. "We're leaving." Most reporters – not all – left the foyer. I left with most of my colleagues. There was an element of protest in the decision, but really not that much: the cameras remained; the substance of Harper's announcement would be on the news that night and in the newspapers the next morning. It's not as though we were detracting from the PM's ability to speak to the Canadian people. But if he would not take questions, reporters were not inclined to stay and be props for what was, by Harper's own decision, no longer a news conference of any kind.

But it turned out that we were asking the wrong question. We thought the question was, "How can we reach an accommodation that reconciles the PMO's need for message control with reporters' concerns about news filtering?" In fact, the question was, "Has there ever been a more stubborn cuss in the history of creation than Stephen Joseph Harper?" And of course the answer was No. Having decided the Gallery needed to be beaten, the prime minister proceeded to beat it like a drum.

He stopped organizing formal news conferences in Ottawa but multiplied his press availabilities in the rest of the country, where reporters were more likely to take an answer from a prime minister any way they could get it. He found ways to make *informal* comments in Ottawa, in ways that gave him complete control over his message. He borrowed a favourite tactic from Brian Mulroney – he would choose to hear a shouted question, if he liked it, while he descended or climbed the stairs between his office and the Commons. He used blogs creatively; Buckler selected sympathetic bloggers, of which there were dozens if not hundreds, and sent them regular news releases, speech transcripts, and sound files. Harper found new ways to deliver his message directly, without any media filter at all. His staff put more sound files of Harper speeches on his website than ever before. They even put them on Apple's iTunes online music-sharing service so Canadians, or some tiny, incomparably nerdy subset among them, could download the prime minister's words and listen to them on the iPod while jogging.

And Harper gave more and more private one-on-one interviews – to the conservative *Western Standard*, to the conservative Ottawa talk-radio station CFRA, to *La Presse*, which was not particularly conservative but whose editorialist had endorsed him for prime minister, and even to outlets that were not sympathetic to him as a matter of doctrine, including the CBC. Sometimes his choices of outlets were pure mischief. Edward Greenspon, the editor of the *Globe and Mail*, had ordered his reporters across the country to stay off Dimitri Soudas's scrum lists for fear that the prime minister's man might be selecting which reporters would get a question. So Harper had his staff offer an exclusive one-on-one interview to the *Globe*'s Ottawa bureau chief, Brian Laghi, knowing Laghi could not say no. Nor should he have. But Laghi's boss should either have refused to run the interview, or admitted that his boycott of the PMO scrum lists was now a hollow sham. The calculated goal of offering the *Globe* an interview, a PMO source confirmed to me, was to make a moral pretzel of Greenspon's policy. It worked a charm. The paper would have no part of wholesale selection of reporters' questions. But when it came to *retail* selection of reporters' questions, the *Globe* was happy to oblige.

All the while, when he believed he was addressing a congenial audience, Harper denigrated the character of Gallery reporters. His office distributed talking points to MPs calling journalists lazy. He told a London, Ontario, TV station that no Liberal would have been treated the way reporters treated him. In *Report Magazine*, a conservative Edmonton publication, he penned a guest column in which he complained about "the usual gang of anti-Conservative pundits" who "seem totally absorbed by where we hold press conferences and which cocktail parties I do or do not attend."

There is room to argue the ethics of this nasty little spat seven ways to Sunday. I do not believe there was nearly enough effort made by many of my colleagues, especially among newsroom managers, to understand how long-term trends toward fluffy, gossipy Ottawa coverage turned us into sitting ducks as soon as we tried to argue we were standing up for *any* kind of journalistic principle. We had razed forests to tell Canadians about Paul Martin's chef and Jean Chrétien's golf balls and Harper's formidable gut and the odd little fishing vest he wore in Cancun and the way he shook his daughter's hand when he dropped her off at school. And we were supposed to be the guardians of – what, precisely? At *Maclean's*, almost alone among the Ottawa news bureaus, we caved early and abjectly: we considered Harper's rules silly, but we did not believe it was our job to act sillier.

But the net result of Harper's concerted campaign to shame his journalistic tormentors was that by June he had beaten the Gallery in a rout. You could get Harper in your monthly magazines, Harper in your local paper, Harper on the radio, Harper on the Net, Harper on your iPod, Harper skywriting *Surrender, Yves Malo* across the sky on a broom. Just about the only people in Canada who couldn't get a word out of Harper were the people who had moved to Ottawa to cover him. This state of affairs would be easy to repair: all we had to do was grovel. Nothing short of that would save us. Nice.

⇧

You will note that I have belaboured the Gallery's travails at considerable length. Mostly because it's just so much fun, for me if not for you. But also because the whole mess reveals certain habits of Harper's mind. He can be stubborn and vindictive. Note that these are hardly unique traits. Indeed, they're almost endemic to the political leadership class, not just in Canada but anywhere: you do not win consistently over time, as a rule, unless you get out of the habit of backing down and into the habit of making your opponents hurt for the sin of crossing you.

Second, and more idiosyncratically, Harper is convinced that forces in Canada are stacked against Conservative success. Today it is reporters. Not so long ago it was the people of Ontario. Remember the barely coherent harangue Harper wrote for the *National Post* after Stockwell Day lost the 2000 election? Its thesis was that Ontario would always reject an Albertan and that Alberta must give up on Ontario and the rest of Canada. Within five months after Harper wrote that diatribe, Stock Day was the least popular politician *in Alberta*. In hindsight the lesson of the 2000 election is that just this once, Ontario was a little quicker on the uptake because it was not distracted by native-son pride. But Harper couldn't see that. He was too busy looking for someone to blame.

Finally, and most importantly, Harper is less frequently motivated by vindictiveness and a victim complex than his opponents would like to believe. In fact, if his first five months as prime minister were a success – and they were more than that, they were not far from a triumph – it's because he kept his darker instincts in check. No, not just in check. He *overwhelmed* his darker instincts with some of the finest instincts any Canadian leader has shown in a generation: strategic genius, careful planning, discipline, a constant desire to expand his coalition and to reward voters' faith with concrete and demonstrable results.

So why did it turn a little sour near the end of that remarkable run? I believe for the same reason he blew his lead in 2004 and then nearly blew it again in 2006. He ran out of scripting.

Five priorities – taxes, parents, crime, clean government, health care. All, except health care, checked off by May. Two bigger themes, federalism and foreign policy. Both on the road to substantial realignment by May. A few files hanging fire, especially environmental policy, with no progress likely before autumn. Suddenly, and probably only temporarily, Harper had no big story to tell the Canadian people. This had happened before, and he reacted the same way.

With less message, he became fixated on the messengers. With less momentum, he became certain great forces stood in his way. With less control, the control freak in him started to freak out. Fortunately for Harper none of this was a permanent state of affairs. By June he was telling people privately he was ready, after two leadership races and two national election campaigns in less than five years, to take some serious downtime. His staff would have the summer to prepare a fall agenda, complete with new scripting. The agenda would be his again in the fall. But when his control and concentration had flagged, Harper had given vent to impulses that had hurt him before and might yet – who knew? – bring him down.

Or not. The Conservatives stood strong in the polls, a little ahead of their January 23 results, a little short of the majority Harper coveted. Unemployment was near record lows, the dollar near record highs. Harper had inherited that good news from the Liberals, but he'd take it, thanks very much. Except in Afghanistan, far from the concerns of most Canadians, the country faced no grave crisis. Harper had united two of Canadian conservatism's three sisters and was pursuing the third, the cutie with the French accent, with an ardour and a chance of conquest no one could ever have expected. His opponents were in disarray, their odds of rallying only so-so. He was well positioned, which was good to know, because the way he saw things, the real work had barely begun.

The assault on the history books lay ahead.

14

NOTHIN' BUT BLUE SKIES?

⇧

To understand who Stephen Harper is, it helps to know who he isn't. For starters, he's not Strom Thurmond. Probably this shouldn't need saying. But I keep hearing from readers who believe, or claim to believe, that racial segregation, an abortion ban, the institution of a state religion, and an aggressive program of chastity-belt distribution for all Canadian women under thirty are just over the next hill.

Before the January 23 election I became very cross with a reader who emailed me to announce that with Harper in charge it would be only a matter of time before they were teaching creationism in the schools again. And that it would be my fault, because I hadn't done enough to stop him. Actually, what got me angriest was the hash this reader was making of constitutional law: school curriculum is a matter of provincial jurisdiction. But besides that, the reader's note demonstrated

how deaf some left-of-centre Canadians are to the differences
of tone among the various strains of conservatism. Social conservatives know Harper isn't really one of them. Legislating
right moral conduct isn't his game.

"This is the interesting story of Stephen Harper," Pierre
Poilièvre, the young Ontario Conservative MP who once
worked as an assistant to Stockwell Day, told me one day.
"Everyone thinks he seduced the centre. It's actually the way
he tamed the right.

"Let's get this straight. He's now taken the most left-wing
position of any conservative party in the world on gay marriage. He's adopted the position of European socialists that
gays should have civil unions – full marital rights without the
word *marriage*. Harper has ruled out any abortion legislation.
He has basically moved the party onto an agenda that is centrist and acceptable to mainstream people.

"And he's done it almost without a peep from the right –
from the people who founded the Reform Party, who had
made the bombastic and even embarrassing remarks that had
come to typify the Reform era. All of those people have gone
along with this swift, centrist move while making almost no
sounds at all."

Why? Why are social conservatives so willing to let Harper
pursue a not-particularly-socially-conservative policy? One
school of thought, of course, holds that the hard-core right
wingers know Harper is one of them. They're just biding their
time. Once he gets his majority, the masks will fall and the *real*
Harper will become visible. This theory will certainly be a
centrepiece of any Liberal leader's campaign to block Harper
from gaining seats at the next election. "Oh sure, you haven't
seen any hidden agenda . . . *yet* . . ."

But for my money this analysis misunderstands Harper too.

First, because I don't believe his political beliefs are wildly out
of the Canadian mainstream. But second, because *even if they
were*, he has never been interested in implementing wrenching
change if it means doing lasting damage to Canadian conservatism's electoral chances. The "penchant for incremental
change" he valued in Progressive Conservatives so long ago
has become an integral part of his own political philosophy.

Which is another way of saying that he's not Brian Mulroney
either. When an obscure environmental group gave Mulroney
an award in the spring of 2006 as Canada's "greenest prime
minister," the wily old crooner delivered an epic speech in
tribute to his own cleverness, a favourite topic. Harper was on
hand to deliver a few closing remarks for the benefit of anyone
who hadn't already passed out from Mulroney exhaustion.
Harper said that one of the things he liked about Mulroney
was that the former prime minister was always quick to offer
advice – and not particularly broken up if Harper declined to
take it. I'm quite sure this was Harper's way of letting everyone
know he often ignores Mulroney's advice.

And why shouldn't he? The spur for Harper's entry into
electoral politics was dismay at Mulroney's practice of federalism and fiscal policy. But philosophy aside, just look at the
scoreboard: by the time Mulroney was finished, his party had
split into three and the Liberals had a decade-long free ride
ahead of them. Harper has learned to be too polite to say so,
and he has too great a stake in keeping Tories who revere
Mulroney inside his big conservative tent. But as he and Tom
Flanagan wrote in *The Next City* nearly a decade ago, the
flaming wreckage Mulroney left behind makes him a loser, by
their definition of conservative success.

Stephen Harper's project has never been to burn out. That's
why January 23 was not the highlight of his career, he hopes,

but merely set the stage for the long-term project. Indeed, the real test of his success won't come until after his career ends, because his goal is to make Canadian conservatism competitive, over the long term, with Liberalism.

To what end? I asked an associate of Harper's what he hoped Canada might look like in a few years. The answer reflected Harper's blend of strategy and policy. "Taxes will be down. Ideally André Boisclair will be a defeated leader in the election campaign and the PQ will be in some kind of internal turmoil. That's an uncertainty at the moment, but that's the play." In this post-Harper Canada, "criminals are spending minimum sentences in prison, and there is an organizationally strong, united Conservative Party; a divided, discredited, possibly bankrupt Liberal Party; and a resurgent NDP."

In some ways it's a modest set of goals indeed. A functioning two-party-plus system isn't a legacy project for most leaders in Western democracies; in most Western democracies, it's a *given*. Minimum prison sentences? Sure, if you like, but it actually doesn't differentiate Harper's aims much from those of Paul Martin and Jack Layton: both leaders promised tougher sentencing in the last election.

Which leaves us with a broken Parti Québécois and lower taxes. Again, it's important to understand that in his pursuit of the former goal, Harper isn't Mulroney. It is a common assumption among sophisticated observers of Quebec politics that at some point, once he has a majority under his belt, Harper will attempt a big-ticket constitutional fix to "bring Quebec into the constitutional fold." Are we back to Meech Lake then? I put that question to two close Harper associates. One looked alarmed. "Oh. That would be reckless."

The other sounded alarmed. A new Quebec round of constitutional negotiations? "Uh, no. No. I mean, no. That way lie demons. None of us have the stomach for that." Which doesn't mean Harper won't try to reform the Senate to make it feel more compatible with a modern democracy. But that's a far more modest constitutional project than the one he is sometimes assumed to be hiding under his hat.

Tax cuts? Here I think the choice of terms understates the scale of Harper's project. The goal is not just to leave more money in Canadians' pockets. It is to think twice before expanding the state into *any* new sphere of human activity. When Jim Flaherty delivered his budget in May, he had a very obscure point he took pains to emphasize in every interview: that program spending as a share of GDP was projected to decline from 13.7 per cent of GDP in 2004–5 to 13.0 per cent in 2007–8. Hardly a revolutionary retrenchment of the state: if Flaherty sticks to this trend line, he'll bring government spending back in line with where it was in Jean Chrétien's second mandate, way back in the late 1990s, before Paul Martin tried to buy political peace of mind with sweetheart deals for every province.

But Flaherty's statistic echoes Harper's comment, in his first unofficial speech of the 2001–2 Canadian Alliance leadership race, way back at that Vancouver airport-strip hotel, that Canada's government spends far more than it needs to. For Conservatives, taxes and big programs are at least as likely to stifle human happiness as to support it. Constraining the growth of the state is a long-term project. So Harper has to keep the Conservatives politically viable over the long term.

Will he succeed? Beats me. We tried to include a crystal ball with every copy of this book, but we couldn't make the packaging work. Many Liberals continue to believe that Harper's January 23 victory was in no way a demonstration of political skill or popular appeal. If it hadn't been for Chrétien leaving a stink bomb when he left 24 Sussex, and the RCMP prank-calling in the middle of a campaign, the theory goes, Paul Martin would still be making history today.

This belief will make the Liberals fight hard at the next election. They're like Apollo Creed, the wounded heavyweight champion in *Rocky II*, itching for a rematch with the punk who caught a lucky break. One presumes Stephen Harper has a little Mickey inside his head somewhere, whispering to him, just as Burgess Meredith did to Rocky: "This guy just don't want to win, you know. He wants to *bury* you, he wants to *humiliate* you, he wants to prove to the whole world that you was nothing but some kind of a – a *freak* the first time out."

In *Rocky II*, of course, the kid proves he wasn't a freak. He has skills the champ was never willing to credit: speed, smarts, a willingness to do the hard work of preparation, the love of a good woman. The challenger winds up cleaning the champ's clock. There are many, many sequels.

Any attempt to predict Harper's chances of similar success, out here in the real world, would be no better than a cheap parlour game. All I know is what Stockwell Day, Joe Clark, Belinda Stronach, Peter MacKay, and Paul Martin have had to learn at their own expense: that you underestimate Stephen Harper at your peril.

ACKNOWLEDGEMENTS

In 2000, Ken Whyte was my boss at the *National Post* and he told me I should write a book. As always, he had some ideas for what it should be about. I could write about the Liberal Party, one of the most consistently successful electoral machines in any Western democracy. How, in the twilight of the Chrétien years, would it renew itself for a new generation of political hegemony? Or I could write about conservatism in Canada: why was it so consistently uncompetitive?

I promptly forgot about all of this until the 2006 election. Ken was now my boss at *Maclean's* magazine. We resuscitated an old pet project: an unusually ambitious blow-by-blow account of a national election, modelled on the legendary *Newsweek* election issues, to be published so soon after the returns were in that people would be impressed and buy lots of copies. The final product filled about thirty magazine pages and hit the newsstands three days after the polls closed. We sold lots of copies.

And that would have been that, except I began to realize that there was more here than just an election post-mortem. Here was a chance to examine *both* of the themes Ken once suggested for a book. For the last five years, Canada's main political movements have been playing against type. Under Paul Martin, the Liberals lost much of their characteristic focus and competence. Under Stephen Harper, Canadian conservatives finally showed at least the potential to win national elections consistently. How did that happen? To me it boils down to two men, Harper and Martin. *Right Side Up* is the quite surprising story of what happened when their paths crossed.

The long *Maclean's* article, substantially updated, became the basis for three chapters in the middle. The rest is new.

This is my first book. I have many people to thank. Ken Whyte put the bug in my ear and grumbled only a little when I vanished from the pages of *Maclean's* for weeks on end. He is the most intelligent and creative Canadian journalist of his generation, a fantastic boss and a valued friend. Douglas Gibson at McClelland & Stewart gave this book a home, bought me good lunches, encouraged me endlessly, weathered my grumpy spells. He is a pillar of Canadian publishing; that he turned out to be a hell of an editor was an excellent bonus. Jackie Kaiser, my agent, offered wisdom in the ways of Toronto's publishing world. Also, patience. Boy, did I take her up on that latter offer.

I received extraordinary co-operation from participants in the drama recounted here, regardless of party or faction. Because most of my sources preferred to remain anonymous, I can't thank them by name. But I am grateful for the co-operation of political professionals who surely knew I would not always be gentle, but who wanted to help get a big story right.

Several *Maclean's* reporters contributed work to the long election article. Much of that work did not make it into this book, which is more of a personal account and less of a team effort. But I did rely on Steve Maich to make sure my description of the income-trust unpleasantness would be coherent. And much of the campaign-insider reporting from the 2006 election is by the redoubtable Joan Bryden, to whom I still owe cases of Diet Coke from our days at the Southam News bureau on Sparks Street. It was a great pleasure to work with her again.

Joan was one of four superb Ottawa journalists whom I am happy to thank both as colleagues and as friends. Graham Fraser and Susan Delacourt, down the hall at the *Toronto Star*'s Ottawa bureau, offered all the counsel and sympathy a first-time author could want. John Geddes, the *Maclean's* Ottawa bureau chief, never mentioned the extra workload my absence imposed on him. I also found John's writing about Stephen Harper over the years to be an extraordinarily valuable journalistic resource.

Writing a book, you lean on friends and family. In Ottawa, Emma and Phil Welford, Louise Elliott and Paul Vieira, and Lise Jolicoeur and Renée Filiatrault saw either less or more of me than they were used to. They helped me find my sense of humour whenever I lost it underneath piles of interview transcripts. Back home, the extended Wells clan offered quiet support and still more patience.

I kept three books on my work table more as reminders of how good a Canadian political book can be than as references: *Discipline of Power* by Jeffrey Simpson, *Grits* by Christina McCall, and *Fights of Our Lives* by John Duffy. On breaks – too frequent; sorry, Doug – I distracted myself from this Canadian tale by investigating the music of two American originals,

Bruce Springsteen and Morton Feldman. They're in here somewhere too.

This motley crew gets credit for this book's qualities. Any blame for its shortcomings goes to me alone.

Through it all I relied on the insight and support of a talented editor, trusted advisor, legendary organizer, beloved partner: Christina Lopes. Christina, I owe you all this and more.

P.W.
Ottawa, July 2006

INDEX

9/11, 1, 43, 87

Abbott, Jim, 36
Ablonczy, Diane, 23
abortion, 127–28, 142, 144, 232, 314
ACTRA, 193
Afghanistan: Harper's visit, 296, 305–6 ; Ignatieff's stance, 270–71; ongoing Canadian military presence, 44, 270, 301
Alberta: 2001 election, 82; 2004 election, 124; 2006 election, 111; and fiscal imbalance, 292; Day's libel case, 22; Harper's vision for, 20–21; MPs chosen for cabinet, 249–50; wranglings with Ottawa, 20
Alboim, Elly, 84–85, 87, 104, 227
Alcock, Reg, 162, 212
Alliance *see* Canadian Alliance Party
Ambrose, Rona, 249, 299–300
Anderson, Rick, 8, 13
Anka, Paul, 77
Armour, Jim, 61–62, 126, 139, 153
Arthur, André, 241
Austin, Jack, 84
Australia, 1996 election campaign, 156

Bachand, André, 68
Baird, John, 254, 288, 306
Baran, Yaroslav, 125, 182–83
Barenaked Ladies, 213
Belarus, 295–96
Bellavance, Joël–Denis, 101
Bennett, Carolyn, 270
Bethel, John, 110
Bevilacqua, Maurizio, 90
bilingualism, 127, 142, 144

Binns, Pat, 82
Bird, Charles, 109–12, 159
Bird, Richard, 291
Blair, Tony, 43–44, 120
Blaney, Steven, 230–31
Bloc Québécois: 2004 election campaign, 128; 2006 election campaign, 163, 172–73, 181, 199–201, 236; 2006 election results, 241; April 2005 non–confidence motion against Liberals, 147, 149; formed, 15, 123
Boessenkool, Ken: 2004 election campaign, 114–15, 124, 136–37; 2006 election campaign plans, 167; aids Harper's leadership campaign, 70; signs firewall letter, 21
Boisclair, André, 180, 316
Bono, 180
Bouchard, Lucien, 16, 38–39, 123, 276, 290
Boudria, Don, 90, 163
Bourassa, Robert, 98
Bradshaw, Claudette, 163
Brault, Jean, 146, 260
Brison, Scott: 2002 PC leadership campaign, 62–63; crosses to Liberals, 69, 180, 235; hires former reporters, 225, 302; on Afghanistan, 271
British Columbia: 2001 election, 82; 2006 election, 111, 202–3, 212–13, 234; Liberal gains in 2004 and 2006, 251
Broadbent, Ed, 163
Brodie, Ian: 2004 election analysis, 136; 2004 election campaign, 114–15; 2006 election campaign, 202–3, 229, 232; 2006